P9-BTN-534

A DEATH IN TEXAS

A DEATH IN TEXAS

A STORY OF RACE, MURDER,
AND A SMALL TOWN'S STRUGGLE
FOR REDEMPTION

DINA TEMPLE-RASTON

HENRY HOLT AND COMPANY

NEW YORK

CENTRAL LIBRARY
WATERTOWN

NORTH COUNTRY LIBRARY SYS
Watertown NY 13601

Henry Holt and Company, LLC
Publishers since 1866
115 West 18th Street
New York, New York 10011

Henry Holt ® is a registered trademark of Henry Holt and Company, LLC.

Copyright © 2002 by Dina Temple-Raston
All rights reserved.
Distributed in Canada by H. B. Fenn and Company Ltd.

Library of Congress Cataloging-in-Publication Data
Temple-Raston, Dina.
    A death in Texas : a story of race, murder, and a small town's struggle for redemption / Dina
    Temple-Raston.—1st ed.
        p.   cm.
    Includes bibliographical references and index.
    ISBN 0-8050-6652-7 (hb)
        1. Byrd, James, d. 1998. 2. Murder—Texas—Jasper. 3. Hate crimes—Texas—Jasper.
    4. African American men—Crimes against—Texas—Jasper. 5. Jasper (Tex.)—Race relations.
    I. Title.
    HV6534.J363 T45 2002
    364.15'23'09764159—dc21   2001039052

Henry Holt books are available for special promotions and premiums.
For details contact: Director, Special Markets.

First Edition 2002

Designed by Fritz Metsch

Printed in the United States of America
10   9   8   7   6   5   4   3   2   1

Grateful acknowledgment is made to the following for permission to reproduce photographs: numbers 1, 4–7, 9, 30, 32: Jasper Country Sheriff's Office (J.C.S.O.); 2, 3, 8, 10, 16, 21, 22, 26–29, 31,
34–42: Associated Press; 11, 12: courtesy Ronald King; 13: Rider Stockdale; 14: courtesy Joe
Tonahill; 15: courtesy Mike Lout; 17: courtesy Greater New Bethel Baptist Church; 18: courtesy
Reverend Kenneth Lyons; 19, 20, 25, 33: Kathy Lane; 23, 24: Los Angeles Police Department.

To all the good people of Jasper

CONTENTS

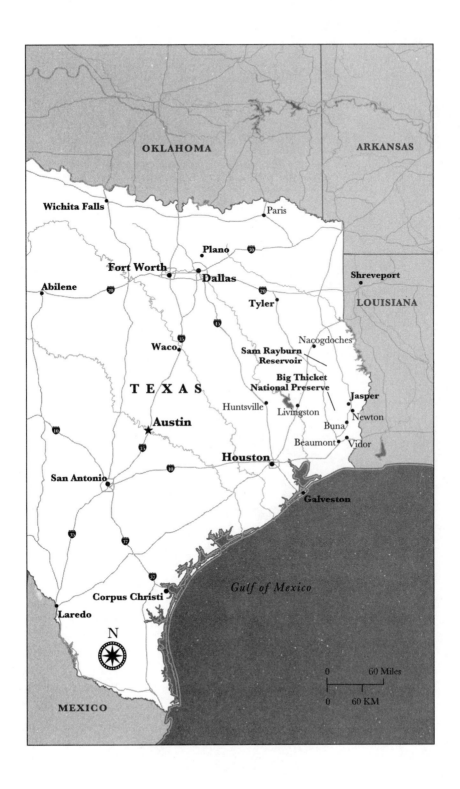

OKLAHOMA

ARKANSAS

Wichita Falls

Paris

Plano

Fort Worth

Dallas

Shreveport

Abilene

Tyler

LOUISIANA

Waco

Nacogdoches

Sam Rayburn
Reservoir

T E X A S

Big Thicket
National Preserve

Jasper

Huntsville

Livingston

Newton

Austin

Buna

Beaumont

Vidor

Houston

San Antonio

Galveston

Corpus Christi

Laredo

N

Gulf of Mexico

0   60 Miles

0   60 KM

MEXICO

A DEATH IN TEXAS

PROLOGUE

"If I owned Texas and hell,
I'd rent out Texas and live in hell."
—GENERAL P. H. SHERIDAN

June 7, 1998

DEATH HAS A way of making even slow people hurry. It scares them into seeing things the way they are, instead of the way they wish them to be. Even small deaths people don't expect to notice, or welcome deaths, which end hard-luck lives or long, painful illnesses, sweep mourners backward through rooms they have been avoiding for years. So when the black community in Jasper, Texas, awoke one Sunday morning to hear one of its own had been killed in some awful way on Huff Creek Road, the phones began to ring. Ladies who had come to church early, ahead of the Sunday services, abandoned the hymnals in messy stacks and began counting noses. They called relatives, and friends, and friends of friends to see if their men were home, safe, or whether it might be one of their kin dumped on the side of an old logging road.

It was a little after 9 A.M. when Sheriff Billy Rowles received the call from the dispatcher about the body. His first thought was a routine hit-and-run—a commonplace accident on the unlit roads on the outskirts of town. Deputy Joe Sterling, a baby-faced officer, had come on the line a little breathless.

"It's a bad one, Sheriff," he said over the crackle.

Rowles held the radio closer to his ear as his truck roared up Highway 190 toward Houston. He had a golf tournament to go to, Police Olympics, and, as a competitive man, he was determined to play and intended to win.

Yet something about Sterling's voice bothered Rowles.

"Joe, should I come down there? I'm on my way to Houston now. Shall I come down there?" Rowles said. He was already eyeing the exits and crossovers looking for an opportunity to turn the truck around.

"No, no, don't do that, Sheriff, we've got it under control," Sterling said, steadying his voice. "We'll be fine. Curtis just rolled up. I'll let you know if we come up with something."

Rowles had a feeling he shouldn't wait. Moments later, he had swung his truck around and was headed back to town.

Back on Huff Creek Road, Curtis Frame, Jasper's best investigator, was just stepping out of his car. He'd been to more evidence schools than the rest of the police department combined and wasn't shy about letting people know it. He was about six feet tall, burly, and bald. (If he was going to be bald, he had decided, he would do so emphatically. He shaved his head completely.) He smoked cigarettes nonstop, fanning away the smoke self-consciously as he exhaled, sensitive to the fact that even in Texas nonsmokers outnumbered smokers. His leather belt and holster creaking, hardware jangling, Frame walked over to the body. All the equipment on his belt forced his arms out from his sides. Sterling fell into step with a similar gait.

"Sweet Jesus, there's nothing left," Frame said to the younger officer as they looked at the torso. The knees and genitalia had been ground off. The head and right arm were missing. The little that was left of the body lay near the gate of one of Jasper's oldest black cemeteries, one of those neighborhood resting places that had come to dot the East Texas landscape. Slave owners and, later, company executives had donated these little patches of land to the communities so workers would have somewhere to bury their dead. Some of the graves had headstones; most did not. Those who had passed were memorialized instead by spirit markers and makeshift crosses in which love was meant to make amends for the inability to pay for a more proper burial. Sterling took in the scene around him and then followed Frame with his eyes, watching him fish a box of rubber gloves out of his squad car. The investigation, Sterling thought, had officially begun.

Huff Creek Road was usually deserted, but for Sundays. That was when a parade of the faithful, dressed in their churchgoing finery, made their way to the white clapboard refuge of Rose Bloom Baptist Church. During those Sunday mornings there wasn't much conversation, just the sound of a small army of feet crunching across the tall dry grasses in the meadow—a march to one of the few places where unlettered people could find solace from the poverty all around them. That's why, even before the caravan of police cruisers and television station vans turned Huff Creek Road into a drag strip of shiny cars, a crowd of simple country people had already started to gather. They emerged from small houses in the woods in various states of dress—the women in flowered smocks, the men in sleeveless undershirts and dingy button-downs. They came out just to see who it was, or even what it was, laid out in front of the unmarked graves of the cemetery. The event had shattered a quiet Sunday routine. Clothes were half pressed, hair half plaited, children half washed.

The bystanders were a rainbow of the Huff Creek community: from yellow-skinned blacks with freckles to those who were as dark as coal. This had been the black part of town for as long as anyone could remember. It was here in 1867 that great-grandparents had first heard—more than two years after the end of the Civil War— that the Union had won and they were free. The delayed dispatch, made by a Union major general on June 19, 1865, was known forever after in Texas as "Juneteenth." Some people in the black community said the tardy announcement was the first of many historic delays in Jasper. It began with the Civil War, continued through the heady days of integration, and could be seen today in the struggle for real equality among the races. Jasper, they said, had always been a place where things seemed to happen long after their appointed time.

The roadside crowd of stout women and broad-shouldered men shaped by the labor of felling trees spoke in quiet voices. Why had it happened here? Why was the body in front of the cemetery? If this accident (or was it a murder?—no one was willing to venture a guess) had occurred on Farm-to-Market Road 1408, or on one of the dusty tram roads that shot off into the pines, no one would have discovered the body for weeks, maybe months. Instead, here it lay, as if it had just decided to pick itself up out of one of the unmarked graves in the cemetery and settle into a new resting spot on the pavement outside. The appearance of inaction from the group of onlookers, their gaping stares from the body to the graveyard to the squad cars and back again, masked the drama of their thoughts. Was someone trying to send Jasper a message? And if so, what was it?

*   *   *

JUST FIVE HOURS earlier, James Byrd Jr. had stepped out into the steamy East Texas air to walk down Martin Luther King Boulevard toward home. The evening had begun the way most evenings started for Byrd: he had been sitting with friends on a porch drinking Busch beer enjoying a quiet summer night.

"You watch. James Byrd, he's going out in style," Byrd said, leaning back in his chair, a little tipsy. "The name James Byrd is going to be on everybody's lips. James Byrd."

"You gonna win the lottery? Because that's the only way anyone is going to remember you," said James Brown, one of Byrd's best friends. "If you're going to win the lottery, you can buy me a car. You gonna buy me a car?"

Byrd laughed, sang to himself a little, and winked at Brown. "You listen to what I'm saying. When I go, everyone is going to be calling me Mr. Byrd. Not Byrd-man or Toe or James. They'll be using Mister."

"Then you better be buying up those lottery tickets," Brown said, handing his friend another bottle. "Because that's the only way you'll be making a name for yourself."

Things might have been different if James Byrd had taken the ride Brown offered him later that night. Byrd had decided instead to have just a couple more drinks before walking home from Willie Mays's party. Brown and Byrd had been there together, singing, playing music, having a good time. Byrd didn't want to leave. He was having fun. He was always trying to have a good time.

Liquor had become a way for the forty-nine-year-old Byrd to put a fuzz on the world, his friends said. With no job, no prospects, and a small disability check, Byrd was living life by skimming along the surface, making few waves, harboring even fewer aspirations. His parents had virtually banned him from the house years before because his drinking upset them. The Byrds weren't rich, but they had standing; they were elders in the church, and their son cast a shadow over everything they had achieved. Also, Byrd was aggressive when he drank, and that made him unpleasant to be around. The Byrd family felt wounded every time they saw James. His six sisters and one brother had grown up, gone to school, and moved on to good jobs in Houston. James had been less successful. He was first arrested in 1969 for theft and was in and out of prison from 1986 to 1996 for a litany of offenses, including forgery, theft, and habitual theft. He had only left Jasper once, to go to Houston, and returned a year later more broken than when he had left. It was not long before he had become the town drunk, a fixture people grew used to seeing shuffling along alone late at night. By June 1998, he was on parole. Had he stayed out of trouble, his parole would have ended in January 2003.

The headlights of the gray sidestep truck must have blinded Byrd momentarily as it turned onto Martin Luther King Boulevard. It swung around, tires squealing in protest, and pulled over on the gravel shoulder ahead of him. There were three men inside: Shawn Berry, the twenty-three-year-old manager at the Twin Cinemas downtown; Bill King, an ex-convict; and a third man James did not know. Berry leaned out the driver's side window and asked Byrd if he wanted a ride. Byrd nodded slowly, struggled into the truck bed, and leaned his back against the cab. Berry handed him a beer through the window. The truck lurched back up onto the road and headed for the woods on the far side of town. James Byrd must have been dimly aware, just for a moment, that he lived in the other direction. But in small Texas towns where there was little to do, speeding down country roads with a cooler of liquor was as good a diversion as any.

*   *   *

THE SOUND OF Joe Sterling's voice still nagged at the sheriff as his truck came around the bend on Huff Creek Road. The golf tournament, Rowles had quickly decided, would have to wait. Dressed in golf shorts and a polo shirt, Rowles stepped down from the cab, put on his cowboy hat, and walked over to Sterling. The two walked wordlessly over to the body. Something about the way it was dumped made Rowles look twice. Curtis Frame had noticed the same thing. It was not lying askew on the side of the road the way one would expect a hit-and-run to be. Instead, the legs were set out straight with the feet together, and an arm, the only one remaining, rested across the chest, as if the entire body had been laid out in a coffin only God could see. The peacefulness of the corpse, after what looked like a savage dragging, was odd.

The onlookers kept growing in number, drawn from a land that otherwise seemed to have no one on it. And as they watched from behind yellow police tape, the talk was that this was no accident. A rumor of a cross burning surfaced. Was it the Ku Klux Klan? The spectators shook their heads. The names of those local black victims who had died suspicious deaths in the past rolled off their tongues like chimes: Ray Peacock, Loyal Garner, Kenneth Simpson. They shuddered to think that another name would be added to the list.

This body, however, was so torn up no one could match it with a name. The authorities couldn't confirm its identity even after finding a wallet in the trail of evidence with an identification card photograph inside.

Rowles looked at the trail of blood that ran like a tire skid down the middle of the road. While a hit-and-run was a likely explanation for what had happened, Rowles had been in law enforcement long enough to allow his mind to wander down other avenues. Sweet Jesus, he thought, don't be Klan. Don't be a racial killing. Only the week before, Jerry McQueen, a local contractor, had been found beaten to death at his family's private hunting camp just outside Jasper. Donald Kennebrew, a black man who worked for McQueen, was being held for the slaying. The investigation had been quick and clean, but Rowles worried about the fallout. The white community in Jasper was outraged. McQueen was well liked, and Kennebrew had brutally beaten him to death with a piece of pipe. The details of the killing quickly made their way to the coffee klatches at Texas Charlie's Bar-B-Que and the Belle-Jim Hotel, where everyone agreed this was not the type of thing that happened in nice quiet towns like Jasper. And now there was another body, another death.

As Billy Rowles followed the trail of blood and evidence on foot, he mulled the dreaded possibilities. He took off his big white hat and placed it next to a set of keys for investigators to mark. Three feet farther up the road he put a tin of Skoal chewing tobacco next to a set of dentures. He saw more keys, then loose change, puddles of blood, and more than a mile down the way, an arm, James Byrd's head.

Margaret Tukes, who had known James Byrd for years, said later she couldn't recognize anything about his face when she saw his head and right arm lying in a roadside ditch more than a mile away from the rest of his body. "I had to go and see it, see if I knew who it was. I have brothers out there, and when the devil's loose, it doesn't matter who he catches," she said. "I was worried they had caught one of them. And you know, it hardly looked like a face. I know James, but I couldn't hardly recognize him at all. You know we were lucky the head landed in the black family's yard. Otherwise, mark my words, this all would have been covered up."

Rowles was running out of things to take out of his pockets to mark the evidence.

"I thought this was going to be the easiest hit-and-run I would ever solve. It looked like it was going to lead me right to the culprits," he said later.

When the trail stopped and turned off Huff Creek Road onto a sandy logging trail, however, Rowles swallowed hard.

"This was no accident," he said aloud to himself. He spied a footprint in the dusty track and radioed back to Curtis Frame. "Rope off this scene, close it off; let's get a cast of this footprint." There were tire tracks too.

Up at the top of the dirt logging road investigators began gathering evidence of a struggle. The ground was torn up. There were cigarette butts stamped out. Beer bottles. Rowles tried to take it all in. Then Curtis Frame called him over.

"Look at this," he said, handing the sheriff a Zippo lighter. The symbols for the Ku Klux Klan were etched on one side; below it the word "Possum."

"This country boy's in trouble," Rowles thought, and his heart began to hurry.

CHAPTER ONE

DANTE'S INFERNO

JASPER LIES ON the eastern edge of what Texans call the "Big Thicket," a triangle of woods that runs south to Beaumont, north to Corrigan, and ends on the banks of the Trinity River. For more than 160 years, ever since the first families arrived in Jasper on horseback to live in the sparsely settled area between the Neches and Sabine Rivers, the piney woods provided most everyone, regardless of race, a means to eke out a living. One hundred years earlier, the woods had been so thick and breezeless, a candle would not flicker in the trees. The place so teemed with life that hunters could hardly step outside their cabins without stumbling over the river's washtub-sized loggerhead turtles. In those days it was easy to go fishing for the table, and a man could bag wild hog, bear, and deer just by pointing a gun and pulling the trigger.

Jasper's young boys were taught at an early age the way to handle a gun and kill an animal. In a town where winners were few, hunting in the Big Thicket provided an opportunity for every man to be bigger than he really was; it provided an opportunity for boasting, whether it was about who had the biggest arsenal, the biggest truck, or the biggest buck dragged lifeless from the trees.

The weekend rituals became predictable. Men of every hue woke early on Saturdays and drove down undulating backroads, ruminating aloud about the life expectancy of deer and how they intended to shorten it. They disappeared into the forest, whooping and caterwauling, sometimes pumping their rifles victoriously over their heads. In September, when deer-hunting season started, all that firepower in the woods made the place sound like a battlefield. By daybreak, the first pickups pulled up to Jasper Quality Meats and Smokehouse on South Wheeler and deposited the animals in the side alley. The men stopped only long enough to pose for photographs next to a rack of antlers. Bo Jackson and his employees stacked does and bucks like cordwood beside the shop, which, by midmorning, looked like an abattoir. Jackson, in his stiff blood-soaked apron, skinned the deer and sliced them into steaks for $47.50. Field dressing, the quick gutting of animals most hunters did in the field, was an extra $3.75. Jackson often got three hundred deer in the first weekend.

Deer-hunting season was the one time of year when local Jasperites, who endured the day-to-day condescension of visitors from the city, displayed their sagacity. They waited all year for this role reversal, when they were judged by how much life they could take out of the woods and not by their tobacco-stained teeth or the nubs above their knuckles. The Big Thicket was an equalizer. It made people from Dallas and Houston feel awkward as they clomped through the bramble, busting twigs and tripping over roots. The Jasperites, those country Bubbas city folk ridiculed, walked noiselessly through the trees like Indians, skimming over the ground beneath skies as gray as smoke.

Over the years, the visitors' discomfiture, viewed on the sly from beneath sleepy, half-lowered lids, had become one of Jasperites' richest delights, an unexpected tidbit among scanty rations. Jasperites particularly liked to recount visitors' reactions after the first crack of gunfire tore through the wooded stillness. As the report echoed from all directions, instinct told the city dwellers to take cover. The visitors' minds flooded with stories of accidental shootings, bullets gone astray, human movement among the trees mistaken for prey. Finally, they stood stock-still, eyes darting, bracing for the moment when the bullet found its mark. Would the shot hit them between the eyes, or would it be a flesh wound that would make them moderately late for work on Monday?

When silence descended again, the visitors laughed uneasily. It was not just the gunfire that made them nervous. After several hours in the woods, it dawned on most city people that this Faulknerian, testosterone-loaded horde all around them could be lethal. The competition in the woods, man against forest, man against animal, man against man, danced on the edge of deadly. That was about the time Jasperites let the city folk in on the secret: there were so many trees in the forest, bullets did not often hit accidental targets. The real problem with woods this thick was that if a man was shot, or a bear surprised him in the bramble, or there was a murder, no one would ever know. These woods were so deserted one could be left for dead a month before anybody would find out.

And nestled in these woods, where the only sound was the soughing of pines, was Huff Creek Road, a spooky, deserted stretch of asphalt bound by a thick strand of pine on either side. It was so quiet one could drive its entire six-mile length and never run into another driver, car, or flicker of life.

Cedric Green lived in a trailer on the edge of the Huff Creek community, just over the county line in Newton in a small black settlement called Jamestown. Green was a small square man with a barrel chest and broad shoulders. He worked in the scrap yards and had become sturdy moving heavy iron and steel pieces around the yard. It was before 8 A.M. the morning of June 7, Green bounced over the curb where the dirt part of Huff Creek Road played out and the pavement began. He was in his signature orange truck, which, had anyone sworn to it, would have had to be described as more metal-colored than orange. Everyone in Jasper best knew Green by that ancient Ford. The truck was so renowned it had become a landmark: because there were no street numbers around Green's trailer, it was a description of the truck parked out front that helped visitors identify his house.

That morning Green was tooling along the roller-coaster road with the window open so he could smell the pines. He turned up the radio. Rock and roll from KJAS, the local Jasper station, sputtered through the speakers. Green was going against the usual flow of Huff Creek traffic. Most Jasperites turned onto Huff Creek from the Jasper city end, from Farm-to-Market Road 1408, instead of the back way from Jamestown. It was a sharp left off the main drag. One hundred feet down the pavement one crossed a tiny railroad tie bridge fording the trickling dribble of water from which the road got its name.

Huff Creek had always been a mecca for drunk drivers, partly because it was so deserted and partly because such isolated roads permitted anyone who had had a few too many to skirt sheriffs' cruisers and get home without a DWI. For that reason, casualties along these old timber routes were commonplace. It was not unusual to see vehicles wrapped around tree trunks or hear about runaway logging trucks, or raw pine poles rolling off trailer skids and plowing into oncoming cars. In the spring and summer, when the hunters had put away their rifles, the deer bolted across the road as they pleased. Drivers hit so many, they were referred to as "fast food."

Cedric Green accelerated through the curves, shooting glances out of the corner of his eye at his five-year-old son, who sat beside him on the seat. Green let his eyes rest on the primitive little black churches that dotted the landscape—shoeboxes on stilts. He caught glimpses of the old "colored" cemeteries that sped past him through the side windows. They appeared every few hundred feet, it seemed, with their rough-hewn headstones, plastic flowers, and roll call of sweetly docile and abbreviated names: Colemans, Parks, and Adams. As Green came up over a hill at speed, he noticed something on the side of the road. A deer carcass? He swerved to miss it, nearly plowing into the culvert on the other side. His son stood up on the seat to see what it was. Then Green, looking in the rearview mirror, saw shoes. "Son, don't look," he said, covering the boy's face with his hand. He swung the truck around and pulled into the first driveway scraped out of the dirt. He knocked on the door, asked to use the phone, and called the sheriff's office. "A man's been killed up on Huff Creek, by the Rose Bloom Cemetery," he said.

Green went back to the truck and sat with his son. He was out of breath.

* * *

ACROSS TOWN IN a one-bedroom apartment, shades blocked out the midday sun where Bill King and Russell Brewer slept. They hadn't bothered to undress from the night before and were asleep facedown across the bed as if they had been struck from behind. In the living room, a small square space littered with free weights and dirty clothes, Shawn Berry was similarly dozing.

The trio of young white men roused themselves sometime after lunch and drove down to the Jasper Car Wash, where, witnesses said later, they scrubbed Berry's gray sidestep truck with an attention to detail they had rarely exhibited in the past. They hosed off a thirty-foot logging chain, blasted the bed with water, and then roared up Highway 59, muffler rattling. No one would have noticed had it not been that these three boys were among the least likely to care about the cleanliness of the truck they drove. The three were headed out to nearby Burkeville for a barbecue—they were providing the steaks—and a pickup volleyball game. Neither King nor Brewer had much fun, though. King said he had hurt his arm riding a motorcycle the day before. Brewer said he had hurt his toe.

"At the time I didn't think anything of it," said Pat Behator, a friend of King's who was there.

*   *   *

GLORIA MAYS'S GOSPEL Inspiration Hour aired on KJAS radio every Sunday between 9 and 10 A.M. A mixture of gospel music, scripture reading, and prayers for the community, the show had a devoted following. Every Sunday, the station got forty or fifty phone calls on its prayer line. Residents called to ask listeners to include the sick or dying in their prayers.

Mike Lout, owner of KJAS, and Mays were taking turns answering the phone and jotting down prayers to say on the air when a call came in from the Huff Creek community.

"There's a man's head in a ditch off Huff Creek Road," the caller said.

Lout thought nothing of it. "This is the rumor-est damn place in the world," he said later. "I think it is because they don't have anything to do. So I didn't think anything of the call."

Five minutes later, Gloria Mays took another call from a frantic woman, also from Huff Creek, who said police had found a body without a head. "Then I knew something was up," said Lout. "There was something going on out there."

At Evergreen Baptist Church, where beauty salon owner Unav (pronounced Una-vee) Wade attended services, a member of the congregation had burst into the room at the back and breathlessly said the head of a black man had been found in a yard on Huff Creek Road. "No one could hardly go through with the service," Wade said. "And no one knew who it was."

Sheriff Billy Rowles's arrival at the crime scene more than an hour later seemed almost beside the point. In the time it had taken him to drive up to Huff Creek, the shoulders of the road had filled. Ambulances and police cruisers were parked helter-skelter along the pavement. The coroner, police photographers, and state troopers were snapping on rubber gloves and walking the crime scene. Sheriff's deputies were roping off the area, and inside the yellow tapes investigators were at work. Hunkered under the trees, grim policemen, deputies, and agents were dropping the contents of James Byrd's pockets into brown paper bags and photographing puddles of blood. Others circled evidence with bright orange paint. The forest sounds had been replaced by the crackle of static over two-way police radios.

By the time Rowles had walked the three-mile crime scene, seen the cigarette lighter with three interlocking *K*'s, and had taken in the evidence of a struggle up at the top of the dirt timber road, he was thinking the worst. "I was a brand-new sheriff. I didn't even know the definition of a hate crime," he testified later. "What I knew was that somebody had been murdered because he was black. Once we saw the KKK emblem on the lighter, that's when we started having some bad thoughts."

There were other disturbing signs. There were no skid marks, the usual evidence in a hit-and-run. Typically, once a man has been hit, drivers stop to see what they have struck. What's more, the bloody trail down Huff Creek Road didn't run parallel to the tire tracks. It went from one side of the road to the other, zigzagging like a water-skier jumping a boat wake. "It was going through my mind—somebody's dragging something," Rowles said.

The investigators took plaster casts of the tire tracks on the dirt tram path off Huff Creek Road. Bagged beer bottles. Dropped CD cases into paper bags. Picked up a socket wrench. As the evidence began to accumulate, one thing was clear: the suspects had done a poor job of covering up their crime.

*　　*　　*

THE DISPATCHER AT the sheriff's office rang Dorie Coleman's Mortuary on Fletcher Avenue around 11 A.M. There was an unidentified body on Huff Creek Road that needed to be picked up. The dispatcher did not need to say it was a black man; that was understood. There were two funeral homes in Jasper that served the black community and two homes that tended to the white. The race of the deceased determined who was summoned. Coleman's

Mortuary and the Robinson Community Funeral Home, the two black establishments, alternated their pickups. The dispatcher kept track, and on that June morning it was Coleman's turn. Rodney Coleman, the mortician's son, took the call.

The younger Coleman climbed into the car and went by Greater New Bethel Baptist Church to pick up his father, who was a deacon and preparing for Sunday services. On this quiet Sunday morning it took them only ten minutes to drive to the crime scene. As they pulled up, they saw that an army of deputies had stationed themselves at the corner of Farm-to-Market Road 1408 and Huff Creek Road to guard against the curious. They waved the Colemans right through. Another deputy stood at the bridge in that locked-knee stance officers took when they knew they would be on their feet for a while.

"Follow the line," he said, pointing to the bloody stripe that wound along the pavement. The Coleman men exchanged glances and eased the car in over the bridge.

Dorie and his son had picked up so many bodies over the years that the process had become routine. They rolled the car up to where they saw Billy Rowles, Judge Ronnie Billingsley, and death investigator Phil Denny standing and turned off the engine. The white men were standing on the pavement looking down into a culvert. The head and arm of a black man lay below. Denny nodded toward the head and arm in the ditch and asked the Colemans to go ahead and "do the removal." Dorie Coleman knew just about every black man in Jasper, but he didn't recognize this one.

As they climbed back into the car, the two Colemans had simultaneous thoughts. "We right away thought this was some guy from Houston who crossed some skinheads," said Dorie Coleman later. "Once we had the head and arm in the car, we must have sat around for an hour waiting for the detectives to finish. Then we followed them up the road. There was evidence marked all over the pavement, so we drove slowly. We hadn't even got to the body before Rodney and I decided it was a hate crime."

The Colemans picked up the torso in front of the cemetery and drove it back to the funeral home. They hardly said a word in the car. The phone rang again about forty minutes later. It was Curtis Frame. He wanted to bring by a couple of men from nearby Newton to try to identify the body. A friend of theirs had been missing for several days, and they thought the body might be him. When the three arrived, Frame unzipped the body bag and the two Newton men peered in. It wasn't their friend. Frame took a fingerprint and thanked Dorie Coleman for his time.

"If you find out, sure would like to know who this is," Dorie Coleman said.

Half an hour later, Frame was back on the line. "It's James Byrd Jr. We got a positive ID from his prison record. It's James Byrd Jr."

Dorie Coleman was shocked. "I knew James, I knew James well, and the face—it didn't look anything like him."

*   *   *

IN THE SPRING of 1998, the entire country was riveted by two things: the mythic battle between St. Louis Cardinal home-run king Mark McGwire and Chicago Cub Sammy Sosa, and the nightly prime-time reports of an entanglement between a middle-aged president and a smitten twenty-one-year-old intern. The baseball story was a simple one; both McGwire and Sosa were congenial in their competition, supportive of one another, and provided an opportunity for fans embittered by the 1997 baseball strike to begin to believe in heroes again. The Clinton-Lewinsky scandal managed, by contrast, to do just the opposite. The president claimed never to have had relations "with that woman" just as Monica Lewinsky's confidants were being flown to Washington, D.C., on a daily basis to tell their side of the story to an independent counsel. It took no time for the summer to become a season of promiscuous opinionizing. The story set friend against friend, provided fodder for off-color jokes of the kind your grandfather told when your grandmother wasn't around, and turned Lewinsky into a verb. The center, as Joan Didion once wrote about the 1960s, was not holding.

*   *   *

MOST OF THE men in Jasper found their way to the Aubrey Cole Law Enforcement Center for one of two reasons: either to report a crime or to deny being mixed up in one. Official authority in the rural South had always tended to concentrate in the sheriff's office, and Jasper was no different. The Jasper County Jail and sheriff's office were housed in an unremarkable cinder-block square with fifty cells on one side and a struggling vegetable garden, tended by trusties in their black-and-white wide-striped jail pajamas, on the other. The jail was flat and bland and looked like a packing crate. The view was equally unremarkable: it looked out over the dust of a concrete factory and a patch of scrawny trees on Burch Street. The parking lot, with its thirty spaces, was usually full of trucks and sheriff's cruisers. The county jail was always a bustle of activity.

Truth was, Jasper offered few alternatives. There were no bars; the town was dry. Restaurants circumvented the regulations by selling "club memberships," which permitted them to serve liquor to anyone who set down a five-dollar membership fee. Getting a six-pack for the cooler was more difficult. Residents had to drive ten miles up the road to Solley's dry goods store just outside of town. Every couple of years there was a push to change the liquor laws, but it was always defeated by citizens who figured the unemployment rate and abject poverty in Jasper made people angry and dangerous enough without adding liquor to the mix.

What's more, summers were notoriously difficult in the South. Jasper's residents' chief concern became finding ways to escape weather that seemed straight out of Dante's *Inferno*. The summer of 1998 was worse than most. It brought to Jasper forty-one straight days of temperatures above one hundred degrees, weeks of drought, and shortened fuses. Summer unemployment in Jasper had tipped up to 17 percent. The price of a barrel of oil had dropped to ten dollars, erasing any incentive for companies to drill for more. Lumber prices also declined, which meant more layoffs at the mill. The double hit put hundreds of Jasper's young men at loose ends just when the kiln of a Texas summer was firing up. Disaffected Jasperites spent hours seated before huge, whirring fans and inefficient air conditioners that did little more than push around the suffocating heat. They filled their days grumbling about their plight and tinkered with windows and screens to see what combination of open and shut worked best at what time of day. At night there was little relief. Jasperites haunted different rooms of the house or trailer in search of a breeze. The long slow days began to drive the entire town to distraction. There were only so many barbecues to attend, volleyball games to play, and motorcycles to ride before heat-inspired restlessness was bound to take over.

The first explosion roared through town at the end of May 1998. Almost as soon as the sun rose, entire families would begin making plans for relief. Driving up to Sam Rayburn Park for a swim in the reservoir was a common escape. Carolyn McQueen came home from shopping with the feeling that something was wrong. Her husband, Jerry, had not called to say he had arrived safely at the family hunting lodge. Her son had left a message on the machine saying his father had missed a Saturday appointment at the school. The younger McQueen, with his new driver's license, decided to drive up to the hunting property, seven miles west of town on Highway 130, to make sure his daddy was all right.

The McQueens were a quiet, upper-middle-class family who lived in the nicer part of town known to locals rather derisively as Silk Stocking row. It was there that the district attorney and the mayor lived in big new houses set back from the street on wide landscaped yards. It was an island of prosperity in a place like Jasper. Carolyn had married Jerry young and had opted to stay home and raise their children while her husband built up a concrete contracting business. Most Jasperites considered Jerry McQueen one of those few homegrown Jasperites who had succeeded. Billy Rowles was on the fifth hole at the country club when his pager went off. The young McQueen had found his father murdered in the woods.

By the time Sheriff Rowles had driven to the hunting camp, seen the body, and returned to the McQueens' house, Carolyn had known about her husband's death for hours. Rowles began with the usual questions. Who might want to kill her husband? Did she know if he had any enemies? When did she last speak to him?

He had no enemies, she said. She didn't know who might want to kill him. She broke down in tears.

Joe Sterling, the same baby-faced and soft-in-the-middle deputy who would be on the scene for the Byrd murder, was the lead investigator for the McQueen killing. He figured the motivation was drugs, something that had become a scourge in Jasper. In the mid-1980s, cocaine and crack had replaced marijuana as the best-selling commodity in the East Texas drug trade. In Jasper, crack caught on mainly in poor black neighborhoods and the Quarters and the poor, mostly black, Pollard Street housing project. Few whites got into crack; they preferred marijuana or speed.

By Monday afternoon, Sterling had zeroed in on Donald Kennebrew, a longtime black employee of McQueen's. Known to have a crack problem and financial woes, Kennebrew had not shown up for work that morning, and his family had not heard from him for days. By Tuesday, sheriff's officers had tracked down Kennebrew at a local motel and brought him to the station for questioning. It took thirty minutes to get him to confess.

After McQueen had paid Kennebrew his regular wages the previous Friday, Kennebrew had quickly spent his entire check on some rocks of crack cocaine. The next day, down from his high and ravenous for more, Kennebrew had driven out to the McQueen hunting camp that Saturday morning to ask his boss to advance him some more money. It was something McQueen had agreed to do in the past, but this time he refused. Kennebrew went back out to his truck, smoked another rock of cocaine, and returned to the camp with a piece of rebar, one of the heavy iron strips used to reinforce concrete foundations. He bludgeoned McQueen to death and stole his wallet. He still had McQueen's billfold on him and was still wearing bloodstained clothes when the sheriff's deputies picked him up. Kennebrew was so addled by the crack that he didn't know Jerry McQueen was dead. As murders go, this one was easily wrapped up. Carolyn McQueen, distraught over her husband's death, wanted Kennebrew to plead guilty and avoid a public trial. Kennebrew agreed, promised not to appeal, and got a life sentence. It was a terrible black-on-white murder everyone hoped would just go away.

If there was any solace in the case, it was that this type of murder didn't happen often in Jasper. There were more bad accidents—accidental shootings at the hands of jealous boyfriends—than premeditated killings. McQueen was a family man, was popular in the community, and was one of Jasper's best employers of both black and white men. And now one of his black employees had killed him. While that wasn't immediately alarming to Rowles, he did think that such a murder would do little to help people get along in Jasper.

"The McQueen murder was shocking to a lot of people because it was a whodunit," said local radio reporter Mike Lout. "We have murders and shootings in this town all the time, but they are never whodunits. In Texas people say, 'Hell yes, I shot him; I should have done it ten years ago.' They don't weasel around." The McQueen murder was different. In the hours after the murder, detectives were questioning anyone who had known McQueen. In the white community, the talk around town was all speculation, not only about who had been called in for questioning, but who was likely to be summoned next.

In the east end of town, however, there was frightened gossip. There was immediate speculation about Kennebrew's well-being. Some wondered aloud about rumors that he had been beaten while in jail—a holdover from the good ol' boy justice blacks had come to accept. There was frightened gossip. This was a grudge beating.

McQueen's murder certainly set the tone for the coming storm. It took the breath out of Jasperites. Imagine someone killing McQueen for drugs. No one could remember anyone having ever exchanged a cross word with McQueen. And then, exactly a week later, James Byrd's body was found on Huff Creek Road.

*   *   *

MIKE LOUT REPORTED the news from a small soundproof room in his house on a Jasper hilltop. Out the window he could see the rodeo grounds on one side and a Baptist church on the other. The events that qualified as news in Jasper were usually minor. A car stereo stolen, a man's trailer missing, growing speculation of a bowling alley moving into town. Covering small-town news well, Lout said, meant that his most important sources were the beautician, the barber, and the bartender. And he made sure he was on good terms with all of them.

Lout was, in the fullest sense of the word, a small-town newsman. In a single day he would attend chamber of commerce meetings, accidents, city council gatherings, and anything else that might be fashioned into a news item for KJAS. He was often up at night to cover house fires or car wrecks. He complained about long hours but never had a police scanner out of earshot. He loved his work, and, with all its warts, he loved Jasper, too.

Reporting on neighbors and friends may be one of the toughest journalism assignments. If Lout displeased someone with his stories, there was no avoiding them. He would run into them at the Wal-Mart or on Courthouse Square. And anyone with a complaint had little trouble finding Lout. He was a fixture in town, who had as many supporters as he had detractors. Newcomers counted on Lout to let them know what was going on. Old-timers said he was just trying to stir up trouble.

Lout was a born-and-bred Jasper boy. At fifteen, he had landed his first radio job at Jasper's own KTXJ. He cut the grass, burned Teletype, and did whatever needed to be done around the station. He graduated from Jasper High School in 1974. Technical jobs in Orange and Beaumont over the next decade helped teach him how a radio station actually worked and inspired him to start his own operation with three friends in 1987. They called it KJAS. The business plan had included hiring a newsman, but money was short, applicants were few, and Lout filled in, only to discover he loved it. "Mike steps on toes; he's like that," local journalist Mike Journee said.

Two years after it started, the radio station went off the air after Lout got in a dispute with his partners and pulled the plug. "I climbed up the tower and took back the antenna," he said. "The station ceased to operate." Lout returned to jobs in public relations in Beaumont and Port Arthur and in the meantime bought everything he needed to resurrect the station on his own. A transmitter came from Charlotte, North Carolina. Everything he pulled together was either used or broken. He secured an FCC permit in 1996 and returned KJAS to the air that November, opening with the national anthem.

Most Jasperites awakened to Mike Lout's cheery good mornings. He was the main source of their local news, and his reports came over the airwaves like clockwork. He sat every day behind a desk in his house, scanning the newspapers, recording the day's weather, and rewriting news stories on a typewriter. Every Monday at 8 A.M., he read Jasper's weekend crime report, a compilation of the petty crimes and fires that make news in small places: "There were a couple of bedspreads missing from the Holiday Inn on 96; the police think they have some leads. . . . There was a UFO sighting last night, and this might have gone down as just another story had two law enforcement officers not seen it for themselves. . . ." Lout always finished the weekend crime report the same way: "And the good guys are winning." With those words, nearly everyone in Jasper knew it was 8:05, time to snap off their radios and tackle the day.

In 1998, the biggest news story Lout had ever had landed in his lap. Before the Byrd murder, Jasper had been a town where journalists asked themselves whether it was really their place to report the news because stories in small towns caused big stirs. After the murder those questions stopped.

"The Byrd deal did a lot of things to Jasper, and not many of them were good," said Lout. "But in terms of media, and the way we covered news in this town, Byrd's murder completely changed things. It was the difference between daylight and dark. All of a sudden, we weren't holding anything back."

CHAPTER TWO

JASPER, TEXAS

JASPER WAS ABOUT as deep as Deep East Texas could get, seventy miles closer to Natchez, Mississippi, than to the capital city of Austin. Sitting at the easternmost edge of the state, at the top of the long skinny county that shared its name, the town of 8,600 was more Dixie than Lone Star. It sat just under an hour's drive from Vidor, Texas, the capital of Klan country, where until the early 1990s one could still see signs warning "Niggers Get Out of Town After Dark." At one time a modestly prosperous timber town, Jasper had been reduced to a curious thing, a place near noplace. By the end of the twentieth century, its poverty showed like the wrists and ankles of adolescents exceeding their cuffs. The entire community, from the Aarant family to the Zunigas, filled just 79 pages of large type in the Southwestern Bell phone book. The yellow pages, in the same thin volume, added only 129 pages more. Each year the directory seemed to get slimmer, proof positive of what everyone already knew: Jasper was a town in decline.

Downtown, such as it was, was announced by a small congregation of buildings split right up the middle by a slash of U.S. Highway 96. The four lanes of blacktop, 150 miles northeast of Houston, pulled visitors past shells of empty drugstores and family-owned storefronts that once sold everything from gingham to plow points but where more recently one could roll a marble from one end of the building to the other and touch nothing at all. The surviving businesses bore names Yankees found quaint: the Bent Can Discount Grocery, the Guess What Gift Shop, Bobby's BoKay florist, and Texas Charlie's Bar-B-Que ("All you care to eat Pork Ribs $4.99"). The signs were an attempt to make amends for what was otherwise a visual display of constant disappointment. Stores were boarded up. Buildings were perpetually for lease. Residents shuffled up the side of the highway with downcast eyes. By the 1990s, Jasper had become a place where most people stopped just long enough to lick a postage stamp.

Once clear of downtown, past the handful of ranches passed from one old-family generation to the next and the all-white Sam Rayburn Country Club, one could see through the clear-cut patches of virgin forests to gentle undulating land. This wasn't the Texas of the movies, the Lone Star State of cattle herds, cowboys, and rodeos, of sun-swept towns, tumbleweeds, and dust bowls. This was the Texas of the longleaf-pine belt—a place time had forgotten. In 1998, one could still buy a lollipop for a penny and a can of soda from a vending machine for a quarter. Loggers still talked about felling the largest-ever section of pine log in Texas back in 1927 at Blox Front. It took fourteen mules to haul it out of the woods, they said, pointing to the fuzzy black-and-white picture hanging on the wall of the three-room Jasper Public Library. The four shelves marked "Jasper History" were filled with picture books from the 1920s, when times in Jasper were good, lumber was plentiful, and there was enough prosperity to go around.

According to local legend, Thomas Lewis Latane Temple stepped off the train in neighboring Angelina County, suitcase in hand, in the summer of 1893, ready to turn the piney woods into a business. Temple, a native Virginian, had studied the lumber business in Texarkana and, at the age of thirty-four, had his heart set on building a timber empire. He bought 7,000 acres from J. C. Diboll, a large landowner in the area, and built his first sawmill. The small manually operated circular mill cut its first slab off a log at the end of 1894. From that modest beginning the Temple family built Temple-Inland, one of the largest manufacturers of lumber in the United States. Temple-Inland came to own half the timber in the county, and over time Jasper's fortunes became inextricably linked with the mill and the timber industry. It swallowed nameless toilers into its depths at daybreak and then gave them up, at sundown, with the weary, shoulder-bent gait of a hard day. The bone-crunching work amid the trees broke men, twisting their shoulders, rupturing their guts, and softening their spines.

The men disappeared into the pines with chain saws that made their teeth chatter. It was hot, dirty work requiring strength enough to heave great logs over the eight-foot sides of dump trucks or onto rubber skids that moved so quickly they swallowed fingers with startling regularity. The men would return home at dusk with their arms coated with sap and their hair tangled around chips of bark.

Generations of Jasper's men worked in logging camps that bore the names of the town's oldest families—Kurth, Gilmer, Seale, Martindale—people who had come to town with skillets strapped to their oxen one hundred years earlier with the idea that they could head west to make fortunes largely predicated on simply having arrived there first to claim the woods as their own. Those people who weren't the Direct Descendants accepted destiny as requiring them always to work for someone else. And they found it reassuring that they cut trees on land owned by citizens they actually had a chance of bumping into at the grocery store or waving to on the street.

In the very early days, families' lives revolved naturally around the sawmill. Lumbermen lived mostly without hard currency, buying staples with credit vouchers at places like the Kirby Company Store. Wives knew precisely where their husbands were, which tract of land they were clearing, and the men with whom they worked. The women could, in their mind's eye, place their husbands in the trees and imagine their trucks parked on a particular stretch of road, sure that if something awful happened (dead wood falling unexpectedly from treetops, a cut in the tree read wrong), the Jasper bosses for whom they worked would find a way to put it right. After all, the bosses lived in Jasper and were expected to care for the community.

Those simple assumptions still dominated life in Jasper in the 1990s. There weren't video arcades or discos or nightclubs to disturb the rhythms of country life. Instead, a night on the town consisted of families going downtown to the Swan Hotel on Main Street and splurging on a piece of Karo pecan pie or grabbing a couple of cold ones from the Coca-Cola warehouse on Milam Street and sitting on the stairs outside the courthouse to watch the foot traffic go by. Men might slip off later to join one of their private drinking circles to play cards or dominoes in the back of P. E. Lindsey's general store or on wobbly card tables weighed down by bottles at the Veterans of Foreign Wars building on Highway 59. By and large, such a simple, predictable existence suited almost everyone just fine.

Glacial progress in the timber industry complemented the slow pace. Most of the work, until the mid-1980s, was done by hand and with brute force. While both white and black men hewed railroad ties and cut pulpwood, it was the black lumbermen who hoisted, stacked, and manually loaded the wood. The black workers knew they were chosen for the task because stacking ties was dangerous work. Fingers and hands were often caught between the logs, crushed or ripped clean off, and presumably black fingers were more expendable than white ones. Just as one could tell the age of a tree by counting its rings, one could make a good guess when a lumberman had begun his career by looking at his hands. Most who worked in the mills before 1985 had some nubs in lieu of digits. After 1985, automation transformed the industry, saved fingers and hands, and lowered skyrocketing worker compensation costs.

Timber work was, by nature, a dangerous business. Twenty years ago most of the fatalities came in the mom-and-pop mills, small operations in which people logged the hundreds of acres that had been in their families for generations, employing brothers and sons and cousins. Those were the days when men took their boys into the woods to teach them how to read a cut on a tree to make sure it would fall right and when chain saws, used skillfully, could drop a fifty-foot yellow pine in ten minutes. The modern automatic cutters—big tractorlike contraptions that grabbed the tree around the trunk with great mechanical arms—could do the same work in thirty seconds. The steel arms hugged the tree as a saw sliced through the trunk like a hot blade through butter. As the cutters dropped the trees on the ground, the branches snapped like popcorn and fell with such force the earth seemed to lose its breath. The efficiency of the high-tech cutters drove small mills, which couldn't afford them, into bankruptcy. By the mid-1980s, Temple-Inland and its rival, Louisiana-Pacific, owned most of the timberland around

Jasper, and small mill owners either sold their holdings or slowly went bankrupt. The big companies found ways to use everything off the logs: boards off the sides; ties out of the center; barks and edges for the chipper, to make paper. The only timberland that stayed in local hands was held by families that didn't need the money from the big mills and could stand their ground against offers other Jasperites simply couldn't refuse. As a result, the established families had an aura of sorts. They seemed untouchable.

Jasper's discontent could be traced back to the late 1980s, when the fall in lumber prices and the escalating cost of workers' compensation in the timber industry became a lethal combination. Some companies were unable to pay both their workers and the insurance premiums. So they sold out to bigger mills that enjoyed economies of scale.

When Louisiana-Pacific closed the city's plywood plant in 1992, it was a body blow. Four years later, they shuttered a stud factory, putting hundreds more on the dole. Workers lost health insurance. Customers evaporated. Stores liquidated their stocks and closed. With each passing year, the closest jobs, if they were there at all, got farther and farther away.

In 1993 salvation seemed to appear briefly, in the form of oil people. The companies descended on the town like gypsies promising its residents untold riches. Jasperites saw their town growing into another Giddings, a hamlet in Central Texas that boomed in 1986 as a result of wells that tapped the prolific Austin Chalk pools of oil. People in Jasper imagined a steady pounding of pumps, the rattle and clank of drilling rigs, the incessant grinding of heavy truck gears. Early estimates said Jasper would grow from a town of 8,000 to a bustling metropolis of 25,000 in just five years.

In 1995, the combination of falling oil prices and the high cost of production ended such delusions of grandeur. It didn't take long to find out there wasn't enough oil in Jasper to fill a sinkhole, and the oil companies fled. They left in their wake broken wells, half-built shopping centers, and the uncomfortable feeling that great expectations would never be realized in a place like this. Folks watched helplessly as chain stores liquidated their stocks, shut off the lights, and disappeared back down Highway 96 from where they came.

Older Jasperites blamed the disappointment on the entire town's readiness to abandon timber for a newfangled industry. Timber had been the mainstay in Jasper for more than one hundred years, and that, they said, wasn't about to change. Making the best of a bad situation, Jasperites focused their attention on the new innovations the big lumber companies imported.

The latest great hope came in 1997 in the form of oriented strand board, or OSB, a type of particleboard. The lumber companies said it would be the wave of the future and would bring, eventually, more jobs to town. But to start with, the highly automated OSB plants required fewer people. There were layoffs, one hundred, two hundred at a time. OSB, locally known as SOB plants as the layoffs continued to climb, needed one third of the workers traditional mills required. To reduce logs to the consistency of cornflakes only a handful of men were required. They used hooked metal poles to pull the logs into the blades. The rest of the process required only a couple of computer experts in air-conditioned booths monitoring the board's baking temperatures.

It was just another in a long string of disappointments. Residents came to the conclusion that life was full of mischance and they might as well give up trying to change their lot. Eventually, Jasper settled on an old idea of itself, and visitors could see precisely what that idea was by simply looking around. Standing on the corner of Milam and Austin Streets, one was transported to another time in which everything—women, children, blacks—had a distinct place and, it seemed, would hold that same position for just about forever.

Segregation was of the unspoken variety. Over the years, blacks in Jasper drifted together, living on the edge of the woods, where the only whites they ever saw were mean-spirited boys in pickup trucks driving the back roads so the sheriff wouldn't catch them drunk. Whites drifted to other parts of town, clumped together in patches. Eventually, the racial makeup in Jasper became roughly fifty-fifty, black and white, with a demographic profile that defied news stories about America's unprecedented prosperity. In the late 1990s, the average family of four in Jasper had an income of $20,000, slightly more than half the national average. Jasperites hoped for reinvention when companies like Visador, which made steel doors, and the Tyson Chicken plant, where women boasted of gutting a chicken in twenty seconds flat, came to town. But getting something off the ground just seemed harder here. In 1998, the overall unemployment rate was 15 percent, nearly three times the national average.

The difficulties in the timber industry and the joblessness meant that in many front yards one saw broken men sitting limply on fold-out chairs, and entertainment was watching eighteen-wheelers rumble through town and disappear into the yellow woods. The men would still be at their fold-out-chair stations at dusk, watching the trucks re-emerge from the forest, grinding through their gears and leaving in their wake the sweet-and-sour perfume of sap and diesel.

*   *   *

DEEP EAST TEXAS had always been insular, and the attitude was rooted in history. When the Louisiana Purchase failed to clearly designate the new western boundary of the United States in 1803, the United States and Spain agreed the swath of land along the Sabine River—the current Texas-Louisiana state line—would be neutral ground. Until the official boundary could be determined, both countries agreed not to enforce their laws there. The area became a no-man's-land, a safe haven for murderers, rapists, thieves, and fugitives from authority. Most Texans said East Texas wasn't really Texas. Residents behind "the pine curtain" had failed to come out of the woods during the great westward movement. They were, people in Houston said, different.

Nearly two hundred years later, not much had changed—partly becaues Jasperites were so concerned with just getting by. Events that occured in Houston, Birmingham, and New York occurred in a world far removed from the piney woods and double-wide trailers of Jasper. The town's residents watched the civil rights marches in Birmingham on their television sets and drew away from the violence, hoping that the black nationalist storm would somehow blow itself out before it reached the edge of their woods. And when the time came, and the law required the whites to allow the blacks to come in the front door, Jasper did just that.

In 1954, *Brown v. the Board of Education* fell on Jasper like a fist. After three centuries of black oppression, the Supreme Court of the United States had decided, on May 17, 1954, that African-Americans were entitled to everything whites already had. Blacks had to be treated as equals everywhere, beginning in the public schools. Overnight, segregation in the schools was decreed unconstitutional and against the law.

In the white South there was gloom and in Jasper there was disbelief.

It took fourteen years to integrate. There was some wiggle room in the Court's decision, and Jasper's white community didn't want to rush things because, frankly, they were worried about whether everyone would get along just because the Supreme Court said they must.

"Negroes" was the word whites used in polite company then; "black" was the word they used in public in the 1990s. Behind closed doors, however, "nigger" was part of the vernacular, used both as a noun and an adjective. As a noun, to describe an individual in the black community, it usually had an adjective added to it: "good nigger," "fucking nigger," or "poor nigger." As a descriptive word in its own right, it was more benign: people could "nigger-rig" a fence (a type of jerry-rigging) or pick "nigger navel" flowers (a variety of African daisy with a black button center). By the late 1990s, the word wasn't used cavalierly when the races were mixing, but when whites were together, and alone, the word came out naturally, without raising any eyebrows at all.

By the late 1990s, racial relations were complicated in Jasper, just as they were throughout the Deep South. In these sparse rural areas the races had interacted—professionally, not socially—closely for generations. Dating back to slavery, blacks and whites were able to trace the intersection of their families in a way northerners couldn't even begin to understand. Blacks in Jasper still introduced themselves by exchanging the names of the antebellum white families that "brought their people over," while whites interacted with blacks whose ancestors had once been owned by their great-granddaddies. That history bubbled below the surface and created an awkwardness that couldn't help but strain relations.

Racial epithets aside, in the years leading up to the Byrd murder white Jasper liked to think of itself as warm and tolerant and enlightened about race. The fact that whites seldom mixed with blacks and called them "niggers" behind closed doors seemed beside the point. To say race relations in this town were worse than in any other rural community would be merely looking for trouble where there was none, they added. "We all get along just fine" was the refrain. They were convinced prejudice was buried in the ancient unmarked graves of their forefathers up by Sam Rayburn Reservoir or beneath the crowded headstones in Jasper City's cemetery.

In fact, Jasper City's cemetery may have been the best counterexample. The headstones in the front of the yard had one thing in common: they all marked white graves. The largest was the eighty-square-foot expanse of pink granite that Joe Tonahill, the town patriarch, had erected in memory of his wife, Violett (which residents said would have had the ever so practical Violett spinning in her grave because of its garishness). Hewn from the same pink granite that adorned the capitol in Houston and the criminal courts building in Dallas where Tonahill had defended Lee Harvey Oswald's killer Jack Ruby, the headstone rose from the ground in a great eruption of rock virtually shouting in twelve-inch letters, TONAHILL. The black graves, marked with colorless stones and plastic flowers, were behind a fence in the back of the cemetery—segregated for eternity.

*   *   *

WILMA DOUGHERTY, A pint-size eighty-year-old white woman, embodied the Jasper everyone knew. She had lived in a little house behind the old Jasper High School for nearly seventy years and watched the school's desegregation from her back porch. Her husband of fifty years, A. P., kept the books for the Louisiana-Pacific mill.

Wilma, like many people in Jasper, had a secret fascination for the Byrd murder. It was like a gruesome accident one could not help looking at. So when her niece offered to drive her up to the crime scene on Huff Creek Road, Wilma could hardly wait. The whole "Byrd deal," as it was known in town, reminded Wilma of the days of the Black Cat Society in the 1920s. That's when white boys in Jasper donned hoods and drove by young "niggers" walking by the side of the road and hit them with baseball bats. "It wasn't to kill them or anything; it was just for fun, I guess," said Wilma. "It was like that then. You don't hear about that kind of thing now. I'm sure it happens, but you don't hear about it."

"Nigger knocking" was the first thought that occurred to most whites in Jasper when news of the murder on Huff Creek Road filtered down from the woods—some white boys took a black man for a ride and meant only to leave him cut and broken on the side of the road and then things had mistakenly got out of hand. They had too much to drink and had taken a bigoted southern tradition too far, they told themselves. They never dreamed, in the summer of 1998, that the killing of a black man would threaten, like nothing since the *Brown* decision, their quiet southern way of life.

But in the quiet, paneled rooms of Jasper's elite, the offices of Joe Tonahill and Henderson Real Estate, James Byrd's dragging murder was immediately seen as trouble. They saw the consequences of this act immediately. As a general rule, murders in Jasper were motivated by a lethal combination of alcohol, lost love, and betrayal. This killing had all the hallmarks of something else, something darker and more sinister. It was too big to have the white community simply close the door on the subject. "All this happened in Jasper," one prominent Jasperite said with simple brutality, "because some no 'count white boy killed a no 'count nigger."

*   *   *

ANYONE LOOKING FOR Sheriff Billy Rowles in the morning was likely to find him eating a breakfast of biscuits and gravy at the Ramada Inn on Highway 190. Rowles went there knowing he would run into a handful of his men as well as some local police officers and, inevitably, KJAS radio station owner Mike Lout. The informal breakfasts allowed Rowles to catch up on everything that had happened since he left the office the night before. It gave Lout fodder for his crime report. And it provided Jasper's law enforcement an opportunity to talk politics and local gossip and to laugh a little before the day's events picked up in earnest.

There was an odd overlap in law enforcement in Jasper City. The police department, led by Chief Harlon Alexander, was responsible for anything that happened in the town proper. Billy Rowles's sheriff's office enforced the law in the many unincorporated towns of Jasper County. Essentially, anything that happened outside the town limits, like the James Byrd murder, was the sheriff's purview. The awkward arrangement—the difference of a mile could put a crime in one jurisdiction or another—made for good-natured competition between the departments. Rowles tried to make sure that a police officer or two joined the Ramada breakfasts to keep the rivalry friendly.

Deputy James Carter was always at the morning breakfasts. In 1998, he was Jasper's only black street deputy. Carter was a hero in his community and an irritant to some of the older whites, who still found it hard to deal with the fact that a black man could arrest them. It wasn't easy for Carter either. He had put in his time and done a good job but was still viewed by most Jasperites as colored first and a deputy second. Billy Rowles found himself doing little things to make it clear he did not see Carter that way. He tried to include Carter in everything he did. In fact, Carter was in many ways the perfect deputy—levelheaded, smart, and always quietly assessing the moment. Carter, for his part, genuinely liked and trusted Billy Rowles. That was no mean feat given the checkered history of Jasper sheriffs with blacks. Carter was comfortable enough in his relationship with his boss that he had taken to razzing him, teasing him in a respectful but affectionate way.

"They found some sort of inflatable sex doll in the park," Deputy Carter told Rowles as he walked into the Ramada for breakfast one morning.

"It is over at the police station now, under the Captain's desk," Mike Lout piped up, stoking the good-natured competition that flourished between the police department and the sheriff's office.

Rowles guffawed and wondered aloud about how he could get that in his weekly crime report for the *Jasper Newsboy*. "Was the doll anatomically correct?" he asked.

Carter nodded and smiled.

"Was it wearing any identifiable clothing?" he said.

Carter laughed. "No, Sheriff, no real clothing to speak of."

Rowles continued. "Did it look like it had been abused?"

The table erupted in laughter.

"Plenty abused," Carter replied.

"Did we find an owner for the said doll?" Rowles asked.

"No, but I have some ideas," Carter said, sending the assembled crew into boisterous laughter.

Billy Rowles liked mornings like that. Early breakfasts in which the men could assemble and find some humor in their work. It did not all have to be warrants and arrests and drug busts. When the men let him, Rowles picked up the tab for the meal in hopes that they would keep showing up and keep starting their mornings with a good perspective rather than a bad one. It said a lot about Billy Rowles that he found this important. "Billy's like his daddy," said his aunt Do Bagesse, a former army truck driver and one of the Rowles family matriarchs. "If he had two chickens, he'd invite half of Buna over to share them. He loves being around people."

Rowles was six feet tall and weighed 180 pounds. While he was not heavily muscled, there was a lot of strength to him. The bounce and quickness of the high school athlete was still visible. He was a neat, attractive package of a man past fifty, with a sad-faced countenance reminiscent of the actor Tommy Lee Jones. Rowles dressed the part of a good sheriff. He wore a big white hat and was partial to leather vests and Wrangler khaki slacks. He was exacting, too. He pinned his shiny sheriff's star with precision over his heart. For a sheriff, he was gentler and quieter than folks expected. When he took off his oversized cowboy hat and laid it on the desk beside him, he looked more corporate executive than Texas lawman.

There was a lot about Sheriff Rowles that people in Jasper didn't know. Most could trace his job history back several years, to when he was a highway patrolman, and from that there was only one story: Rowles had shot and killed a man who had lunged for his gun after a routine traffic stop. What many people did not know was that Billy Earnest Rowles was a born-again Christian. He didn't wear his religion on his sleeve, but his office was dotted with framed passages from the Bible that provided him with solace.

"You know, you'd look at Billy and think he liked Westerns and shoot-'em-up movies," said Jamie, Rowles's wife of more than thirty years. "The truth is he's really romantic. His favorite movie is *When Harry Met Sally*."

All uniforms make the people in them seem easily understood, and no one knew this more than Billy Rowles. In an attempt to go against type, he made it a point to drive slowly along the dusty dirt roads and dead ends of the woods, with his truck window rolled down and his elbow stuck out, talking to anyone he might meet along the way. Police work had made Jasper transparent to him. State detectives would call him occasionally to ask for information about Jasper residents, and Rowles could rattle off, without a moment's hesitation, where they spent their time, what kind of car they drove, and who they were dating. Being sheriff was about a lot more than just arresting people. Sheriffing required the patience of a pastor, and Billy Rowles had developed just that.

"Are you sure she was actually kidnapped and doesn't want to be there?" Billy Rowles said into the phone one morning. A mother had called asking the sheriff's office to retrieve her daughter from her boyfriend's car.

"Well, ma'am, we could pull the car over on suspicion of kidnapping and get her off by herself and ask her if she wants to be there. But she's of age. She can make this decision on her own, and if she wants to be there, there's nothing we can do about that."

There was more talk on the other end of the line.

"We'll be happy to do that, if you would like. And if you were asking my advice, that's what I would do if I was you. Yes. Right. Well, if you can give us a description of the car and maybe a license plate number, we'll be happy to do that. Yes, ma'am. Absolutely."

Rowles got a similar call one afternoon from Kylie Greeney's mother. She had found some disturbing photos of her daughter about a month before the murder. She asked Rowles if he would come by and talk with her about them. Sitting in her small living room, she showed Rowles and James Carter some sexually explicit photos of her young daughter with an ex-con named Bill King and several other kids taken inside the Twin Cinemas, obviously after hours. "When these photos were taken my daughter was underage." Mrs. Greeney began, obviously shocked by the graphic nature of the photos. "And I know this guy is a racist," she added, pointing to the fuzzy images of Bill King. "And my daughter doesn't."

Rowles was a little shocked. He didn't really know any of the people in the Polaroids except Shawn Berry, a twenty-three-year-old manager at the theater. Mrs. Greeney was obviously upset. Rowles said there wasn't much he could do. Kylie was seventeen now, even if the photos had been taken when she was only sixteen. Rowles knew very little about John William "Bill" King aside from the fact that he was an ex-con who had returned to Jasper from prison about six months before. So far he had kept his nose clean, and Rowles hadn't had an occasion to run into him. He did make a mental note, however.

"Her mama was having lots of trouble with Kylie," said Rowles later. "In fact, Kylie was moving out when we walked in. They had been feuding, apparently, and they were feuding about Bill King. Mrs. Greeney didn't want her daughter around someone like that," she said. It all happened less than a month before the Byrd murder.

When he cruised around town in his oversized truck, voices called to Billy Rowles: friends, acquaintances, sometimes people who were looking for trouble but thought they could throw Rowles off the track by starting a conversation and acting casual, as if they had nothing to hide. Crack dealers and pushers and users on Pollard Avenue, near the housing projects, would walk up to the cab and chat, to prove by their nonchalance that they weren't up to anything. And for those few moments, while they good-naturedly teased the sheriff, they felt like regular citizens, Rowles said. He did not believe their stories about keeping clean or standing on the corner just to enjoy the evening. But he knew they wanted him to pretend that he did. It made them feel good, and Billy Rowles understood that. And to everyone, as he gently touched the accelerator, the sheriff said the same thing: "Stay out of trouble, you hear?"

Rowles's easygoing nature belied his history. A lesser man would have more likely emerged from Rowles's childhood as an inmate at Jasper County Jail instead of running the place. Born in Beaumont, Texas, right outside Jasper City, Rowles had a tough time growing up. His parents separated when he was in the seventh grade, and the young Rowles opted to live with his father, an unusual occurrence in the 1950s when mothers were awarded custody as a matter of course. Rowles went with his father out West as his father landed contracts to lay floors at military installations across the country. He spent summers in Colorado Springs, a year in Brigham City, Utah, and started high school in Glasgow, Montana, where he was all set to be quarterback of the football team and "be the man," he said. Then his father got another job somewhere else and took his son with him.

All the moving meant Billy Rowles made friends where he could find them. He joined sports teams. Played basketball. Worked at football. And the younger Rowles learned to take his direction not only from his father but from a host of coaches and male role models who demanded the best from him. Those mentors helped Rowles to grow up responsibly despite his father's single parenthood. Certainly, Billy Rowles took part in small crimes and misdemeanors, as most young boys do, but at the same time he was usually singled out by the adults around him as a leader and a boy who could be trusted. So much so that when the young Rowles begged his father not to make him leave San Antonio High School his junior year, a short time after his parents formally divorced, his father set him up in an apartment and came back to San Antonio to visit him only on weekends.

Because Rowles spent most of his school years farther west, the race battles raging in the South during the 1950s and 1960s were something that happened in a world very distant from his own. The N-word was never used in the Rowles household, and by the time the younger Rowles was back in Texas for his sophomore year in high school, he had been mixing quite easily with whites and blacks. Rowles had also, by that time, found his girl. "There was a little blond girl sitting on the steps of the school when I walked up the first day," Rowles said. "I asked her where the principal's office was, and she showed me. She was fourteen, I was sixteen, and I knew we would be married."

A newspaper clipping from Rowles's senior year hinted at how directed and sure of himself the young man had become. Under a photo of Rowles in a basketball jersey, he had laid out his ambitions: he would marry, do two tours in Vietnam as a marine, and then become a highway patrolman. He married the little girl on the steps in 1966, two years after he joined the Marine Corps and shipped out on the USS *Bennington* to Vietnam. They moved to Camp Lejeune, South Carolina, in July 1967. Rowles became part of the First Battalion, Second Division of the Marine Corps and went to the Mediterranean to fight in the seven-day war. He ran helicopter rescue missions. His third tour he was part of a grunt infantry squad thirty miles outside of Da Nang. "I saw ugly stuff on the third tour. It was just like that horrible stuff you see in movies," he said.

Rowles wasn't back from Vietnam more than a month when he applied to the Texas Highway Patrol Academy. A veteran with a purple heart, he had little trouble getting in. He graduated from the academy in December 1968 and became part of Texas governor Preston Smith's protection squad. Two years later he became a highway trooper. He remained a trooper for twenty-seven years and would still be one, he said, if Aubrey Cole, who had been sheriff in Jasper for as long as anyone could remember, hadn't surprised everyone and decided to retire in 1992. Eight candidates, including Billy Rowles, ran for the vacant seat. Roscoe Davis, a former Texas Ranger, won in a runoff. Rowles was devastated. The man who beat him, however, was no slouch.

Roscoe Davis had been an officer for the Texas Department of Public Safety for twenty-five years. He was a decorated patrolman and then for more than a decade was a member of the legendary Texas Rangers, the Department of Public Safety's elite criminal investigative unit. Davis had been the state's chief investigator in the Loyal Garner case in the Sabine County town of Hemphill, forty miles north of Jasper. It was a case that was infamous in East Texas as proof that there had always been two kinds of justice in the Big Thicket—white and black.

On Christmas Day 1987, Loyal Garner, a black man, drove down the wrong road in East Texas and was pulled over by a white police chief. He was taken to jail and, after demanding to make a phone call, was beaten unconscious by police officers.

When they found him barely alive the next morning in his cell, Garner was hospitalized and died. Although witnesses swore to the beating that caused his death, the policemen were quickly acquitted by a hometown jury. Roscoe Davis had early on suspected a cover-up. Ironically, the case that made him so famous had landed on his desk only by chance. Davis usually covered Jasper, Tyler, and Newton Counties, south of Hemphill. Ranger Don Morris, based in Lufkin, would normally have been responsible for Sabine County. Morris was out of town on a hunting trip and Davis took the case to back him up. While he claimed to hate politics, Davis knew the outcome of this case was good for his campaign for sheriff. It helped him beat Rowles in the run-off.

Looking back on it, Rowles said his defeat was the best outcome: "I wasn't ready to be sheriff."

In 1996, though, Billy Rowles had matured and become more politically astute. With four years of quiet campaigning under his belt, he ran against Davis on a platform of harmony—not only among Jasper's black and white communities but among its law enforcement officers as well. Murders had been left unsolved as police officials and sheriff's officers elbowed each other out of the way trying to get credit and take charge of various investigations. There were only five officers on the Jasper force, but they took umbrage when folks from the sheriff's department offered to lend a hand. What's more, Jasper citizens said they were tired of a sheriff who tried to limit his hours at the office. Jasperites were searching for a more paternal figure. That was what Billy Rowles offered.

Billy Rowles, who campaigned door-to-door on horseback, sought to end the divisiveness, and his platform was compelling to voters. He won the 1996 election by a landslide.

Being a reasonably new sheriff made Rowles particularly careful in the way he handled the Byrd investigation. He hadn't been in office long, yet he found himself swamped with a stack of unsolved cases that critics of the sheriff's office said were the result of mediocre crime work. Billy Rowles, like Jasper itself, was struggling just to stay in the present. As he worked to sort out old cases, he had to make time for the intangible duties of his job: walking the neighborhoods, listening to the complaints of discrimination, and determining which were simple grousing and which demanded his immediate attention.

Eventually, Billy Rowles put himself on twenty-four-hour call. He listed his phone number and made sheriffing more than a full-time occupation. His wife, Jamie, who was a jailer in the nearby town of Orange, said she understood. "Being sheriff isn't something you can leave at the office," she said. Rowles's aunt Do was more blunt. She said she wasn't going to vote for Rowles if he ran again. "I'm tired of having to share him with everyone else," she said.

"Billy Rowles was trying something new" when he was elected in 1996, said Jasper district attorney Guy James Gray. "After years of folks talking about unsolved murders and the police being at odds with the sheriff's office, he decided to make everyone try to work together. He hired a black deputy, and he tried to get out in the black community more. People were suspicious at first, but Billy sensed from the beginning that was important, so he did it."

"People are always underestimating Billy because he's got this aw-shucks way about him," said one former state trooper. "Some people think he's some typical Texas sheriff who's a little slow. He was really aware of those kinds of impressions when all these murders happened. Everybody would be watching. He didn't want people to think that Jasper was some hick town with some Boss Hog sheriff with a pot belly who was going to cover all this up and sweep it under the rug."

Billy Rowles was fighting history. For a long time East Texas criminal justice was ruled by white cops, white grand juries, white jurors, and white judges. At best, the system tolerated black defendants, if they made it past the white cops who often administered their own justice at the side of the road or in a jail cell. The Loyal Garner case only fed those suspicions. That was why the black community viewed Rowles with circumspection. Law enforcement in Jasper had a long-standing reputation for prejudice. Black residents complained that they were detained for imaginary driving violations more often than whites. They accused law enforcement officers of arresting only the lower-level black drug dealers while permitting the white kingpins to go free. Most of all, they vividly recalled the days in which police chief Alton Wright would stop blacks in their cars just to beat them up. Many of his victims were handcuffed when they were beaten.

"We knew about it when we were kids," said Jasper district attorney Gray. "And we thought of Alton Wright as a bit of a coward. I wouldn't say we were sticking up for blacks; it was more the idea of anyone beating on another who was handcuffed."

It was a different time then, said Linda Wright Powell, his daughter. "He was a hard man but he was a good man. He tried to be as fair as they would let him be."

Vander Carter, a strong, handsome, fifty-seven-year-old black machinist at Tom Hart Lumber Company, was a frequent target. "I remember the last time he pulled me over. I was so tired of his picking on me I got out of my car and said, 'Chief, reach for your gun because I'm fixin' to fight back this time. You can't do this to me no more.' He was shocked. I've always been a mean cat and I'm a big man, and he decided once I refused to take it, I wasn't worth hassling no more. So it stopped. Sometimes you just have to stand up for yourself. Problem here is that folks don't do that until they are plumb fed up."

Against that backdrop, Billy Rowles became the embodiment of all that was right and wrong in law enforcement that had gone on before him. There were stories and revisions and revisions of revisions. Billy Rowles's difficult arrest of a robbery suspect in 1975 evolved into a tale of police brutality against a black man on the side of the road. Rowles was off-duty and driving through nearby Buna, Texas, when he noticed a group of men carrying guns out of a house. He made a quick U-turn, thinking he had caught them in the midst of a robbery, and watched as the men escaped into the woods. Rowles called for backup. Officers needed to look for three white men, one of whom was wearing a black watch cap and a camouflage jacket, he said. Additional officers arrived on the scene and were searching the suspects' car when Rowles spotted a man walking along the road in his direction.

"That's one of them," he told the assembly around him.

When Rowles informed the suspect he was under arrest, the problems started. "He took a swing at me, and I knocked him on the ground," said Rowles. The suspect turned out to be on parole for murder and had stolen guns from seven counties. Even so, he brought a civil rights suit against Rowles. The suit was eventually dismissed (lawyer Joe Tonahill handled the case for free), but it provided the threads of a story about Rowles beating a black man. Only problem was, the suspect was white.

Another incident, almost ten years later, made the rounds in Jasper's rumor mill.

In the autumn of 1984, Billy Rowles was a highway patrolman, and he was chasing what he believed to be a drunk driver. A car "nearly hit me head-on, and I tried to pull this drunk kid over," as Rowles recalled it. "My lights were on, and one way or another I found myself following him down a little-bitty dirt road at least a mile from any house. At the time I thought he was fixin' to hit the woods on me." Rowles climbed out of his cruiser, and before he knew it the kid had burst out of his car and had kicked Rowles's hat off his head. "He was one of those kung fu guys, you know, just kicked my hat right off." The boy wasn't planning to light off into the woods at all; instead he was after Rowles's gun. The story, as Rowles told it, was every patrolman's nightmare. The kid managed to get Rowles's gun out of its holster, and the two began to struggle. "We were on the ground rolling around, and he kept taking the butt of my gun and hitting me on the head. He hit me so hard once, I saw stars," Rowles said. "Then he started chewing on my throat like a mad dog, trying to get to my jugular vein."

Rowles began to lose consciousness and with one final push tried to overpower his assailant, struggling for his gun. "I just rolled left and pulled the trigger," said Rowles. The shot grazed Rowles's arm, went through his uniform shirt, and hit the suspect in the head. "He was sixteen, died in my arms, and the last thing he said to me was 'Call an ambulance.' "

"I met his mama a couple years later at a golf club where she was working," said Rowles, slowly. "She asked me if I was Billy Rowles, and I said I was, and then she started screaming at me, saying I murdered her boy. I didn't know what to say. The manager came out and apologized and said he'd fire her. I asked him not to do that; she'd been through enough already. The whole thing just made me feel like shit. It still does."

A grand jury investigated the shooting, and Rowles was cleared. The suspect was white. But the story in Jasper is that Rowles shot and killed a black man. "There's nothing I can do to fight those rumors but act properly and replace those stories with good new ones," said Rowles. "Truth is, I have never laid a hand on a black person as a law officer in my entire career."

CHAPTER THREE

"AIN'T NOTHING WE CAN DO"

AT DUSK, THE silhouettes of the pine trees rose above Jasper like enormous bars. The shadows, crisp as toast, moved along the trees just beyond view, making Jasperites jump. When the sun slipped below the tree line, it was as if a velvet curtain had fallen, muffling sounds and light. It was then that the bushes seemed to move silently, like great dark cats, and the wind rushed with a great swoop across the roof of the woods, echoing off the hollows. At the foot of the trees, the shotgun houses trembled, vulnerable and weightless in the desolate darkness. The silence was broken only by the sibilance of wind in the dry grass or the barking of distant dogs. Nighttime made the woods frightening and sinister, as the tyranny of superstition took over. One never knew where death might lurk, the black community said. The hooting of owls or yawing of night birds seemed to presage bad luck. The musky scent on summer nights? That was the smell of danger. When darkness fell, the woods were haunted, and it would be an insensitive person who did not know this.

The world always appears more menacing—without street-lights, sidewalks, or indoor plumbing—on the rim of modern society. As Jasper residents stumbled along the dark macadam state roads, they braced for any eventuality. Would it be a smite from God or the random beating from slim, mean white men who had hands like stumps? They worried about vast networks and secret brotherhoods lurking in the woods: men who would burst into their homes and send them running for their lives into the night.

James Byrd's murder, "the way he was done," only solidified their deepest suspicions. Days and even months after his death, black residents felt as if they were being watched. They wondered aloud whether it was safe to walk outside. Every night sound was magnified threefold; every scrape of feet on the gravel could have been a Klansman seeking revenge. Most disconcerting of all, the community elders asked themselves in whispers whether just two years before the dawn of a new century, they would be forced to refight the battles of the old one.

"A lot of people kept very quiet until James Byrd was murdered," said Elmo Jackson, a black man who had tended bar at the white country club for two generations. "The way James was killed, though, made it impossible not to say something. We heard about it after church, and I remember we were shocked. You think, this can't happen here, this can't happen in your town, and then it does. And then you get to thinking."

So the black community began to dwell on the nigger needling that went on in Jasper's white homes. They mulled opportunities lost. They counted how many black bank tellers worked behind the window at Jasper's banks (one); and how many blacks had opened a store on Courthouse Square (one); and how many of their own sat on the city council (two); and saw, as if for the first time, a great injustice. There was, of course, the black mayor, R. C. Horn, who beat three white candidates in 1997 for the job. But Jasper's black community saw him less as an ally than an empty gesture of appeasement. What had Horn ever done for the black community that whites hadn't tacitly approved first? The question drew blank stares and shrugs.

"He's powerless," said Unav Wade, the first black business owner on Courthouse Square. "It isn't his fault. It is just the way things work around here."

After James Byrd was killed, however, the harder questions came. The black community asked itself why it had been content to simply gather the crumbs that fell from the table. Was it really safer, they wondered, to cloak themselves in anonymity, to create a world apart from the whites and their bigotry? Or should they have faced it head-on?

*   *   *

DRIVING INTO THE wild beautiful landscape of Jasper, roaring past old cemeteries and tar paper shacks with children squatting helter-skelter in the yards, one could not help but wonder whether God had decided to make them pay for the loveliness all around by demanding everything else.

Nowhere was this more evident than in East Jasper. It was a part of town full of churches and ramshackle houses, with porches and doorways disintegrating in the Texas air. It was an unchanged, unchanging picture that could have been taken anytime in the last one hundred years. People in East Jasper practiced hard economics, searching a system with too few jobs for ways to make ends meet. By their thirties, most women became grandmothers; by their fifties, great-grandmothers. Two-parent families had become an endangered species. Teen pregnancy was the norm.

Charlene Adams was forty years old in 1998 but looked more like fifty. She woke every day with the sun to walk to a job in Jasper's white community. She left Independence Quarters in East Jasper early so that she could cook breakfasts of ham and eggs for people who expected her to be at work in the kitchen before they came downstairs in the morning. Her days were spent sweeping white employers' floors, tending their gardens, and caring for their children. She and East Jasper women like her returned home at dusk, picking their way slowly down the roads (which have monosyllabic names for easy reading and pronouncing). Charlene Adams worked for one family five days a week and found odd cleaning jobs to fill her weekends. She made three hundred dollars a month.

Charlene was one of the lucky ones. Most of the women in Jasper had trouble finding work. They made do on a fragile mix of assistance checks, homegrown vegetables, and hand-raised fowl. Most of the men in the community had long since given up. They spent their days drinking beer, nursing bitter discontent, and waiting for an act of God to change their circumstances. Televisions played nearly twenty-four hours a day in these trailers. When marijuana and cheap forms of cocaine entered the mix, they caused an explosion in meanness: bloody fistfights, shootings, misery. With times so hard, little things, like neighborliness, evaporated. Instead of favors there was a barter economy. Those with cars charged those without for rides to the store. Washing machines stood in the middle of dirt yards, where residents could wash their family's clothes—if they paid fifty cents a load.

"That's the way it has always been," said Charlene Adams, sitting on swaying wooden steps outside her trailer. "Things ain't never gonna change. We'll always be poor. The whites, they will always be rich. Ain't nothing we can do."

A car thundered by, towing a rising wake of gray dust that cloaked everything with a fine grit. Percussive hip-hop pounded from inside. Charlene shaded her eyes and waited for the cloud to settle. "Ain't nothing we can do."

*   *   *

AMID THE GENERAL poverty there were some black people who managed to make a decent living in Jasper. They were the self-motivated. Entrepreneurs like Unav Wade, who ran her own beauty salon, Unav's, on Courthouse Square, and the schoolteachers, nurses, and funeral home directors. They lived in sensible five-room, one-story affairs floating in large, ragged lots like small ships in an ocean. Photographs of Martin Luther King Jr. or Bobby or John F. Kennedy hung on the walls beside family portraits and high school diplomas. For Jasper's black community, this was about as good as it got.

Driving downtown, one couldn't help but notice that the people who owned and managed most of the city's businesses—the restaurants, motels, antique stores, groceries, and gas stations— were white. There were no black bank managers, car dealers, or salesmen. Black men only got the jobs white men didn't want, the saying went. As a result, they were the ones who rose at dawn to put creosote on telephone poles for Texas Electric (work so hot

Jasperites said just standing next to a pole in the Texas sun would blister your skin) or haul pulpwood out of the forests. They mopped floors at the schools, flipped catfish fillets at the restaurants, and collected the garbage—all for minimum wage.

Good jobs could be found at the hospital. The wages were good, members of the black community said, though they were quick to mention they had never been treated there. The reason was simple: Jasper Memorial Hospital was a small place with little beyond basic care. What's more, it was a private institution, and most of Jasper's black community were uninsured. The closest public hospital was in Galveston, hours away, so if they got hurt Jasper's blacks usually bandaged their wounds, got friends to take them to bus stops on the outskirts of town, and rode for hours for treatment.

Charlene Adams was diagnosed with breast cancer in 1997 and underwent a mastectomy and a year of chemotherapy—all at public expense. Once every two weeks she would get a friend to take her to catch the bus to Galveston and ride for hours along Highway 190 to receive her chemotherapy. She didn't understand why the medicine the doctors were giving her was making her so sick—they didn't explain it. Most of all, she didn't understand that if something went very wrong, the emergency room at Jasper Hospital was open to her—even though she was black and poor. So when her two-year-old granddaughter drank a can of lighter fluid, Charlene hesitated. She had trouble rounding up a neighbor to drive her to a doctor. When they finally did take the little girl to Jasper Memorial, there was little doctors could do. They medevac-ed the child to Galveston. "They had to take her to the black hospital," Charlene Adams said. The child was on life support for five days before she died. One of Charlene's employers bought a marker for the grave.

The buying of the marker harked back to antebellum traditions, a strange mixture of whites feeling superior and at the same time protective of black residents. Even in the twenty-first century rich town ladies still descended uninvited on the rickety doorsteps of their maids and housekeepers with a "pounding"—a pound of flour, a pound of sugar, a pound of butter, and a pound of beans—handing the food across the threshold and scarcely daring to breathe the odors inside.

Pounding invasions aside, Jasper's black and white communities kept to themselves as much out of habit as out of misplaced southern courtesy. "We were raised to stay among ourselves," said Elmo Jackson from his cinder-block house behind the county jail. "Even after integration, we didn't think of mixing so much. It is like a sleepwalking; you just did as we always had done. We'd stay out of their way without thinking, and things keep going on the way they always have."

The social code still dictated a subservience that had disappeared most everywhere else; breaking that code—forgetting your "place"—opened blacks up to retaliation. That unwritten law overshadowed everything they did. Jackson said: "Things haven't changed that much. We still have to remember our place."

*   *   *

IN 1977, RAY PEACOCK, eighteen, was killed when a white teenager named Rocky Phelps hit him with his pickup. The Peacocks, and specifically Cecil Peacock, a sixty-eight-year-old stooped woodsman, said it was murder, motivated by race. Ray Peacock went to college in Beaumont and returned every weekend to his family's small wooden house in Shankleville, a rural community in neighboring Newton County. On one of those visits home, someone phoned the Peacocks to tell them the family's cows were wandering loose on State Highway 87, a two-lane road near their home. Ray Peacock volunteered to go round them up. An hour later, at about 11:30 P.M., his car was found on a grassy shoulder of the road. His body was 225 feet from the car, facedown, with no apparent wounds, according to the sheriff's report. The next night, Rocky Phelps and another white youth came forward to say their pickup had hit someone in the fog. Phelps insisted—and the sheriff agreed—that it was an accident.

"It was foul play," said Booker T. Hunter, founder of the Jasper branch of the National Association for the Advancement of Colored People, who had helped the Peacocks comb through the mud and grass the morning after the killing to look for clues.

For twenty-one years, the Peacock killing served as another example of quiet oppression, a lesson to remind the black community what would happen if they forgot their place. As time often does to recollections, the story evolved over the years. In Jasper's black community it had been embellished and revised. The narrative added a courtship between the young Peacock and the white sheriff's daughter. He was found by the side of the highway with his genitals missing, they said. Drugs, said the white community. Murder, said the black. Years later another black man was found tied up and mysteriously drowned in a public pool by Sweet Briar Gardens public housing complex. The black community felt it was a murder. Suicide, said the white community. Klan, whispered the black. By the late 1990s, such rumors had ignited mistrust among the races that smoldered beneath the surface. Lingering doubts and resentments about deaths, real and imagined, made efforts to change the dynamics of race in Jasper all the more difficult.

Blacks in Jasper did talk about standing up for their rights, particularly in the aftermath of events like the Peacock murder, but it was always in the context of "someday." In general, they found that merely talking about civil rights and equality seemed to make the whites meaner. It was better to wait for equality to rise up on its own, naturally, they decided, rather than force the issue.

"It just brought more animosity," Eddie Land, a former timber man in his high seventies, recalled. "It changed their attitudes. Before, what the white people used to 'give us,' now they would only 'sell' to us. There weren't a lot of black folks who were following civil rights here because it just caused problems. So we didn't pay it much mind."

It was only after the death of Martin Luther King Jr., after the television news put race riots in the past, that Jasper's black community felt they could openly embrace the black leader. Wailing rose in every black church in Jasper from the cinder blocks of Greater New Bethel to the clapboards of Rose Bloom Baptist. Choirs in their scarlet robes swayed and clapped and sang out their grief in a way that eased nearly two hundred years of frustration and sadness. In life, King was a man blacks in Jasper watched like a feature film, only vaguely aware that what he was trying to accomplish in Birmingham could someday find its way to Jasper. It was only after his death that his photographs appeared on every living room wall in the black community. The father of civil rights was remembered in sepia likenesses, and pen-and-ink drawings, framed and placed on mantles like a family member who didn't come visit often enough but was loved all the same.

When heroes did emerge, they arrived unexpectedly and quietly from places as far away as Illinois and California. Professor J. H. Rowe, a pioneer black educator who arrived in Jasper in 1924, was one of those men. It was hard to find anyone in Jasper, black or white, who did not have something good to say about 'Fessor Rowe and his rule at the Jasper County Training School. It was

Rowe who instilled a feeling of self-worth into a generation of schoolchildren who had been raised to sharecrop and stand ankle deep in soft earth picking cotton or tobacco for white landowners. School enrollment went from 116 in 1924 to 600 in 1936. There were only 4 graduates in the class of 1925, but during the next eleven years, 167 students left with diplomas.

Rowe, with a gold watch chain draped across the vest of his black serge suit, lit the way for a community that had been swallowed by the forces of poverty. His seven-room frame schoolhouse sat on a two-acre tract on the south side of town, where blacks were supposed to get their separate but equal education. Rowe was strict. He instituted a dress code and counseled parents to save their money to buy land.

"There were no shirttails out, shoes had to be shined, and our hair had to be cut neatly," said Reverend Kenneth Lyons. "On Fridays, boys had to wear a tie. Mr. Rowe was trying to give us self-esteem, to let us know we could be somebody and should have respect for ourselves. No one had done that until then in Jasper. Mr. Rowe was a role model for blacks in Jasper. He was responsible for us moving ahead. Most black families that have land and nice homes in Jasper got them because Mr. Rowe told their parents they should buy land and build on it. He had boys in the shop building screens and doors and furniture for the black community. They were always doing things for the people in their homes. They would come and fix your windows. Mr. Rowe changed how Jasper's black community saw itself."

Around the time Rowe arrived in Jasper, Eddie Land was hauling pulpwood out of the forests for Temple-Inland. Pulpwooding was a dangerous, low-cost form of logging. The job required muscle, and Land and other young men in the black community would attend school in the morning and then disappear into the forests in the afternoon to fell enormous pines with long, toothy crosscut saws. They hoisted logs onto trucks, stripped to the waist, their bodies shaped by the work. The teamwork necessary for loading the trucks bound the black community together—the whites called them "pulpwood niggers" and said the young men's prowess on the football field came from the work they did after school in the forests. Land worked side by side with white men, on integrated crews. They drank water from the same Vienna Sausage can, and they worked as hard as one another. "As far as we could determine, we were making the same money," he said.

Land did well at his job. He was the foreman of his team, and the white men respected him because he never asked them to do something he wouldn't do himself. "When it was hot, I would tell them to go to the shady parts, and I would work in the sun," he recalled. "When there was a tough job, I would do it, and, well, they came to respect me and love me, I think. All those white guys were telling me that they wanted me to marry their sisters and tried to set me up. But I wasn't a fool. If I'd have married one of their sisters, they would hang me so high my feet wouldn't touch the ground."

Land met and fell in love with the black woman who would become his wife when he was twenty years old. Maxine was just fifteen. In the early days of the Lands' courtship, there never was a question of mixing with whites or intruding on their world. "When I see a mixed couple even now, I really wonder if they love each other," Maxine Land said. "Do you think they really love each other, or they're just trying to rile everybody up? I really wonder sometimes."

Her greatest fear had always been that Eddie, the man who by 1998 had stood steadfastly by her side for fifty-seven years, would suddenly disappear—either swept away by another love, or as the victim of a wanton reprisal from a white man who held a grudge against blacks. "Would you date a white woman now?" she asked him, playfully touching his elbow.

"I wouldn't even walk with a white woman in this town," Eddie Land said. "There's so much hatred here for that sort of thing you can cut it with a knife. No, no, I stay away from things like that. That's just courting trouble."

*   *   *

JAMES BYRD'S BROKEN body made all these stories of prejudice and double standards more stark. Episodes previously whispered about were suddenly uttered aloud.

Christine Carter, a five-foot-tall schoolteacher who grew up in Jasper and attended J. H. Rowe's "colored" school, saw James Byrd's death as a sign. "What's done in the dark comes to the light," she said. "The Lord had a plan, and James died the way he did for a reason. You'd think all this lynching and violence was done long years ago. After how they did James I was convinced this place was worse than Mississippi, the worst place in the entire world. The black people knew about equality, and the whites never paid it no mind. They didn't care about equal employment or police turning a blind eye to white drug dealers. I think that once the rest of the world knew what kind of bad things were possible in Jasper, once we were labeled, the white folks didn't have a choice. They had to change."

The death on Huff Creek Road sparked something within the black community, too. One could be forgiven for thinking the principal cause of the black community's unhappiness was economic. But what really brought them to the barricades was their desire to live in dignity. The way James Byrd was killed called their dignity into question in the most basic way. Suddenly the black community was no longer willing to carry its second class status around like some clinking leg iron. They decided, decades after Martin Luther King took to the streets of Alabama, that no battles were ever won by spectators.

CHAPTER FOUR

YOUNG MEN, GO HOME

WHEN RUSSELL BREWER called Bill King from a pay phone in Beaumont just before Memorial Day weekend in 1998, King's response was quick—he hung up on him. King was sure it was some silly prison gag: a collect call meant only to spend his money and make him the butt of unit jokes for a day or two. Moments later, the phone rang again. "I really am in Beaumont," Brewer said, laughing. "Now get your sorry ass over here and pick me up."

When things go wrong, there is always a desire to trace events back to a single episode that might have changed everything had it gone differently. Brewer's telephone calls set a grim march in motion. Had he not called back, or had Bill King not driven to Beaumont to pick him up, so many things would have been different. But Bill King did pick up his old prison buddy in Beaumont, and a day later Brewer, who had been out of prison for months, had moved into King's apartment as if it were his own, bringing with him the emotional baggage of years in the Texas correctional system.

Russell Brewer radiated menace. He was sharp-featured and sharp-tongued. Like Bill King, he was relatively small in size. He had tiny feet that would have fit neatly into a lady's shoe, and when he stood up he was not much taller than a twelve-year-old boy. Even so, he had a look about him that would make people instinctively cross the street to avoid him. "He just seemed really angry," said Johnny Rashid, a cashier at the Cash 'N Dash on South Main. "He came in with Mr. King, and I asked them if they were brothers, and Russell Brewer got really angry and told me to go fuck myself. Mr. King was always nice when he came into the store and polite and would talk to me. This other guy, this other guy was just scary."

King and Brewer met in the Beto I unit of the Texas Department of Criminal Justice in Livingston in 1995. The prison lies at the end of a wooded road off the interstate highway, hidden behind a trailer park and rows of shabby houses. The Beto I unit, a cluster of modern low-rise buildings, looks more like a business park than a prison—except when one looks at the windows. They are so small you couldn't shove a cat through them. Beto is considered a "gladiator" unit, filled to bursting with 3,000 young toughs who live through the day wielding a lethal combination of intimidation and one-upsmanship. Prison inmates survive by making alliances with whoever serves them best. Blacks ally themselves with blacks, Hispanics with Hispanics, Asians with Asians. Prison is, without a doubt, the most violently segregated community in the United States. Young whites like King and Brewer have it worst of all. Outnumbered three to one behind bars in Texas, they are attacked by others not only because they inspire resentment but also because if they give in and don't fight back they can be turned into a "ho,"—a moneymaking machine for tormentors who can rent their sexual services to other prisoners. New arrivals have three choices: fight, screw, or "up sixty" (hand over the sixty dollars they are permitted to spend at the commissary each month). Hos are considered the lowest of the low in prison, looked down upon by inmates and guards alike for their inability to stand up for themselves. This rite of passage prompted Russell Brewer and Bill King to meet. They were "peckerwoods," or "woods," together on the unit—slang for men who fight when challenged but aren't tough enough to be admitted into one of the prison's many gangs for protection.

Brewer, thirty-two, was from Sulphur Springs, in Central Texas, and had been in and out of prison for ten years. He was jailed for breaking into a house in July 1987, then paroled the following February. He stayed out of trouble for a couple of years and then went back to prison on a fifteen-year sentence for selling drugs in May 1989. He was paroled two years later. A parole violation put him back in prison in February 1994 until September 1997. When he arrived at the Beto I unit in 1994, he was almost immediately confronted by two Hispanic gang members. The guards had ordered all the inmates in his cellblock to sit down on benches in the dayroom or be punished. Blacks held one bench; Hispanics held another. The whites occupied a third. The whites, members of the Aryan Brotherhood, considered one of the meanest of the white supremacist gangs in the prison system, wouldn't let Brewer join them.

For two days, Brewer leaned against the wall. Then two Hispanic gang members asked him whether he would fight or "ride"—give them money or sexual favors. Brewer told them if they were going to beat him up, then go ahead and get it over with. The Hispanics did not take him up on it, and the whites who witnessed this from their perch on the bench were impressed enough to invite Brewer to join the Confederate Knights of America, one of the less violent white supremacist groups at Beto. The Beto chapter called itself the Texas Rebel Soldiers; its members swore an oath of loyalty to the Ku Klux Klan. They had secret passwords, attended meetings, earned points on a merit chart like elementary school students getting extra credit, and swore to "bear true allegiance to the sacred principles of Aryan Racial Supremacy and political freedom in Government upon which our forefathers founded a new nation upon this continent." While the group may not have been feared (prison officials classified it as a clique, not a gang), it did give members a modicum of protection, a feeling of belonging, and a way to seem more menacing in a world where intimidation was the most important currency of all.

Bill King was "checked"—or confronted—on his first day in prison in June 1995. He said that in the process of standing up for himself, other inmates managed to break his nose. Prison records did not say whether or how King was checked. The guards only reported a scuffle. Either way, the altercation was frightening for the then-twenty-one-year-old King. King said there was no report of a beating because when guards sought to give him medical care he said he had fallen out of his bunk. "If I had ratted out some guy, it just would have happened again. So the floor broke my nose." The beating marked King's initiation as one of a handful of "peckerwoods." What was never clear was whether that was the only beating

King suffered in prison. Had there been other beatings or rapes? Many things went on at the unit that were never reported, and fist-fights and sodomy were commonplace.

The universal sign of a peckerwood—the way the group signed their names and the first tattoos they inked on their bodies—were the two lightning bolts once worn by Hitler's Elite Guard. King, adopting the prison name Possum, wrote the two *S*'s as lightning bolts, to show his "wood" status. (What King didn't know was that the term "peckerwood" originated from southern black slang. Blacks saw the blackbird in the woods as a symbol for themselves, and the redheaded woodpeckers that roamed southern forests came to represent whites.)

Without a gang affiliation, Brewer and King drifted together. Brewer, seven years older than King, knew the ropes of prison life. King, quick and charismatic, impressed Brewer with conversation sprinkled with vocabulary he had never heard before. While Brewer had trouble admitting it, he was strangely attracted to King.

*   *   *

IT WAS DIFFICULT to imagine Ronald King, Bill King's father, as a young man. Tethered to an oxygen tank by his emphysema, he looked as if he had always been old and broken. Years at the mill had made him work-worn, and he was stooped and thinned-down by a respiratory disease that seemed poised to suffocate him at any moment. His skin appeared leached of blood, like boiled meat. Under slicked white hair there were grayish pink glimpses of scalp that he'd long ago ceased to notice.

King came to Jasper in 1973 by way of Louisiana, where he had worked as a millwright for decades. It was a difficult profession—hot, dangerous, and requiring long hours. King's life was all about machines with clanking parts, steel cogs, and tooth-covered blades. And all he saw day after day were rows of men, bent at the waist, doing things with their hands.

Life had always been hard on Ronald King. Born in Picayune, Mississippi, the youngest of four children, he finished high school there before civil rights had gained a toehold. College was never even the flicker of a possibility. Instead King stepped into his father's shoes at the Broadmoor Lumber Mill in New Orleans fixing planers as soon as he graduated from high school, had a brief stint in the military, and then returned to the machines in Louisiana.

The King family's move to Texas was meant to provide a fresh start and a place to retire. Ronald and his wife, Jean, had three grown children and had decided to spend their golden years near the woods. Louisiana-Pacific hired King in Jasper. Stories about King's early days at L.P. were mixed. Two employees who worked with him in the plant said he used the word "nigger" and boasted about burning "niggers" out of their houses in three states. He griped about black millwright Vander Carter getting a newer and faster machine to work on. "It was 'Nigger this' and 'Nigger that' with him back then," they said. Vander Carter remembered an incident in which there was a problem with his machine. People accused King of being behind it. But Carter said King claimed he hadn't touched the machine, and he believed him. "People were always saying things about him; some people plain didn't like him," said Carter. "But the truth was, he was always fine with me. If he was racist, he never showed me that side of him."

King lived about a quarter mile from Carter and around the corner from James Byrd's family. If the Kings arrived in Jasper hating the black race, they were good at hiding it. Jean King was known for baking cakes and presenting them on birthdays to both black and white citizens. She gave Carter's wife, Christine, a pillow for their anniversary.

"I really admired Vander," King said. "I learned to fix machines from my father, but Vander was thrown into the mix without any experience and was able to pick up a lot just on his own. We had come into this kind of work from different directions and were willing to listen to each other and decide the best route to take. He was the best I have ever seen at patching up a machine to get it through the day. I used to do repairs just with getting the machine ready for the following day. It was a difference in style, I guess."

In the mid-1970s, when the last of his children had left the house, Ronald King and his wife unexpectedly adopted an infant boy. Neighbors and friends were confused about where, exactly, the boy had come from. Some had heard he was a distant relation to King by marriage; his mother, unable to care for the boy, sent him to King. "We didn't get him with the intention of keeping him," the old man said of his adopted son, Bill. "We just got him to help out." But the Kings were quickly smitten with the boy and persuaded the birth mother to give Bill up. The old man renamed the child John William King.

"I remember when we took Bill to adoption court. He was nine months old. I remember he had on a pair of red, white, and blue shoes," Ronald King said, as his son sat blocks away in the Aubrey Cole Law Enforcement Center jail, accused of killing James Byrd. "And I remember he was the cutest, happiest, laughing little boy. We just loved Bill to death."

In small towns when one hears something bad about a child, one takes a second look at the family. Are the parents drinkers? Do they beat the children? Many parents are simply blind to the short-comings of their offspring. That was Jean King's problem. Ronald King's wife was always making excuses for Bill, friends and teachers said. The trouble was his friends' fault, she would say. People had Bill all wrong.

"I remember once, I came home from work, and he had been skipping school and staying with his mother," said the elder King in a voice honed by a lifetime of cigarettes. "She tried to hide him in the bedroom so I wouldn't find out. I was the strict one, and Jean was always trying to protect him. I found all this out later, of course, but I remember catching him out of school and being so mad. I guess it wasn't enough."

One could imagine a time when the elder King was tough and hard, but the years had given him a vulnerable air. He was missing two fingers on his right hand, and his left one looked as if it had been soaked in water, it was so pink. He had lost the two fingers in a chain sprocket and carried them to the doctor in a napkin to get them sewn back on. The surgery didn't take, and in their place were just two nubs.

King, with few accomplishments of his own, made it a practice of reciting his youngest son's achievements as if he had been an honor student: he began walking at the age of seven months and was a voracious reader. Bill learned at an early age to look up things he wanted to know. King treated Bill as if he were his own, partly, he said, because "orphan" is one of the saddest words in the English language, and that's essentially what Bill became. His birth mother disappeared from his life. The Kings seemed to be perpetually trying to make up for that.

"We loved him so much. I wasn't a hugger with my earlier kids, but with Bill I just couldn't stop hugging him," said King. "And he hugged me back. He was such a polite boy; he made me so proud."

Even the most well-intentioned parents can't protect their children from everything. Bill King was the adored center of an otherwise difficult family, and it turned him into a man who always thought an exception would be made in his case.

The kindest reading of Bill King would say his abandonment by his birth mother as an infant left him off stride for the rest of his life. "All I know about my mother is that she has a bunch of other children and she's very, very religious," Bill King said. "But that makes you wonder about a person, doesn't it? Being so religious but giving up a son and then refusing to see him when trouble happens. Makes you wonder about religion and what it really means. I corresponded with my brother for a while, out in Utah, but that stopped too."

Still others could blame Jasper, a place where teenagers notoriously had trouble easing into independence. Few white teens there had any plans beyond marrying one of their own and following their fathers into the woods and mothers into the kitchen. When King was sixteen, his adoptive mother, Jean, the one who doted on him, died of cancer. Most people trace the trouble in Bill King's life to that single event. What little minding he had done until then ended altogether after her death. Bill King began experimenting with petty forms of theft, and a short time later he dropped out of high school.

"Bill King went halfway through tenth grade," said Tommy Adams, a black school administrator at Jasper High School. Adams remembers him as an unassuming young man who "didn't mix too well. He used to like to talk to me, though, so when I saw him on TV after the murder, I couldn't believe it. He didn't strike me as racist when I knew him."

King and his childhood friend Shawn Berry decided to drop out of Jasper High School the same day in 1991. Leaving the school doors to slam behind them, they disappeared for a week in King's mother's car, returning determined to stay out of school, tomcat, and just have fun. King became the kind of man who drifted unnoticed in Jasper, doing itinerant day labor, falling into petty theft and inappropriate relationships with underaged girls. Brandy Behator was a childhood friend he subsequently had a romantic relationship with. Kylie Greeney, a girl with a wild streak and the idea she could tame King, was his steady girl, his fiancée, some said, although a marriage date was never set and rings were never exchanged. It was Kylie's mother who had called Sheriff Rowles in 1998 after finding sexually explicit photos of the couple.

Bill King and boys like him in the Deep South were restless and unable to break free of the miseries that had become part and parcel of their lives. There were no jobs. There were no prospects. There was little to do. Poverty sapped the vitality out of growing up. The white community thought the lack of recreation and entertainment for the young in Jasper was the result of perennially empty municipal coffers. The black community suspected there was no bowling alley, no public pool (it had been filled in years ago), and just a small movie house because the white community wanted to limit opportunities for teenage racial mixing. If there was nowhere to mix, it would be harder to do so.

*   *   *

BILL KING HAD resigned himself to a life in which he bounced from one low-level job to another. He had a grocery store job at one point, when he was living with an older sister. He worked construction sometimes, cleared land when the work was available. With little else to keep his busy mind occupied, it was only a matter of time before King got into trouble. He and his friend Shawn Berry were arrested in 1992 for their part in the burglary of a jukebox warehouse. King was driving the getaway car and received an eight-year sentence. It was reduced to several months in a "scared straight" camp aimed at breaking down errant youth the old-fashioned way. Offenders were stripped, shaved, dressed in orange prison garb, and put through army drills in a bid to rehabilitate them. For King, it did little. "It was just like prison really, just less violent," King said. "The guards made you work in the fields and made us march around. It was kind of stupid."

Three years later, after a fight with his sister led to a call to the police, Bill King was back in jail. His probation was revoked, and he was sent to prison for eighteen months. "Shawn did stuff that he shouldn't have too, like drunk driving and things like that," King said. "But my probation officer was stricter than his. And I just couldn't catch a break. So they sent me to prison." He was moved to several institutions until he filed a motion to be sent to Beto, where he later met Russell Brewer. And that's where King learned to hate.

The process of becoming a racist appeared to have occurred slowly for Bill King. It wasn't just prison. What happened to him there was built on a long history of his father's and mother's off-hand racist comments, children at school, and the usual rebellious dilemmas every teenager faced at the same time as their skin problems. Whatever was already there, almost two years in prison made it worse. Bill King returned to Jasper in late 1997.

"He was completely different when he came back from prison," said Louis Berry, Shawn Berry's younger brother. "I didn't know

79

why he was different. He started talking ugly about blacks. I didn't think it would last. I thought it was something he did in prison and would eventually stop doing because now he was out."

Bill King was a series of sums that did not add up. He returned to Jasper "sleeved out"—his arms and back were a solid gallery of tattoos and racist symbols. A menacing version of Woody Wood-pecker sported a Klan robe on one arm and a tiny black man dangled from a tree limb on the other. All the tattoos had been applied through the bars of a cell under cover of darkness. "Hope-fully, by the time I come home," King wrote one girlfriend, "I'll have 65 percent of my body covered. My head, arms, neck, back, side, chest, stomach and dick. I know no one's gonna want to fuck with a . . . peckerwood covered in skin art." He was a small man desperately trying to become menacing and to carve out some kind of place for himself in prison.

King knew that the tattoos were something his father would not approve of. "I know they make people think of me a certain way," he said. "But they just don't understand. This is art. This isn't racist. This is art."

The tattoos were only the beginning. Months after King settled into his prison routine, he began adopting the language of the Aryan movement. He wrote letters about the purity of the Aryan race and declared himself part of the chosen seed line from which superior beings had come. "He wrote me from prison, and the letters got scary and racist," said sometime girlfriend Brandy Behator. "He said mixed couples should hang from the same tree. He said he'd make himself well-known by doing something; I didn't know what he was talking about. But he scared me."

Eventually, he had the words "Aryan Pride" tattooed across his rib cage. "I'm a little racist, I guess," King said. "Everyone is a little racist," he said. "People who say they aren't are lying."

Bill King returned to Jasper thinking he was a recruit in an underground war for the town's soul. In his heart, he thought he was a race hero in the making, a representative of a long and distinguished line of Aryans, willing to put himself in the service of his race.

"In recent years, I have become painfully aware that a war is being waged across the planet earth—and that we (the Aryan Race) are the first, quite possibly the final, line of defense," King wrote from prison. "To pretend we are not at war—to hide behind euphemisms would be misleading and worse, fatal. While it may appear unseemly and disturbing that we are engaged in sometimes illegal activities, it must be stressed that these activities have proven vital to our survival on many occasions. We live in difficult times and moral choices of questionable nature are unfortunately the result."

Though the Aryan language was new to Bill King, he managed to make his letters sound like those of a man nursing lifelong resentments. He thought race mixing would lead directly to the downfall of civilization. He began reading white supremacist tracts and understood himself to be a child of Europe, of the "Northern Race" that would struggle against the racial Armageddon blacks were secretly waging. In the end, maybe Bill King couldn't stand the idea of his falling silent, like a radio running down, when he returned to Jasper, so he created a calling. He began planning an act that would make him a captain in a war that only he and few others could see.

When he took up with his childhood friends after his release, he didn't fit in. He made his old high school buddies, Shawn Berry and Shawn's brother, Louis, nervous with his racist talk and his gallery of tattoos. King toned it down when he didn't get the response he sought and started wearing long-sleeved shirts to cover up his tattoos.

Then Russell Brewer arrived in Jasper. Almost immediately King returned to using prison slang, calling everyone "bro" and spouting tough talk. Neighbors in the small Timbers Apartments complex knew him as an excessively tattooed ex-con, prejudiced but not overly so, trying to get his act together after prison. After Brewer's entrance on the scene, however, the parties at the one-room apartment got rowdier. There were late-night drinking bouts, pot smoking, and screaming matches with various girlfriends. The pair began a petty crime spree. When King and Brewer needed a chain saw and a weed trimmer for a job clearing brush, they stole them. They took fifty bags of potato chips from a motel lobby just for the sport of it. They stole beer from a warehouse. They were just having fun.

*   *   *

JASPER HAS SEVERAL good restaurants, but Patrick's, just north of the city limits, was usually acknowledged as the fanciest, serving everything from chicken-fried steak to chateaubriand. Chef and owner Patrick Lam made fried artichoke hearts, and his waiters set crêpes suzette alight at the tables. Lam, a Flemish Jew, claimed to be the only Holocaust survivor in Jasper. During the first week of June 1998, thieves broke into his restaurant and helped themselves to some of his steaks and shrimp. Lam wondered if it was Jew bashing. The burglars tried to get into the restaurant through a large power vent on the roof and then ended up ripping out a window, casing and all. Bars inside prevented them from breaking in. Undeterred, they finally hacked a hole through a wall.

Once inside, they helped themselves to wine and liquor and then carted hundreds of pounds of fine cuts of meat from the freezers. "I think they were casing the place before I closed," Lam said. "I remember walking out in back and feeling like someone or something was moving in the field. I should have called the police, but I didn't. I thought it was just my imagination."

Nobody was ever charged with the crime.

*   *   *

THE FOLLOWING SATURDAY, June 6, King and Brewer slept late and then drove up to Burkeville to visit Shawn Berry's younger brother, Louis, to drink beer and hang out. But the visit was not a happy one. Louis Berry had invited several friends over for a jam session, and King and Brewer appeared to be spoiling for a fight. Louis Berry was a heavy-metal music enthusiast and had started his own band with several friends. He played the drums, his friend Tommy Faulk was on the guitar, and Gracie, a black man, was the bassist.

The music stopped when Brewer and King began banging on the trailer door. An argument quickly ensued. "They didn't want to come in," Louis Berry said later, "because we had a black man in the house. Bill's attitude kind of upset me. I didn't understand why he was acting that way. He was mad. He said he didn't like black people and didn't want to be around them. So I told him to go."

The battle didn't stop there. Early that evening, Louis Berry arrived at King's apartment to revisit the afternoon's fight. "I told him I was sick of how he was always putting down black people," Berry said. "I guess we had cooled down some by the time I left. But Bill was still mad, I could tell."

Louis Berry thought King was acting tough to impress Brewer. Whatever it was, he felt he had said his piece, stuck up for his friend Gracie, and could leave having done what he set out to do. While he knew he was not going to change King's attitude, at least he had put him on notice for his racism. Later that night, King and Brewer went down to the Twin Cinemas to meet up with Louis's brother, Shawn. They were at the theater when Christie Marcontell, Shawn Berry's girlfriend, came by and tried to patch things up after a fight. Berry told her he was going home to turn in early that night. Instead, Shawn Berry decided to drive his gray pickup around Newton County, up by Toledo Bend Dam, with Bill King and Russell Brewer. The trio were going to try to find a party. They never found one. Instead they ended up driving around back country roads, and drinking beer. Hours later, James Byrd was dead.

* * *

BEFORE THERE WAS talk of mixed-race couples and civil rights and marches in Birmingham, slavery left its print. Startling numbers of people in Jasper, black and white, shared family names: Seale and Hadnot and Coleman and Pickle. The biracial links were created when former slaves took the names of the owners after Emancipation. Those atavistic echoes continued. The old master-servant relations persisted, albeit subconsciously.

"The Seales brought my people over," said the Reverend Kenneth Lyons from his dark-paneled office at the Greater New Bethel Baptist Church. The room was cluttered with magazines and notes and smelled of peppermint candies. Lyons had the voice of a man who spoke to God directly. It was rich and deep, with a dark walnut sound, which, together with his big, round face and toothy grin, made him likable to a fault. The whiteness of his teeth showed up like a match flaring. Kenneth Lyons was the kind of man, Jasperites would tell you, for whom dogs turned belly up. He was known to have gone fishing with friends only to hook a fish and hand the pole to someone else in the boat so they could say they caught it.

Reverend Lyons liked to tell the story of how the Lord beckoned him from a delivery truck. He had a job delivering packages in Houston, and, as he told it, he had "this habit of getting into accidents."

"You know, they liked me fine at the company. I had a good attitude, I was always at work on time. But every week it seemed I was running into a pole or backing into something," he said. " 'Kenneth,' they told me, 'Kenneth, we like you, but our insurance premiums are going crazy with you in the truck.' I thought I was driving real careful, and no matter how hard I tried, I'd end the week with a wreck. The Lord was trying to tell me something. I just wasn't listening. I've been driving over twenty years since I started preaching," he said. "And not one wreck."

In reality, preaching was in his blood. He could trace his earliest Texas roots to Uncle Dick Seale, a man who came out of his slave mother's womb in North Carolina in 1798 with such a powerful scream that women in the slave quarters found a piece of rock candy to put in his mouth to shush him. Uncle Dick had been the stuff of legend ever since. Once, during a parade, Dick began to cry, howling over the noisy throng lined up on the streets. His mother tried to quiet him but could not. Then the crowd parted, and a man on a white horse rode up to her and pressed a coin into her hand. Laughing, he told her to buy the baby some chocolate, that he had a long life ahead and should not waste his childhood shedding tears. When the man departed, a trader came to Uncle Dick's mother and told her she had received a great honor. The man who had given her the coin was General George Washington. She never forgot the scene or spent the coin, legend has it.

In 1835, Uncle Dick was sold to Joshua Seale, a man who had ridden with the troops in the American Revolution and had sent his son to the Battle of New Orleans as a drummer boy. When Joshua Seale hired a tutor for his children, Uncle Dick asked if he could learn too. His master agreed on the condition that Uncle Dick not neglect his work in the fields, according to William Seale, the great-grandson of Joshua Seale and now a White House historian in Washington, D.C. As his knowledge grew, Uncle Dick's standing among the slave community did too. Uncle Dick was a character, traveling from North Carolina to Texas with the Seales, who would make a plantation, buy more slaves, build a house and sell it as an improved site, and move on. Joshua Seale saw Uncle Dick as one of the family and promised him early on that once they had settled, he would set him free. By the time the Seales moved to Jasper County in 1849, Uncle Dick was considered part of the Seale clan and was known as "Uncle Dick" by whites and blacks alike. In the woods, he was called to the deathbeds of blacks and whites to deliver prayers and read from the Bible. He became the overseer of fifty-five other Seale slaves and took a devout Christian wife, Aunt Phyllis.

It was about 1853 when Joshua Seale told Uncle Dick that he would build him a church for the colored people. The church was built from finished lumber from the Seale mill, beneath the beech trees, and dubbed Dixie Baptist Church. On a Sunday in 1875, at the age of seventy-seven, Uncle Dick delivered his last sermon at Dixie Baptist. He spoke of the past and remembered that he had been born in a slave pen in North Carolina. A week later, his congregation laid him to rest near Joshua Seale.

"The front pews had been reserved for the white folks," town patriarch Joe Tonahill's wife, Violett, wrote her father in 1967 after attending the dedication of a historical marker at Dixie Baptist. "I was escorted to the front row. Promptly at two the ceremonies began with the choir. And if you have never heard a negro Baptist choir sing, you've never lived. It has a definite beat and I defy any-one to keep from swinging his foot in time to the music."

Photographs showed the church's two towers, its recessed porch, and its hard pine pews. The Dixie Baptist Church stood for more than one hundred years—from the 1860s until 1966—until it burned to the ground when children burning leaves accidentally set it alight.

"My great-grandfather, Joshua Seale, was a tough man, but he loved Uncle Dick like one of the family," said William Seale. "He made his sons work in the field under Uncle Dick's supervision, and the truth is, while my great-grandfather would be a racist by today's definition, life was hard enough for everyone back then that there was a certain camaraderie that came from working together. They just couldn't have imagined selling a member of the household. There is a family relationship there that gets clouded by the issue of slavery. There were people who were mean to their slaves, but there were others who loved them very much."

The harder times seemed to come after the Civil War, when southern families could no longer own their workers like pickup trucks. That's when whites and blacks had to find a new way to relate to one another, Lyons said.

Kenneth Lyons's grandfather, Leonard Barnes, was born in 1896, the first man born free in his family. Barnes ended his family's trial with slavery without looking back. When he was a teenager he fell into line with other black men from Jasper for a paying job at the sawmill stacking lumber. He, too, became legendary, after he challenged a white man at the mill for addressing him as "boy."

Lyons left Jasper when he was a young man, traveling as far as he could go, to California, in the army. It was the first time he saw that whites could treat blacks as equals. And the first time he realized that prejudice in Jasper was the exception, not the rule.

"I left Jasper on a bus in 1959 and couldn't go in the front door of any restaurant," said Lyons. "I came back a year later, and I could. I had to ride in the back of the bus when I left, and by 1965 I was allowed to ride anywhere I wanted to."

Lyons struggled with the fact that, by virtue of his color, he was forced to sit in the balcony at the movie theater, confused as a child as to why he couldn't sit closer to the screen. As teenagers, Lyons and his black friends would leave fifteen minutes before the feature was over so they could get a head start on the white boys and there wouldn't be any trouble. At the Jasper Drive-In, now gone, the Jim Crow laws meant that blacks were obliged to park behind a fence. "I was willing to accept that we couldn't sit together at cafés or at the movies," he said. "But at the drive-in our cars kept us apart. They wouldn't even let our cars be together."

*   *   *

"MOST PEOPLE DON'T want to be hated," Reverend Lyons began his sermon on Sunday, June 7. "That's why we have people who go along with things. To go along with the crowd rather than be hated. But when you do that, you do more harm to yourself."

Lyons had no idea how close to the truth he had come. What he did know was that his congregation was anxious. Though there were few details about the murder on Huff Creek Road beyond the rumors that the body of a black man had been found, the pulses of those who sat in the hard pews of Greater New Bethel Baptist Church were already quickening.

"When you surrender all to Jesus, you could lose some friends; sometimes your own household turns against you. When Jesus preached he didn't try to undermine anyone. He didn't move in on anyone or take any position from anyone. Because of his holiness he revealed their sins. He revealed to us who they really were. They decided to put him to death without a cause."

The congregation provided the requisite nods and sang hymns at the top of their lungs. But somehow the unfolding events of the day made it difficult to take the sermon to heart. The churchgoers could only mimic Lyons's secondhand notions about coming together. In their hearts they were torn between the contradictory impulses of reconciliation and revenge. The churchgoers tried not to think about what was going on up on Huff Creek Road. The only overt reference to their shapeless anxieties came in Lyons's blessing at the end of the service. "Young men," he said, "go home."

*   *   *

LATER THAT DAY, after all the hymnals had been stacked and the church floors swept, Lyons, Rowles, and other community leaders began bracing for the worst. Their biggest fear: reprisals and violent, summary justice. Fifty-five years before, almost to the day, the city of Beaumont had erupted in racial violence after a white woman accused a black man of raping her. On the evening of June 15, 1943, more than 2,000 dockworkers and another 1,000 spectators marched on Beaumont City Hall to demand vigilante justice. Even though the woman could not identify the suspect among the blacks held in the city jail, the workers broke up into small groups and began breaking into stores in the black section of downtown to exact their own revenge. With guns, axes, and hammers they terrorized black citizens in Central and North Beaumont. Many blacks were assaulted; several restaurants and stores were pillaged; a number of buildings were burned. More than one hundred houses were ransacked. All told, police arrested more than two hundred people. Fifty Beaumonters were injured, and two people, one black and one white, were killed in the melee. Another black man died several months later of injuries sustained during the violence.

Lyons remembered hearing about the 1943 terror in Beaumont from his mother. Billy Rowles remembered the stories from his father.

Mayor George Gary mobilized the Eighteenth Battalion of the Texas State Guard late that night, and the governor put Beaumont under martial law. A force of 1,800 guardsmen marched into town to try to keep the peace. To those forces authorities added one hundred state police and seventy-five Texas Rangers. They imposed an 8:30 curfew. The city was sealed off as citizens, both black and white, sat crouched inside their houses with guns loaded, waiting for a spark that would ignite the situation. Mayor Gary shuttered all the liquor stores and closed the parks and playgrounds. He canceled the black community's Juneteenth celebrations. Blacks were not permitted to go to work, and the Jefferson County Fairground was converted into a stockade to accommodate the overflow of prisoners from the city and county jails. Martial law was finally lifted, five days later, on June 20.

The Beaumont riots had more to them than a simple rape accusation. Beaumont had become a boomtown during the war, when people moved to the city in 1941 to take jobs in the shipyards and war plants. The population quadrupled over the seven years from 1941 to 1948, and the influx acted as a type of forced integration because there weren't enough facilities to keep the races apart. In the factories, blacks began to have access to semiskilled and skilled jobs, which put them in direct competition with white workers. Tensions between the races were serious enough that in early June 1943 separate commuter transportation had been put into service to end racial violence on overcrowded buses.

Food shortages added to the tension. The government had issued food allotments and ration cards, but it hadn't accounted for the dramatic increase in Beaumont's population by 1943. With wholesalers' quotas still based on 1941 population figures, there wasn't enough food to go around. There were severe shortages of meats and canned goods. Three days before the riot, the head of the regional food administration had wired Washington, D.C., saying the food shortages in Beaumont threatened to spark violent protests. To make matters worse, a chapter of the Ku Klux Klan active in the city was planning to host a regional Klan convention on June 29, just ten days after the black community's Juneteenth celebration.

The alleged June 5 rape merely threw gasoline on an already smoldering fire. A black man was accused of assaulting an eighteen-year-old white Beaumont telephone operator, the daughter of a Louisiana shipyard worker then working in a Beaumont plant. The black man was subsequently shot and killed by Beaumont police while resisting arrest. When a second alleged rape occurred on June 15, violence ensued, and Beaumont then joined Detroit, New York, Los Angeles, Mobile, Philadelphia, Indianapolis, Baltimore, St. Louis, and Washington, D.C., as one of the sites of bloody race riots in the summer of 1943.

"We'd heard a black man had raped a white woman in the good part, the north end, of Beaumont," said Dorothy Bagesse, who was a teenager in Beaumont during the melee. "We heard the blacks were coming into town by rail to take it over, and we were scared."

Durwood Cox was a carpenter at the shipyard and remembered the riots as if they had happened yesterday. "They closed up the yard and told us to go home," he said. "A lot of the guys dropped their tools and rushed out saying, 'We're going to kill those niggers.'"

Cox climbed on his motorcycle and headed for the northern part of town. He lived on the edge of the black community and imagined the worst for his wife and new baby.

"I offered a guy a ride on the back of my motorcycle and took off toward downtown," he said. "I was getting down by the hotel— back then there was only one—and the guy on my bike pulled out a piece of lead pipe and as we drove by a black man, just clubbed him. I got him off the bike right quick, but that's the way the violence was in town that night."

Cox stopped at home long enough to pick up his wife and baby, his car, and two shotguns: a 20-gauge and a 30/30. The group set off to his mother's house and met his brother-in-law, Cecil Rowles, Billy's father, there.

"We were so nervous," Cox said. "Grandmother had a nightmare in the middle of the night and woke up screaming, and Cecil was up and out the front door with one gun, and I was out the back with another. If a nigger had been out there, he'd have been shot. Instead, it was just two white boys pointing shotguns into the darkness in their shorts."

Years later, Billy Rowles remembered asking his mother about the riots. "She said Daddy didn't go out that night and instead came straight home from a union meeting," Rowles said. "A man named V. J. Withers was daddy's boss at the shipyard, and he was mad that Daddy didn't go. Years later when I met him, he said my daddy was a sissy. That really shocked me; I just adored my daddy. Then I found out V. J. thought Daddy was a sissy because he didn't go out that night. 'When we went to get them niggers, your daddy wouldn't go with us.'"

It was a disease that was all too common at the time. Otherwise reasonable people went stark raving mad when anything involving a black came up. The memory haunted Rowles. "As soon as it became clear this Byrd deal was a racial killing, well, I thought about what happened in Beaumont. I was worried something like that could happen here, and I thought about how my daddy would have handled it," he said.

Fifty-five years after the smoke had cleared from the most infamous race riots in Texas, Billy Rowles was climbing the stairs of the Byrd family's front stoop with Deputy James Carter. He cleared his throat before pushing the bell. That June morning had been an emotionally mauling one. As the doorbell chimes echoed through the Byrd house, Rowles suddenly felt as if he was going to cry. He swallowed hard and waited for the door to open. James Byrd Sr., a small man with gray thinning hair and a resigned expression, opened the door and gazed at the sheriff. With Billy Rowles on his doorstep, there was no question the rumors they had heard all morning were true. His boy, James, was the one they had found on Huff Creek Road. Behind him, in the living room, Stella Byrd, James's mother, let out a howl.

"I didn't hesitate and just told them abruptly, 'Your son is dead. . . . Now what can I do for you?' I assured them that we would find the killers. I didn't say it was a dragging. There were a lot of emotions. I broke down afterward and just cried."

*   *   *

THE LIGHT OUTSIDE was just starting to dim Sunday evening when Billy Rowles fell into a chair at the head of the table in the small corrugated building behind the Jasper County Jail. Curtis Frame, Joe Sperling, and nearly a dozen officers from both the sheriff's and the police departments had gathered to compare notes on what they knew about the murder so far. Before them on the conference table were various pieces of evidence gathered from the crime scene: a cigarette lighter, tools, a heavy metal CD, a socket wrench with the word "Berry" engraved in cursive on the side. The men were trying to think of anyone in town with the first name "Berry."

Already bits of information were beginning to filter into the office. Steven Scott, who lived over on Martin Luther King Drive, had seen James Byrd, obviously drunk, staggering down the road. A short time later, he noticed a gray sidestep pickup drive by with Byrd seated in the back. The truck had several passengers in it, he said, and was loud. James Brown had last seen Byrd at Willie Mays's party around 1 A.M. and expected Byrd had been walking home about then.

"Doesn't Shawn Berry have a loud sidestep truck?" Sterling piped up.

Curtis Frame nodded.

Rowles raised his eyebrows and nodded. "Let's pick Shawn up for questioning," he said. Not more than fifteen minutes had passed before Officer Larry Pullman's voice came over the police radio. "I've got Shawn Berry's truck going south on Ninety-six," he said, his voice rising. "And he's got expired tags. I'll pull him over and bring him in."

That's a lucky break, Rowles said to himself. Now we just need about a hundred more.

CHAPTER FIVE

JOE TONAHILL'S TEXAS

ON DAYS WHEN the tedium of quiet country lawyering began to grow old, Joe Tonahill would close his eyes and imagine himself back in Judge Joe Brown's Dallas courtroom, sitting at the defense table with Jack Ruby. The trial opened on February 17, 1964, and ended almost a month later with a guilty verdict. After more than thirty years, Joe Tonahill remembered the fidgeting of bodies in the gallery, the jury's reaction as prosecutors rolled television footage of Ruby shooting Lee Harvey Oswald at point-blank range. "I asked Joe why he would want to get into this, and he said it would be such a challenge," Tonahill's wife, Violett Smith Tonahill, wrote her father in late 1963. "I don't want him to get involved because you never know what the 'side effects' will be. He seems to think Ruby was temporarily insane, which, obviously, is the only defense."

Tonahill recalled the greedy curiosity of the people who gathered outside the Dallas courthouse that winter. Women in smart dresses and men in crisp black suits and thin striped ties took their places in the courtroom's straight-backed pews. They looked on with bemusement as Tonahill and his cocounsel, Melvin Belli, tried to defend a man 4 million viewers had seen shoot another on live television.

Joe Tonahill remembered it all in slow motion. When the guilty verdict was read, news photographers burst through the gates around the bench and climbed onto the judge's desk for a better picture. There was a roar from the courtroom gallery and a second concussion outside as spectators watching on closed-circuit television heard the decision for themselves. Tonahill staggered in the rush.

After the verdict there were interviews, appeals, decisions, conferences. At the time, it was the longest murder trial in history. A year later, in 1965, by the time Jack Ruby had been diagnosed with cancer, Tonahill had won an appeal. Witnesses had lied. Evidence had been prejudicial. "There was enough wrong with the case that a first-year law student could have gotten him off," Tonahill said. "But he died waiting to be retried. He died in Parkland Memorial Hospital, same as Jack Kennedy."

As the years went by, the trial became a highly personal, emotional touchstone for Tonahill and, by extension, for Jasper. It was something Tonahill kept coming back to for images and metaphors, and just having him in town made Jasperites feel a little special, as if Tonahill's place in history might rub off, just a little, on them.

More than thirty years later, Tonahill's office had become a private museum of the Ruby trial. Behind the brown vinyl couches in his front office, yellowing charcoal courtroom sketches dotted the walls. In his private chambers, the red leather law books on the credenza were from the same year: 1964. To visitors, Tonahill still provided eight-by-ten glossy photographs of the defense—him, Belli, and Ruby—mapping strategy. A nearly life-size photo of Ruby killing Oswald dominated one wall.

In the years after the trial, Tonahill busied himself building a kingdom in the way only national figures are able to do in small towns. He bought and sold land; opened a bank. He roosted atop a fortune comprising oil wells, several thousand acres of timber, a 560-acre ranch called Sherwood Forest, and a roster of buildings on the south, east, and north sides of Courthouse Square. His local acquisitions, paired with the international fame brought by the Ruby trial, became a force that profoundly shaped how people behaved toward him: he had become the sun around which Jasper revolved.

As the years passed, Tonahill and the city's other white elite slowly molded Jasper into a town of their own liking, a place that retained a purity that modernizing America no longer had. It was a town where Tonahill was known by one and all as Poppa Joe and where life remained, in many ways, frozen in his favorite year.

Joe Tonahill was a burly man—the quintessential old-time southern gentleman, with dewlaps and a shock of white hair. Born in 1913, Tonahill had grown up without money, following a father who worked a succession of unrelated jobs throughout the South. When he finally got a diploma from Port Arthur High School in Texas, young Joe, as most strong boys did then, went directly to the oil fields.

Joe Tonahill might have set himself on the same path as his father if he had not had a terrible accident. Three years into a roughnecking job, Tonahill was working in the Conroe Field for Humble Oil (now Exxon) when a natural gas backup caused a monstrous explosion. Had Tonahill not dived out the window of a workers' shack to safety, he would have been killed. As it was, he suffered third-degree burns over his face, arms, and hands and spent two weeks in the hospital recovering. "We didn't get any settlement or judgment from the company, and it was then and there that my father and I decided I ought to go to law school. What happened to me just wasn't right," Tonahill said.

While a student at the Washington College of Law in 1939, Tonahill met Violett Smith, daughter of Virginia representative John Smith. The romance of Joe and Violett was the stuff of legend in Jasper. Violett was a tall thin auburn-haired beauty who enjoyed the privileges of being a representative's daughter. Joe was a young law student who refused to accept no for an answer.

Her father asked Tonahill only one question eight months later when he asked for her hand: "Can you live without Violett?" he said. The young lawyer, who was making $150 a month, shook his head. "Then she's yours," Smith said. With Violett, the congressman made a separate pact. She could move to Texas, he said, only under the condition that she wrote him a letter every Sunday.

Everyone in Jasper, white and black, had a Joe Tonahill story. Meeting him in the grocery store was deemed a brush with greatness. Violett Tonahill's granite tombstone dominated the town cemetery. Lawyers who wanted to do well in Jasper were expected to do their time in Tonahill's law offices. County judge Joe Bob Golden had once been Tonahill's law partner. District Attorney Guy James Gray had been an associate. Sheriff Billy Rowles retained him when Rowles was the target of a civil suit. Reverend Lyons remembered caddying for him at the Sam Rayburn Country Club. Elmo Jackson talked of serving him hamburgers after his golf game. Tonahill was as close to royalty as Jasper could ever hope to have, and the Ruby trial was the most exciting court case Jasperites ever expected to be a party to, however tangentially. And then the Byrd murder happened. Joe Tonahill, for more than a year, was no longer the sun around which Jasper revolved. Instead, everyone was focused on a young man named Bill King.

*   *   *

"GUY JAMES, WE'VE got a bad one," Billy Rowles said. He looked at the clock on the wall. It was 11 P.M. Sunday.

District Attorney Gray didn't ask any questions. Rowles sounded worried, and that unsettled him. "I'll be right there," he said, fishing for his watch on the nightstand. He knew if the sheriff was calling this late, something was very wrong.

Gray's history in Jasper was easy to trace. His father had been a basketball coach at the high school and a rancher, and his mother had been an elementary school teacher. His paternal grandfather was a judge in neighboring Newton County. Guy James Gray liked to say a Chevrolet led him to his calling. The short version of the story was that his father bribed him. "Daddy said he would buy me any car I wanted if I went to law school, and I told him okay, but it had to be a Corvette," said Gray. What Gray got instead was a Ford Fairlane. He went to law school anyway.

He returned to Jasper ready to set the world on fire. He joined Joe Tonahill's personal injury practice in 1973 and began looking for opportunities. ("Joe has another young lawyer coming to work tomorrow," Violett Tonahill wrote her father in September 1973. "Guy James Gray from here. He thinks this boy will make a good trial lawyer in time.")

Gray spent only a year with Tonahill before he decided to go into politics and run against the incumbent district attorney, Bill

Martin. He lost by two hundred votes, largely, he said, because he was "an unmarried, twenty-six-year-old know-it-all who had no business being D.A."

Tonahill remembered Guy James Gray as a bright, ambitious man. "There was no stopping Guy James," said Tonahill. "He was a man with ambitions and the smarts to make it happen. I knew we'd never have him in the office for long."

While politics came naturally to the new graduate, it was never easy. He was acerbic, and some people in Jasper thought that all those years at Texas A&M—"that liberal school," they called it—had taken most of the essential Jasper-ness out of him. He had become, his critics said, a city slicker. What rankled Jasper's elite even more, however, was Guy James Gray's willingness to break the code of conduct that had governed city policy and politics for generations. Gray was a maverick, and it made the white establishment nervous.

"I was never part of the clique inside Jasper, part of the Tonahill, Dickerson, Lindsey cabal that had always controlled sheriffs, commissioners, and other officials in town," Gray said. "By the 1980s you couldn't get by practicing law by influence, and that meant circumstances were changing for a lot of people like Joe Tonahill. And they weren't happy about it. They tried to keep things the way they had always been, but progress was getting the better of them."

Guy James Gray might have made fewer waves in Jasper if there was more diplomat and less politician in him. In the end, however, his political instincts won him the job he coveted. He was appointed district attorney by the governor in 1979 to fill an unexpired term. The job didn't come without its complications. There were over eight hundred cases backlogged on the felony docket going back twenty years. Gray worked tirelessly to clean up the office and was largely successful. After his appointment, he ran unopposed for reelection four times, until March 1998, when Ted Walker, a Houston lawyer, ran against him for the post. Gray won—but only by a scant fifty-six votes.

To hear Jasper's black community tell it, they voted against Gray in a united protest against what they saw as a new pattern in the D.A.'s office to prosecute small-time black pushers instead of the white kingpins who ran Jasper's drug trade. The black community watched newspeople interview Gray on local television and commented on how, over the years, he had changed. He had become more of a politician, they said. When they heard him speak, they heard a voice that had taken on the eerie impassiveness of cheap electronics. Gray was no longer a maverick, they said; he was now one of "them," the white establishment.

The fifty-year-old Gray walked into the Aubrey Cole Law Enforcement Center on Burch Street the night of June 8 without any inkling that the "bad one" Billy Rowles had told him about on the phone would change his life and his relationship with the black community in Jasper forever.

*　　*　　*

OFFICERS JAMES GUNTER and Curtis Frame had been with Shawn Berry for hours when Rowles and Gray pushed into the interrogation room around midnight Sunday.

Berry looked as if he had woken up under a bridge. A man who stood less than five feet four inches tall, he spent a lot of his spare time lifting weights, riding bulls, and taking steroids in a bid to be bigger than he was. People who knew Berry said he was kind but a little slow.

He carved rocking horses for many of the poor white children in Jasper and, like his brother, Louis, appeared to get along with both whites and blacks. After Scared Straight camp with Bill King, Berry seemed determined to sort out his life. He got a job at a car dealership and lived in a trailer behind the store. He moved in with Bill King in a bid to save money. He worked at the Twin Cinemas downtown. Berry was dependable enough that John Bailey, who owned the small theater, made him manager. He was bad at choosing friends, however, and tried too hard to fit in. According to Guy James Gray, when Russell Brewer arrived in Jasper, Berry felt his best childhood friend, Bill King, had lost interest in him. Suddenly Shawn Berry was a third wheel, a stranger not privy to a whole part of King's life Brewer understood. And it bothered him.

"In a lot of ways, looking back on it, you could say that Shawn Berry never really had a chance," said Jasper police chief Harlon Alexander, who had had more contact with Berry over the years than Rowles had. "His mama was in and out of prison; his stepfather was a tough character. He had no one to look up to, so he found role models wherever he could. Sometimes they were the wrong ones."

*   *   *

BACK AT THE Timbers Apartments, Bill King and Russell Brewer had heard Shawn Berry was in custody. King thought Berry could be a convincing performer but was unreliable. He panicked too easily. King and Brewer had already worked out an alibi for their whereabouts the night before, and King was sure Brewer would hold out against any interrogation. About Berry he was less sure. The sheriff's office was fishing, King thought; they must be talking to other suspects. At the same time, King would have given his right arm for just five minutes with Berry, to make sure he didn't talk. If Berry broke, they would all end up in Huntsville prison, at the Walls, as death row was known, and they would get lethal injections for sure. King paced around the apartment.

Shawn Berry was feeling equally cornered. There was nothing behind him, he thought, but wall. Rowles leaned forward.

"I bet your stomach hurts, Shawn. I bet it does real bad," Rowles began.

Berry dropped his shoulders and then appeared to be trying to hold himself back. The signs of his effort were classic, Rowles thought as he watched him. Berry uncrossed and recrossed his legs, covered his mouth with his hand, yawned, needed to go to the bathroom a lot. Rowles knew that guilt tended to reveal itself. Its presence was found in movement and gesture and tone of voice. Berry had already said they were out the night before driving his truck. He said he knew Byrd. Beyond that he had not yet ventured. The grilling continued for hours. Berry kept to his story. He said he had spent Saturday night with Bill King and Russell Brewer, but he denied knowing anything about any murder.

In the meantime, Rowles sent a squad car out to watch King's apartment.

"Shawn Berry and Russell Brewer have IQs of about 80," the sheriff said later. "They weren't smart enough to do this on their own. To lay the body out in front of the cemetery where everyone would see it—that was Bill King's doing."

As the hours ticked by, Gray suggested they see if they could get Bill King and Russell Brewer to come in voluntarily for questioning. "That way we didn't have to worry about the legality of an arrest and charges," said Gray. "And it worked."

Almost too well. Moments after Rowles and Gray had decided to try to bring King and Brewer to the station, the two men emerged from King's apartment on the way to twenty-four-hour Wal-Mart across the road. It was 2 A.M. The sheriff's officers stopped the pair, asked if they would be willing to go to the station. They even offered them a ride. King and Brewer, neither of whom had a car, took them up on it.

"I thought Brewer looked guilty as soon as I saw him," Rowles said later.

In the waiting room of the jail, Brewer couldn't seem to sit still. King, on the other hand, was smug. Saturday, June 6, the three of them were looking for a party and a couple of girls they knew, King told Sheriff Rowles early Monday morning. He described the road where they drove, mailboxes they had knocked down for fun, and even admitted to picking up James Byrd. Of course, the last time he saw "Mr. Byrd" was when Shawn drove away with Byrd after having dropped him and Brewer off at his apartment. "What happened after that I don't rightly know," said King.

Rowles was impressed with Bill King's poise, with his peppering the account with details that could be verified. At the same time, though, Rowles was sure nearly all of it was a lie. King talked for more than two hours, into the wee hours of the morning. He told Rowles all about life for a virile young man in Jasper, the girls he had laid, the women he had impregnated, and about his life in jail. When he finished, King leaned back in his chair with a self-satisfied smile and asked Rowles if he had any other questions.

"Do you mind if we search your apartment?" Rowles said evenly.

"Not at all," King said, straightening his mouth. "Where do I sign?"

Rowles handed him a voluntary consent-to-search form. King smiled. "I've got nothing to hide; go ahead and search," he said. Twenty minutes later, officers found more than a dozen steaks and boxes of frozen shrimp in King's freezer. Rowles called in restaurant owner Patrick Lam, who had reported the break-in from a week before. Lam identified the meat that officers found in King's apartment as his. Rowles booked King and Brewer on suspicion of burglary, and the ball started rolling.

Meanwhile, in the interrogation room, Shawn Berry had started to crack. It was 4 A.M. by then, and Rowles told him King and Brewer had been arrested. The sheriff told Shawn Berry about prison, and how much better King and Brewer would fare because they knew the ropes and had been there before. The jail time, he told Berry, would be much harder for him. Of course, he had one opportunity to get himself out of this mess, Rowles said: write a confession. "Tell us what you know, and I will make sure the federal prosecutors I call down here come to your cell first," Rowles said. "Otherwise, I may just start with King and Brewer, and there's no telling what they are going to say. It's your choice, Shawn."

Berry began to tear up. Rowles had him. He left the room as Berry began to write. Berry's statement was incomplete but said enough. He and King and Brewer had been driving around, drinking beer, and had picked up Byrd on Martin Luther King Boulevard. They drove him up to Huff Creek Road, beat him up in a clearing, and dragged him with a logging chain three miles before dumping his body at the side of the road. Berry said he didn't know they were dragging Byrd until it was too late. His written confession and the implication of Bill King and Russell Brewer in the murder made it clear that this was a hate crime from the start. For Sheriff Billy Rowles and for Guy James Gray, that was key.

Hate crimes, which can carry stiffer penalties than simple assaults or other violent offenses, are usually defined as violent acts motivated by some form of discrimination. Forty-five states in the United States have enacted hate crime laws, which generally protect victims on the basis of race, religion, and ethnicity, and, in some states, sexual orientation. Proponents say a hate crime, which is inherently subjective, can be summed up in two words: "motive matters." While there was no hate crime in Texas, there was a federal statute under which the trio could be tried.

Soon after Berry provided his statement, Rowles was back in his truck on the way to Beaumont, seventy miles away. He had an appointment with the hate crimes unit at the FBI. "I knew this whole deal was too big to do on our own," Rowles said. "This wasn't a time to get turf-y or decide we could handle it on our own. I wanted their help. I needed their help. Looking back on it, it was the smartest thing I ever did."

*   *   *

BY TUESDAY MORNING a crowd had formed outside the Jasper County Courthouse. Residents had heard that the three men accused of the Byrd murder would arrive soon. Newspeople of every description had descended on Jasper: members of the major wire services, photographers, television cameramen, reporters from around the world. Many of them had only just arrived, cornering Jasper residents for interviews as they walked along Courthouse Square. Billy Rowles and Harlon Alexander had set aside ample space on the sidewalk in front of the courthouse. From the looks of it, one would have thought the congregation in the square had gathered in expectation of a movie star or a famous politician. High school friends of Bill King's and Shawn Berry's had wandered down to the square. Others, from the black community, just wanted to catch a glimpse of the trio.

"They should just set them free and let us take care of them," said one black resident. "They wouldn't make it two blocks before we'd rip them apart. Like the Bible says, 'An eye for an eye.' The death penalty is too good for these guys."

No one expected violence as the three men were led into the courthouse. What they anticipated was shouted abuse. But when the group caught sight of the accused with their escort of brown-uniformed sheriff's officers, they were struck dumb, as though they were amazed to find King, Brewer, and Berry in human shape. Clad in orange prison jumpsuits, bullet-proof vests, and hand-cuffed, the men blinked against the television lights and flashbulbs. King smirked for the cameras. Brewer stared at the ground. Shawn Berry tried to hide his face.

*   *   *

IN THE DAYS after the arraignment, back on Huff Creek Road people shuddered in their shacks of gray wood, convinced that James Byrd's murder was only the beginning. They imagined Jasper was returning to a time of "nigger words," unexplained deaths, and suspicious fires.

The police stepped up patrols along Huff Creek, driving through the pines just as the gloaming above the woods turned the sky into a monochrome slate. Bats no bigger than sparrows began to flick and dart in the dusk as the people of Huff Creek Road melted out of the woods in what had become a daily ritual after the murder. Wordlessly, residents went down the road to examine the eerie path of eighty-one circles of Day-Glo paint that had marked the evidence. There were so many circles one could almost hop-scotch from one to the next and cover the entire three-mile length of the crime scene. The investigators' painted trail laid out a virtual map of James Byrd's undoing from the culvert that ripped off his head and arm (marked with a semicircle and the word "Head" in bright orange) to the now faint long bloody stripe that ran from one side of the road to the other.

People in the community recalled Emmett Till's death in 1955. Till was killed in Money, Mississippi. Unused to the ways of the segregated South, the fourteen-year-old Chicago boy allegedly flirted with a white woman, who subsequently told her husband, Roy Bryant. Bryant and his brother J. W. Milam decided to remind the "nigger" about his place. They seized Till from his great-uncle's house in the middle of the woods, in the middle of the night. His body was found floating in the Tallahatchie River the next day. Bryant and Milam were acquitted by an all-white jury in less time than it takes to watch a feature film. A month later, Milam felt invulnerable enough to confess to the murder to a journalist. And he did so with impunity. With an eye on that past, residents called the sheriff's office to ask the county for streetlights.

"I was scared to walk outside after that," said Christine Carter later. "And Vander was always wanting to know where I was going and when I would be back. We were all worried this was the beginning of something bigger. We were all waiting for something even worse to happen."

After James Byrd's murder, the Huff Creek community felt everything around them had been washed in sepia tones. They thought back to a not-so-distant past of lynching and other violent expressions of racism. Vigilante nooses haunted them. They wondered aloud whether Billy Rowles, a white man, would uphold the law or look the other way, the way law enforcement had in Mississippi. Lynching was the work of white mobs who didn't just stop at murdering their victims but also tortured and mutilated them. Just as James Byrd had been. Their victims, carrion left hanging from trees as a warning, were so beaten they became less than human. Just like James. The act of lynching was supposed to win white women respect, emasculate black men, and make white men feel omnipotent. James Byrd's murder, more than anything, brought a community's collective sense of vulnerability back to the surface.

"Right away, Klan ran through our mind," said Reverend Lyons. "Or maybe they paid someone to do it after the McQueen murder. Our main concern was that whoever it was would strike again. Stay home, we told everyone. Don't walk ones, walk twos."

A week later, the circles of paint were still there, but someone, possibly a resident, had carefully gone over the outlines of Day-Glo orange with black paint, turning the screaming reminders of what had happened into whispers.

CHAPTER SIX

SMALL CONSPIRACIES

Father in Heaven Forgive Us.
—SIGN ON TEXAS CHARLIE'S MARQUEE
ON HIGHWAY 96

IT WAS MIDDAY Tuesday, June 9, when the cameras began setting up outside the Aubrey Cole Law Enforcement Center for Billy
Rowles's first press conference. The sheriff's office had taped photographs of King, Brewer, and Berry on the front windows of the
jail. King looked directly at the camera. His puffy baby face
appeared relaxed. The bridge of his nose looked broken. Brewer
bore a striking resemblance to singer Bob Dylan. His face was
scraggly and thin, and his eyes were downcast. Berry looked faintly
like he was posing for a family photo. He stared directly into the
camera with a slightly surprised look. The trio looked younger than
anyone had expected. Less redneck. Less threatening.

When Rowles pushed through the glass doors and faced the reporters, he caught himself. He hadn't anticipated so many people. There were more than two dozen cameras lined up cheek by jowl. More than 150 journalists crowded in. The whirring of the automatic winders on the cameras was deafening. CNN aired the conference live. Mike Lout decided, tentatively, that broadcasting the press conferences live on KJAS would be the right thing to do for the community. That was the only way Jasperites would be able to hear what was going on firsthand. He held an outstretched mike from beneath the television cameras.

Rowles wanted to keep it short. He provided the barest of details about the murder. "On June 7, 1998, at approximately 9 A.M. the body of a black male, minus the head and right arm, was discovered on Huff Creek Road," he began, reading from a script the FBI had provided. The body had been dragged. There was "a trail of some type of brown substance" leading away from the body. The head and arm had been discovered about a mile from where the rest of the body lay. Brewer and King were believed to have had ties with white supremacy groups such as the Aryan Nation and the Ku Klux Klan while they were in prison, he said. Both were on parole. Berry was on probation. The FBI had already sent in agents who were investigating whether this was a hate crime, a federal offense. Rowles provided key details from Berry's statement and added that Byrd might have been alive when the dragging began. Then he took questions. Reporters immediately asked about the Klan. Was this a Klan killing? Was there Ku Klux Klan in Jasper?

"Those boys didn't learn how to hate here," Rowles told the assembly. "There's no Klan in Jasper."

The statement was immediately met by hoots of derision from black residents in the audience. "Yeah, right," said one.

Rowles was immediately sorry he had said it. Later, he reflected: "What I meant is there were no organized Klan factions here. I'm sure there are some Klansmen. But explaining it would only have made it worse; it was too late. It upset me when the black people in the audience scoffed."

He wasn't alone. Among nearly all of Jasper's white community there was a sudden and intense outbreak of guilt. While there was some grumbling on the fringes about all this fuss for Byrd when only a week before Jerry McQueen had been bludgeoned to death, white Jasperites suddenly bowed their heads and asked for forgiveness. They knew that the outside world was watching and judging them. And those outsiders, for the most part, had already found them guilty. Jasper was stained with a vicious brand of racism that could forever make the word "Jasper" shorthand for hate.

In the early days after the murder, an odd closeness grew up between the black and the white communities. The first outward sign came on Tuesday morning, two days after the body was found. Yellow ribbons suddenly appeared on lapels, car antennas, and doors all over town. The idea of wearing yellow strips of ribbon to show unity actually originated many miles away, in California. Unav Wade's eldest daughter, Annegenette Wade, called her mother and told her she was so upset about what had happened in Jasper she had started passing yellow ribbons out in her neighborhood to show support for the community. Unav put the phone back in the cradle, grabbed her car keys, and headed out the door to Wal-Mart. She bought every bolt of yellow satin ribbon on the shelves and cut more than two hundred ribbons for residents to pin to their lapels. That initial supply lasted until lunch. Before she knew it, Jasper's ladies were lined up outside her beauty salon asking for a ribbon, for a pin, and offering a hug. Her youngest daughter, Margena Gardiner, made a return trip to Wal-Mart and other stores around town to buy every kind of yellow ribbon in stock—yarns, cords, satins, plastic. If it was yellow, it went in her cart.

"It was so sweet," Unav Wade said later. "Everybody just got busy. I put one on my door, and then everyone wanted one for their door. I took it all to mean that we all agreed about one thing for certain: this murder was a terrible, terrible thing. It didn't take long for the news media to pick it up."

The tidal wave of yellow ribbons was only the beginning. Blacks and whites would see each other in the stores and spontaneously hug. Whites held doors open for blacks. Hastily called town meetings had white citizens apologizing for racial injustices inflicted years before. A white auto mechanic told a former customer, a black man, that he had charged him for a new muffler and tailpipe when he had actually installed used parts. Traffic lights could be green, but white motorists would wave blacks to cross. More than 1,000 citizens attended a prayer vigil on Courthouse Square on June 15, and called for reconciliation. Billy Rowles counted dozens of confessions of prejudice in the days after the murder. "Dozens of people tell me now how bad they feel for using the N-word," he said.

The people in the black community noticed the changes but viewed them with suspicion. The whites were trying too hard, they said. Obviously they were feeling guilty about more than just a murder. "I was interested to see how long this would last," said Unav Wade.

Behind the scenes, the black community leaders were having trouble convincing black citizens that the Byrd murder should not be met with an explosion of violence and revenge. In a bid to quell those feelings, members of the black community went to their churches and called on their God. They read the first chapter of Peter and the

Book of Matthew. "Take therefore no thought for the morrow," the verse from Matthew read. "For the morrow shall take thought for the things of itself. Sufficient unto the day is the evil thereof." Only the Lord, the black community reasoned, could help them make sense of what happened.

The question was what to do next. The Ministerial Alliance called for community meetings. They organized school assemblies. They called teachers back from summer vacation early to attend classes on tolerance and prejudice.

Some members of the black community ventured to think the murder, gruesome as it was, offered a distant possibility of change in Jasper's balance of power. Perhaps this would be enough to jar whites into less racist behavior. What was certain was that Jasper's elite would not be able to control this situation as they had so many others in the past. This was too big. Too many people were watching. Too many from the news media were here. For the first time in as long as anyone could remember, the white community needed the black community to succeed. If the two races worked together, they could put the murder behind them, send the media on their way, and perhaps even preserve the reputation of their little town. If there was a split, if the black community said what they really thought about prejudice in Jasper, they were doomed.

*   *   *

WHILE COMMUNITY LEADERS made plans for community programs, the rest of Jasper feared what might happen next. Whites braced for reprisals. Blacks waited for another from their ranks to disappear. Theorists called Guy James Gray at home. Most of those who telephoned were citizens wanting to be helpful ("Guy

James? Listen, I'm sure it was a drug deal. Berry was supposed to be on steroids, his being so little and all, and Byrd was selling them."). There were also anonymous people with suspicious minds ("It had to have been Klan. All the hallmarks are there. Vidor people are out in those woods all the time, and it being only a week after the McQueen killing, well, it doesn't take a genius to put two and two together."). And there were people who were officially concerned ("Byrd owed people money; maybe it all finally came due.").

The ghost of the event kept returning, making heads click back a notch as the enormity of it all registered. And Jasperites wondered among themselves—from the blacks in the woods who sat up whole nights wide awake, watchful and listening, to the regulars at Texas Charlie's Bar-B-Que who worried about unrest in the black community and whether they could ever put things right.

The talk swirled in Texas Charlie's, a diner where locals came to stir bottomless mugs of coffee and chew the fat. Texas Charlie's was a big place, with a cowboy feel. Oversized wood booths lined the walls, red-and-white checkered cloths covered the tables, and enormous bottles of Tabasco and big shakers of pepper sat at every station. To a visitor, Texas Charlie's just screamed "Texas." The walls were sprinkled with vintage cards that read: "Finck's Detroit Special Overalls: Wear Like a Pig's Nose" and "A Man Who Thinks Wears Finck's." A jukebox and television sat in the corner. A rack of coffee cups hung above the counter for Texas Charlie's regulars. Nancy Nicholson hailed and hugged just about everyone who walked in, with a faintly artificial ring.

"Didn't take Billy Rowles long at all to solve this case," crowed Charlie Nicholson, who owned the restaurant with his wife, Nancy. Heads wagged in agreement. Everyone wanted to believe all of this would blow over once King, Brewer, and Berry were in jail. "This wasn't about race," the chorus went. "This was about three drunk troublemakers and a man in the wrong place at the wrong time. That's all. They'll go to jail, and everything will be all right."

More nods in agreement. Texas Charlie's clientele was nearly all white.

"Truth is, it was kind of a white people's place," Reverend Lyons said. "It didn't say it on the door, but we knew. Some folks thought that whites got up in the morning and decided about how they could hurt us. But that isn't true. They don't think about us. Period. They've found a way to make it so we're as good as not being there. Signs on the door aren't necessary."

*   *   *

WHILE JASPERITES WERE outwardly shocked when they heard news of the dragging murder of James Byrd, deep down they sensed that this was an incident waiting to happen. If it hadn't been James Byrd, it might have been someone else.

While the rest of the country was enjoying unprecedented prosperity in the 1990s, isolated places like Jasper never experienced the fruits of the boom. Naturally, people got competitive. It wasn't just white versus black or rich versus poor. It was community member against community member, brother against brother, deacon against deacon. The competition sapped the vitality from day-to-day life. It made the white community suspicious of the black community and the black community equally wary of the white. The Byrd murder aggravated those suspicions.

Those smoldering feelings were Walter Diggles's number one concern when he heard about the murder. The executive director of the Deep East Texas Council of Governments, which provided grants and assistance for the indigent in the community, Diggles had grown up in Jasper and was one of its most educated and politically savvy black citizens. Even the most prejudiced members of the town's white community were willing to say that Walter Diggles was different. ("Not really black, if you know what I mean. He's learned to work with whites and can talk to us without letting his color get in the way.") Diggles used his status as an accepted member in both worlds to demand change, whether it was convincing merchants to start job training programs for blacks or cajoling the city council to pave streets in black neighborhoods. Diggles, who followed in his father's footsteps and became a lawyer, lived in an enormous house in the white section of town. The purchase meant that those who might not have otherwise, treated him as an equal, as if he were white.

Even so, Diggles found his ambiguous status was a double-edged sword. Some people in the black community said Diggles wasn't really black anymore. Because he did not feel the arbitrary oppression and abuse that others in the community felt, he had been stripped of his blackness. Blacks in Jasper lived with an unrelenting societal insecurity, a knowledge that the ground beneath their feet could shift at the whim of a policeman or a white person. Because Diggles acted like a regular citizen, he was different. He wasn't scared of the police. In fact, he called them at home. What the black community did not fully understand was that Diggles was accepted by whites partly because he didn't make them nervous.

Forty-five years old, Diggles grew up watching the civil rights movement on television. Because of his father's standing in the community, he played in the homes of Jasper's white elite, and, as was expected, he went to college in Houston, studied law, and returned home. He came back as the executive director of the council of governments. Yet Diggles's triumphant homecoming only put in sharper relief what he intrinsically felt as a child: whites in Jasper were willing to go through the motions of equality, but deep down they still believed that blacks had to remember their place.

Diggles had already starting thinking about the fallout from the murder. If James Byrd's death would serve any useful purpose, perhaps it would be to persuade a guilt-ridden white Jasper to grant a measure of equality, he thought. The black community had a window of opportunity to exact change because the white community was scared of what might happen next.

Four days after the murder, Diggles was in Billy Rowles's office accepting a cup of coffee and taking a seat. Already there were a number of members of the ministerial alliance, including Reverend Lyons, in attendance. The men shook hands, nodded to one another, and turned to Rowles. They all shared the same concern, that outsiders would weigh in, tell Jasper's story to the world, and stir up the feelings of resentment that bubbled below the surface. While no one said it aloud, they were all thinking of the racially motivated events that had rocked and ruined towns around them: the Beaumont riots in the 1940s, the uprising and looting in Hemphill after police officers were initially acquitted in the beating murder of Loyal Garner, the Los Angeles riots after the Rodney King verdict in 1992.

From his pulpit in a big city where few from Jasper had ever been, Jesse Jackson had already delivered a summary judgment. He was outraged, and he vowed to travel to Jasper to provide support for his black brothers who were under siege. The black community in Jasper, however, was not so sure it wanted Jackson's help, and its leaders said as much over coffee in Rowles's office. "We were worried he would just stir things up," said Reverend Lyons. "We wanted to take care of our problems amongst ourselves. We didn't mind him coming so much as not wanting to yield our agenda to his. We were worried he would suddenly be in charge."

The only way to combat that, Diggles told the men in Rowles's office, was to speak with one voice: to push for peace and forgiveness and present Jasper in a positive way. All the men in the room knew there were problems in Jasper—including prejudice—but they were determined not to let outsiders exploit that. Jasper would take care of its own problems, black and white leaders agreed, after the strangers went home. Until the outsiders departed, the message was clear: citizens needed to do what they could to prevent Jasper from being labeled a racist town.

"It wasn't a conspiracy, just an agreement that they would put our best foot forward," said Mike Lout. "And they'd use the national press to make sure that message got out."

It was savvy public relations from a town that strangers were willing to underestimate. At every press conference there would be an equal number of blacks and whites. When a white man spoke, so too would a black leader. Community leaders knew, instinctively, that public dialogue was never real dialogue. Nobody would admit to anything really meaningful in a crowd.

*   *   *

REVEREND BILLY RAY ROBINSON was proprietor of the Robinson Community Funeral Home; president of Robinson's Bail Bonds ("Credit Terms Available"), and, not so coincidentally, chief executive at Robinson's Limousine Service ("Two-Hour Minimum").

Billy Ray Robinson was not well liked in East Jasper. He was considered by most residents a newcomer and untrustworthy. "Billy

Ray is into everything. You have to be careful about Billy Ray," said one law enforcement official.

Billy Ray Robinson ran his funeral, bail bond, and limousine operations from a 3,000-square-foot monolith at the corner of Highways 63 and 190. The building looked oddly like a model home in a luxury subdivision—all fresh brick and leaded glass sparkling in the Texas sunshine—floating on a small island of grass surrounded by bramble and dirt. Three spotless limousines sat parked in the carport shaded by forest green awnings emblazoned with an enormous golden cursive *R*. Inside, the funeral home was hushed except for the soothing hum of air conditioners. The place had a just-moved-in feel to it, even though Robinson had finished construction on the building years before. The two secretaries who kept track of Robinson's many comings and goings sat behind plates of glass in offices that appeared to have few files and even less furniture.

"James Byrd's sisters came out here and asked me to handle the body," said Robinson from his makeshift office in a room at the back of the building. The only decoration on the wall was a mortician's certification. Small boxes sat in the corner. A small conference table with no drawers served as Robinson's desk. There were no papers to be seen, only a single multiline phone which rang incessantly.

"I was always nice to James. I let him sweep up around here and lent him money when he needed it. The family wanted someone who had been kind to James to handle the arrangements, so I did," he said. He had also bailed James out of jail several times, even when Byrd didn't have the money to guarantee the bond, he said.

The black community told the story of James Byrd's transfer from Dorie Colman's to Robinson's funeral home a little differently. Three friends of the Byrd family said Billy Ray Robinson called the Byrds and offered them a deal for the funeral in exchange for being able to say he was the one making the arrangements. Robinson thought it would be good advertising, they said. Robinson denied it. Calling the grieving family would have been unethical, he said.

The Byrd sisters picked out what Robinson called a midrange casket with a mirrored top ("Not as comfortable as our top-of-the-line model, but a solid one"), and a vault added another several thousand dollars to the total. "Interesting thing about blacks and whites and funerals," Robinson said. "Whites like their vaults underground so they have a nice flat burial site. Blacks want the vaults above the ground so people can see where they spent their money. That's what we did for James Byrd, an above-the-ground vault right there in the city cemetery."

Robinson talked about the business of preparing the dead as if he were selling appliances or sporting goods. "Embalming people killed in car wrecks isn't so hard," said Robinson. "Usually what you've got is a head trauma or a broke leg, and, well, we just have to straighten that out; it doesn't cause leaks or anything."

Robinson said Byrd's embalming was particularly difficult because he was in pieces. Lots of embalming fluid leaks required clamping off. The job ended up requiring the same kind of piece-by-piece patience sportsmen had when inflating sections of a rubber raft. "You inflate, or embalm, each section at a time, and then sew it all up when you are through," he said. "You have to be careful with the sewing and not take too much skin; otherwise you cause another leak." James Byrd took eight hours to embalm, a long time by Robinson's standards. "The head and shoulder area were kind of delicate," he said. "I wasn't afraid, but, yeah, it was upsetting. James didn't look like James anymore."

James Byrd was dressed in a suit he had never before worn. The funeral, Robinson said, was going to be a great one, with tents and catered food and awnings.

*   *   *

WALTER DIGGLES HAD grown up watching Jesse Jackson, marveling at his oratorical gift, and now he was awaiting the arrival of the great man in his office. Across town, Reverend Lyons was at Greater New Bethel Baptist Church, where Jackson was scheduled to arrive next. Lyons had what he was going to say all planned out. He would welcome Jackson to his parish and tell him a little about James Byrd and go over some of the details of the funeral as Billy Ray Robinson had set them out. Then the phone rang.

It was one of Lyons's parishioners. There had been a change of plan. Jesse Jackson was at the Byrds' house trying to convince them to move their son's funeral to First Baptist (a bigger, fancier church), he told Lyons quickly, obviously whispering into the phone from another room at the Byrd house. Jackson wanted to deliver the eulogy himself, the parishioner added. "You better get over here," he said.

Lyons put on his hat and drove the quarter mile to the Byrds' house. "I go up to the house and walk in to find Jackson in the den," said Lyons. "I took the Byrds into the bedroom and asked them if they were moving the funeral from New Bethel to First Baptist. No, no, they said. And is Mr. Jackson doing the eulogy? No, no, they said. I looked at them for a long minute and said that I just wanted to make sure. They didn't know how I could have known. If I hadn't done that, I am sure the funeral would have been different."

Diggles had a similar mission, aimed at keeping a lid on the situation. He had to find a way to tell Jackson, gently, what to say to a waiting congregation at a special service for James Byrd at Greater Bethel New Baptist Church.

"I asked Billy if he wouldn't mind having Jesse drop by my office when they went to pick him up at the airport," said Diggles. "So they took him to my office before he went to the special services that Wednesday night. I just couldn't come out and say it. There were too many people, or there seemed to be too much of a rush; I couldn't tell him what I had set out to say, that he shouldn't inflame the situation."

Finally, as the two sat together in the pew at Greater New Bethel, Diggles leaned over and whispered, "Now what are you going to say?"

Jesse Jackson's eyes widened. "What do you want me to say?" he asked.

Diggles had the speech mapped out in his mind as Lyons began a slow introduction of Jackson. "This town has pulled together and needs to heal," Diggles whispered to Jackson. "The facts are that within twenty-four hours of the murder three men were charged with capital murder. This isn't southern justice, this is just plain justice, and you need to tell these people so."

Jackson nodded and smiled as Lyons finished his introductory remarks and turned to welcome him to the podium. Videotape rolled, photographers snapped pictures, and the congregation held its breath. Suddenly Jesse Jackson, the man who had stood on the balcony with Martin Luther King Jr. when he was shot, a preacher who had been a vision on television, was before them in their small church. Jackson took a breath and proceeded to say precisely what Diggles had told him to say.

"God has a way of doing great things in small towns and with ordinary people," Jackson told the more than three hundred people at the service. "I see a new Jasper. The old Jasper has passed away."

*   *   *

RUMORS BEGAN TO fly in Jasper's black community. Another black man had been attacked, went one. The Klan was coming to

Jasper, went another. They were half right. Sheriff Rowles did what he could to assure the community there wasn't another attack, but he was less sure about the Klan. He thought they would be coming, just as they had arrived in Beaumont during the riots decades before. Remembering that history, some members of the black community were thinking now was a good time to pack up and leave, not just Jasper County but maybe even Texas. They wanted to go somewhere where they didn't have to worry about Klan or dark woods where shadows made them jump.

Though few said it aloud, the majority of black Jasperites were skeptical that the sheriff's office would ever get to the bottom of the murder. They were equally circumspect about police chief Harlon Alexander, who was also white. Too many things, they believed, had been swept under the rug, and they had to be convinced this would play out any differently. Even after the sheriff formally charged King, Brewer, and Berry for the murder just a day after their arrest, the black community was dubious.

They weren't alone.

The phone rang in Harlon Alexander's office first thing on Thursday morning. The Dallas Department of Public Safety was on the line with more bad news: the New Black Panthers were planning to come to Jasper to "protect the black community" from any copycat crimes. They wanted their arrival to coincide with the James Byrd funeral that coming Saturday. "I had never even heard of the New Black Panthers," Alexander said later. "I had to have someone explain to me who they were."

Hours after the phone call from Dallas, Alexander was on the phone with Khalid Abdul Mohammed, the group's militant leader. The New Black Panthers of Dallas were formed as a community activist group in 1991. Their ideology draws heavily upon the beliefs of the Nation of Islam movement and Malcolm X. Khalid

Mohammed was openly anti-Semitic. During the mid-1990s, the NBP conducted neighborhood antidrug patrols of predominately black neighborhoods in Dallas and were described as highly confrontational. As Alexander read through the intelligence reports, he had a bad feeling.

"We want to stand up for the black people of Jasper," Khalid Mohammed told the chief.

Harlon Alexander, six months shy of retirement, was the type of Texan who wore his spurs in the house and had reclining LA-Z-BOY chairs in the barn. Famous for his bulldogging and roping prowess, he peppered his sentences with Texas expressions and cowboy metaphors. His legs seemed to be bent to the exact curves of a horse's sides. He held the title record in the Alexandria, Louisiana, Coliseum for the fastest steer ever thrown: three seconds flat. He moved to Jasper in 1945, the son of the founder of the Jasper Rodeo. It wasn't until an injury sidelined him from the rodeo circuit that he joined the Jasper Police Force in 1968. Ten years after signing up, he landed the chief's job. In nearly thirty years of police work, he had never seen anything like the fallout from the Byrd murder. Khalid Mohammed was only the first of his newfound concerns.

Alexander listened patiently as Mohammed made his case for a Panther patrol during the Byrd funeral. The black community wasn't safe, he said. Armed patrols would ensure nothing happened during the funeral. The group was welcome to come, but they couldn't bring their weapons, Alexander replied. Mohammed protested. "We have a legal right to be armed." Alexander repeated the refrain like a mantra; they were welcome to come, but they couldn't bring their weapons. The phone call ended inconclusively.

"The truth was we didn't have a legal leg to stand on," Alexander said. "We talked to the Department of Justice, the FBI, and anyone else with an opinion, and they said that if the New Black

Panthers wanted to carry guns in a nonthreatening manner, there wasn't a damn thing I could do about it. This is Texas. You have a right to carry in Texas."

*   *   *

THE NEXT MORNING, Friday, the phone rang in Chief Alexander's house on Bevil Loop. The Black Panthers were at the county jail and wanted a meeting. Alexander got dressed and climbed into his truck and drove down to what he was sure would be a contentious meeting. He had little wiggle room. "I done been told we couldn't stop them, so I was in a nine-line bind."

Khalid Mohammed was in his black fatigues flanked by lieutenants in various states of repose in Billy Rowles's office. The FBI was in attendance, as was Walter Diggles. Alexander strode in and sat directly next to the New Black Panther leader. Harold Van Moore, a.k.a. Khalid Abdul Mohammed, was a former member of the Black Panthers, Nation of Islam, and former gang member in Louisiana and Texas. The former minister of defense and security chief for the Nation of Islam had the studied look of a man trying to appear a little crazy: his black uniform was folded snugly over his biceps, and his head was shaved clean. He narrowed his eyes at the police chief. All the men in the room were awaiting Alexander's next move.

The former bulldogger surprised them by not yielding an inch. A march to the funeral was nonnegotiable, he said. Members of Greater New Bethel Baptist Church had made it clear they didn't want Black Panthers at the service, so they wouldn't be allowed to approach the church. "We want to take care of things our own way," Reverend Lyons had said publicly. "We don't need Black Panthers stirring things up."

Alexander said as much to Mohammed, never mentioning the tenuous legality of his position. He didn't need to. Khalid Mohammed was ready to deal. He stepped outside with one of his lieutenants and came back several minutes later. "We want to march here behind the jail, and we want a press conference at the jail," he said, laying out the Panthers' final offer. Alexander, so intent on keeping them away from the funeral, jumped on the compromise.

"You've got an hour," he said. They would march after the funeral the next day, Saturday.

*   *   *

LYONS PACED HIS kitchen floor hours before the June 13 funeral. There had been rumors for days that 10,000 to 20,000 members of the Aryan Nation were camping in the woods to respond to the Black Panthers' demonstrations. Rowles and Alexander had called Lyons that morning to say that the Black Panthers would not march to Greater New Bethel Baptist Church until hours after the funeral was over. "I did my usual prayers, and I kept asking the Lord to keep my mind clear," said Lyons.

James Byrd could not have wanted a better box to lie in. It would give him confidence and comfort, the congregation said. And for the rest of the community there was the funeral, a ceremony so grand and large that Jasperites figured it would be remembered forever as the finest in town history. Certainly a town that could bring hundreds out to Greater New Bethel—more than 200 people, white and black, filled the sanctuary, while 200 more stood elbow-to-elbow in the fellowship hall—couldn't be racist. Outside, in the scorching heat, another several hundred people sat under a tent listening to the service on a public address system. The town seemed united.

Inside the church, the coffin looked little in the small, flower-crowded parlor. It was sealed at the service because to have done otherwise would have been too disquieting.

The funeral had already begun, and the music had swelled when Billy Ray Robinson leaned over to Reverend Lyons and whispered in his ear. "We're going to need to insert some other expressions after all," he said. He handed Lyons a list: Senator Kay Bailey Hutchison, transportation secretary Rodney Slater, and Jesse Jackson all wanted to speak.

Lyons winced. The additions were going to seem odd. The programs would not reflect these speakers. It would unsettle the congregation. Moments later, Reverend Jackson announced basketball star forward Dennis Rodman, a native of Texas, had pledged $30,000 to help pay for the funeral expenses. Fight promoter Don King offered $100,000 for James Byrd's three children to defray the costs of their education.

The children, until that point, had been in the background alongside their mother, Thelma Adams. Adams and Byrd had divorced years earlier largely on account of Byrd's drinking, drug problems, and frequent incarcerations. She subsequently moved to Lufkin, where she lived in a ramshackle trailer with the children, making ends meet by taking in laundry. She came to Jasper for the funeral but didn't have enough money for the gas she needed to drive the hour back to Lufkin. During the reception after the funeral, Lyons took up a quiet collection from the congregation.

"We are diminished by this act," Republican senator Hutchison said. "We have seen a family tested." Members of the congregation tried to remember if Hutchison had ever visited Jasper before. They were pretty sure she never had. And certainly she had never visited East Jasper. They sniggered.

Al Sharpton, from New York, lent his own voice to the chorus. "As Brother Byrd's body was torn, America's spirit was torn," he said.

Reverend Lyons, one of the few people on the speakers list who actually knew James Byrd, thought back to his conversations with the man. He remembered one of the last times he had seen him. Lyons was washing his car in his driveway near the church, and Byrd happened by. "Preacher, Preacher!" he shouted, trying to get Lyons's attention from the street. Lyons looked up. "Preacher, what do you preach? Do you practice what you preach?"

"I preach Jesus, I told him," Lyons told the funeral congregation, retelling the incident to shouts of "Amen" around him. "This can be the legacy of Brother Byrd. Preach Jesus because we've tried everything else."

It was, Lyons said later, classic James Byrd. Slightly needling, slightly aggressive, but it was a shot fired from far enough away that the challenge could be issued without ever having to act upon it. James Byrd had come to the conclusion that life had been trying to grind him down almost as long as he had had a life, and whatever he learned and believed came from that. Lyons's stories about Byrd were much like everyone else's. "James wasn't what you might call one of Jasper's upstanding citizens," Lyons said. "I know he was dragged, but the black people knew him before he was dragged. James would drink. He could convince you to lend him money all the time. He even borrowed money from my mother once. Didn't pay her back, either."

Over the years, James Sr. and Stella Byrd had become leaders at Greater New Bethel Baptist. He was a deacon, and she led the Sunday school. Their roles not only provided them with spiritual comfort but made them leaders in the community. Their son, James, threatened that. While their other children made them as proud as they could be—six daughters who were successful professionals in Houston—James had fallen short. And while they loved him, they were disappointed in the way their son had turned out. He was a felon, a forger of checks, unemployed, unwilling to support his former wife and three children, and he used his disability checks to satisfy his thirst for Busch beer. They did what they could to help him but had settled on a regimen of tough love: James wasn't welcome at their house. Sunday dinners were rare. They had called an uneasy truce, in which James gave them a wide berth, and they tried to hide their disappointment.

"They thought that they were doing the best thing for James," said a friend of the family's. "They were hoping if they made him stand up on his own two feet, maybe he would end his drinking and partying and carrying on. But it didn't happen."

*   *   *

THE SATURDAY BLACK PANTHER march had more media, police officers, and Texas Rangers than participating Panther members. The black militia group strode along Burch Street behind the jail and took a left on Martin Luther King Boulevard, swarming into the parking lot of Greater New Bethel Baptist Church. James Byrd's funeral had ended hours before. Police officers escorted the group, per prior arrangement, to Huff Creek Road for pictures. Harlon Alexander made sure a Texas Ranger was standing next to each Panther with a gun.

In many ways the Panthers' press conference in front of the jail afterward couldn't have worked more to Jasper's advantage. The New Black Panthers looked and sounded too radical for either a local or a national audience. "Black Power!" Khalid Mohammed shouted into the microphone as his lieutenant punctuated his words by loudly cocking his shotgun. "Violence and racism by the white man in America is just as American as apple or cherry pie," he continued. "The white man is a cold-blooded murderer." The small audience, gathered largely out of curiosity, jeered. Walter Diggles had had enough. He began to make his way to the podium to end the press conference. Mohammed saw him and ended it himself. Jasper had, for the time being at least, survived a visit from the New Black Panthers.

The *Jasper Newsboy* printed a lengthy account of the James Byrd funeral with a list of the politicians and dignitaries who attended, though most of them had never so much as heard of Jasper only a week before. ("There's nothing like a shovelful of dirt to create legitimacy," said one prominent white citizen of Byrd, a man whom Jasperites had avoided like the plague only a week earlier.) The *Newsboy* said the funeral remarks were conciliatory. Reverend Jesse Jackson called for calm and forgiveness. Kweisi Mfume, president of the National Association for the Advancement of Colored People, called for reconciliation. Transportation secretary Rodney Slater read a letter from President Bill Clinton.

James Byrd was three blocks from his parents' house when King, Berry, and Brewer picked him up that night, and his grand funeral was just a stone's throw from the very spot where he had stumbled along the road. While all the gathered dignitaries talked about reconciliation and harmony, they neglected to note one thing as the last shovel of dirt was patted down around James Byrd's above-the-ground vault: he was buried on the black side of the Jasper City Cemetery, still segregated in 1998.

CHAPTER SEVEN

OUTSIDERS COME TO JASPER

Never saw so many newspeople. This is a big deal.
—ENTRY IN BILLY ROWLES'S DIARY

JASPERITES HAD HOPED that after the funeral the outsiders would leave. That didn't happen. A full two weeks after the funeral, parking spaces on Courthouse Square were still scarce. Patrick's Steakhouse on Highway 96 still required reservations. Sheriff Rowles, who had never seen a satellite truck until the first in a convoy of them pulled into town, counted more than a dozen parked around the old jail. Dan Rather had arrived. The Fox affiliate was taking feeds live. National Public Radio sent its southern correspondent. Court TV was covering the arraignment. The presence of so many journalists, so fast, gave Jasperites an acute sense of their stake in the unfolding events. For weeks now they had been able to present an airbrushed souvenir postcard of a harmonious town where little Toms and Beckys and Jims were getting along just fine, thank you. As soon as this was over, they told themselves, their real lives could resume.

Some of the journalists sensed they were not getting the full story. When they asked questions, Jasperites looked at each other, replying after a momentary, but telling, delay. They had learned, very quickly, how to give the journalists only what they wanted them to know. It was frustrating for the visitors because they had a very specific, and very different, story line in mind. They were readying articles about the Klan, and backwoods justice, and southern sheriffs. And they continued to arrive in a steady stream, in their vans and rental cars, in crisp suits fresh from out-of-state flights.

"After striving for two decades to overcome East Texas' legacy of racism, Jasper suffers a setback," read one *Houston Chronicle* headline. "A Racist Murder Leads Texas Town to Probe Its Bedrock Prejudices," the *Wall Street Journal* banner said. "Race killing in Texas fuels fear and anger," read *USA Today*.

Shawn Berry's statement to police, details of which dribbled out after the funeral, played right into the media's preconceived notions. According to Berry, he offered James Byrd a ride in the back of his pickup around 2 A.M. With Byrd riding in the truck bed, Berry, King, and Brewer drove to B. J.'s Grocery east of Jasper to get ice and beer, and then they headed out of town to Huff Creek Road. It was Bill King who was at the wheel when the truck turned onto an old logging road and the tenor of the evening changed. King said he was "fixin' to scare the shit out of this nigger." The trio got out of the truck, and Berry's companions began beating up Byrd. His affidavit didn't say why the beating began. "At one point, the black male appeared to Berry to be unconscious," according to the affidavit. Berry said he started to run away and then got back into the truck when King drove up to him. "Are you going to leave him out there?" Berry said he asked King. King answered, "We're going to start *The Turner Diaries* early." *The Turner Diaries,* a racist and anti-Semitic novel, described a vicious attack by white Americans on ethnic "undesirables." King and Brewer had read it in prison.

The truck turned back onto the pavement of Huff Creek Road, and Brewer looked behind the truck. "That nigger is bouncing all over the place," he said.

Berry said he was unaware that they had chained Byrd to the truck and said he looked back to see Byrd "being dragged." Berry said he asked to be let out of the truck, and King said, "You're just as guilty as we are. Besides, the same thing could happen to a nigger lover." He said King later took the chain off Byrd, after driving nearly three miles. Before the month was out, Berry had amended his statement. Berry had been lying to minimize his role. He had been driving.

*   *   *

WHEN LAWRENCE BREWER SR.'S son Russell returned to Sulphur Springs from his last stint in prison in 1997, there was one enormous change: a gallery of racist tattoos covered most of his arms. Brewer told his son the tattoos were a sickness. Father and son already had a difficult relationship. The younger Brewer had had drug and legal problems from the time he was eighteen or nineteen years old, and his military-trained father couldn't control him.

Like much of East Texas, Sulphur Springs and Delta County had a history of racial violence. In 1913, a black man accused of murdering a white girl was pulled from a courtroom and lynched. One of the smallest and poorest counties in Texas, Delta County in 1998 was 90 percent white. Even so, by most accounts, Brewer didn't grow up a racist. When he was first processed into state prison at age nineteen, he told authorities he had no objections to sharing a cell with a black man. Brewer's history read much like King's and Berry's. He dropped out of high school and, according to school officials, wasn't even a memorable discipline problem. Anyone looking for Brewer most of his teenage nights was likely to find him perched on the local water tank drinking beer. He had too much time on his hands and paid for a drug habit by staging small heists. By the time he was first arrested in 1986, he had been linked to as many as sixteen burglaries. He didn't seem mean so much as sneaky, people said. He broke into his grandparents' house and stole guns. From his father, he stole a battery charger, and from his younger brother, a pair of stereo speakers. His petty crimes filled two manila folders in the district attorney's office.

Brewer began serving a seven-year sentence for burglary in the summer of 1987 at the Hilltop prison in Gatesville. It was the first of many prison stays. He was paroled in February 1988 but returned to prison a little more than a year later for cocaine possession. He was paroled again in 1991 but was back in prison three years later for failing to report to his parole officer. By the time he was released from the Beto I unit in Livingston, Texas, in the summer of 1997, he was an avowed white supremacist.

In the Beto I unit, Brewer received major punishments for refusing to work, for being absent from his assigned location, and for participating in a riot. When Brewer was finally released, he was told to look for work and report to his parole officer several times a month. He took up with a woman named Tammy Perritt and her young children and was, by all accounts, ready to put his life back together, until she kicked him out. In the spring of 1998, he told his father after Perritt kicked him out that he was going to Houston.

Instead, he said, he went to Jasper, to the only person who had ever loved him: Bill King.

Two weeks later, Bill King's father, Ronald, answered the phone to find out his son was in Jasper County Jail, suspected of murder.

"I just can't believe my boy could have done this," said Ronald King. "He was always so smart. We bought him a set of encyclopedias when he was just a child, and he would look everything up. I bought him a woodworking set, and he was so good at that too. His grades weren't so good in school, but that was because he said he was bored, they didn't challenge his mind. I begged him not to drop out of school. I guess I should have been tougher about it. Maybe that would have changed things."

The trouble that ensued wasn't Bill's fault, his father said. He made the wrong friends, they got into trouble, and his son did, too.

In the weeks before Brewer came to town, Bill King seemed to be settling down. He was getting jobs working construction or clearing land. He wasn't violating his parole. Bill King had lots of good inside him, the elder King said, and that was starting to come to the fore again when "that damn Brewer showed up." "That Russell Brewer reminded him of prison, and he went back to the way he had been acting in there, I guess," said Ronald King. "Because my boy was never like this."

Ronald King sent a note to his son in jail in the days after the murder. Billy Rowles paraphrased it, saying: "Where did the hatred in your heart come from?"

*　　*　　*

THE FOREST FIRES started soon after police found James Byrd's body. They burned all night, sometimes for more than a week, as helicopters and firefighters tried to douse the flames. The fires blackened acres of loblolly pine. The trees were so crackling dry after more than two months of drought and searing summer heat that all it took was a single crack of lightning, a carelessly thrown cigarette, or a spark from an engine to set the woods ablaze.

"It was so hot we couldn't have burned a cross in Jasper even if we wanted to," said Michael Lowe, grand dragon of the Knights of the Klu Klux Klan. "There was a state burn ban on right after the Byrd murder, and we abide by things like that," he said.

Police chief Harlon Alexander had known for almost two weeks that the Klan was coming to Jasper and had hoped that the rally somehow would not materialize. On June 15, two days after the Byrd funeral, Lowe had called the police chief asking for a permit to demonstrate. Lowe wasn't just a racist; he was a felon. He had served six years in a Texas prison in the late 1970s for possession of an explosive device, a conviction that earned him the reputation among lawmen as "the Mad Bomber." He had an eighteen-inch robed KKK night rider tattooed on his back and attributed his recruiting success to his "country boy" approach. Lowe asked Alexander for permission to hold a two-hour rally on Courthouse Square on June 20 or 27. Alexander pushed for the latter date and said they could have an hour. Lowe agreed.

There was something oddly winning about Michael Lowe. He could be self-deprecating and funny, almost as if he were playing a Klansman in a prime-time comedy. "Some people have crosses to bear," he once said. "I've got crosses to burn." He could be mistaken for someone's balding, rosy-cheeked, benevolent uncle. Lowe was one of those men who was always ready to slap another on the back and call him Charlie, a habit that had a slightly counterfeit ring but was disarming all the same. He talked matter-of-factly about ozone and burning permits and the many obstacles that made a simple cross burning a complicated affair.

"We light crosses as a symbol of our bringing truth and light to darkness," said Lowe, whose speech impediment turned the *r* in "robes" into a *w*. The Ku Klux Klan didn't use the term "cross burning" anymore; it sounded too aggressive. Instead they preferred "sacred cross lightings."

"It isn't an intimidation thing; it is a ritual," said Lowe. "Everyone thinks of crosses burning on the front yards of mixed-race couples. Most of the time those are burnings that are self-started, some black couple wanting publicity. It has nothing to do with us."

Publicity was what everyone was after, Lowe said. Cross lightings and rallies brought the media out, something that Lowe was keen to see happen because it turned out potential new members. "It helps our T-shirt sales," he explained. After the Byrd murder, though, bringing out the media in East Texas was easy. "I made time for all the media," said Lowe. "This was free advertising, and we were going to take advantage of it. If the politicians can show up and take advantage of the situation, why couldn't we do so too? Did Kay Bailey Hutchison or Jesse Jackson know James Byrd? Of course not. They were seizing on an opportunity. And so were we."

Among Klan organizers, Lowe was known as one of the best recruiters in the country. Lowe claimed to have more than 5,000 members in Texas alone. (The Southern Poverty Law Center in 2001 put the number at closer to 5,000 Klansmen nationwide.) Lowe's Knights were what Klan experts called a Fourth Position organization. They advocated public appearances and shunned a lot of the outward voodoo that had come to characterize the First and Second Position Klan memberships.

"I don't think we ought to be shipping blacks to Africa or immigrants back to their home countries. My message is to white people: protect our heritage and our culture," Lowe said. At the same time he believed that God was white and didn't create all men as equals. "If we were created equal, why didn't Africans build great cities or become great explorers?" he said. "They would never have left Africa if white men didn't bring them over as slaves."

Lowe's mission, as he saw it, was to put a friendlier face on the hate movement in the South. Like David Duke before him, Lowe sought to reinvent the Klan as one of those groups victimized by an overzealous and liberal federal government. Lowe said the Klan was misunderstood. Just as Bill King said he was misunderstood.

"What the Klan did in the 1920s and 1930s was wrong; there was violence, and it was wrong," said Lowe. "We're not that kind of Klan anymore. I know we attract some people who think we still do lynchings and killings, but the ones that want violence won't stay. We don't want you to join the Knights if you just hate. We're a hardworking group of people who love our families. We aren't Nazis; we're just proud to be white."

Lowe may have been best known for his campaign to keep blacks out of Vidor, Texas, about sixty miles northwest of Jasper. For years, a Ku Klux Klan office sat right on Main Street, and out by Highway 12 the Klan had set up a white school bus where they sold T-shirts, bumper stickers, and membership information to passersby. The T-shirts pictured hooded characters on horseback, the bumper stickers simple Confederate flags or black-and-red crosses or round decals with the face of a raccoon struck out with a red line. ("No 'coons, get it?" said one vendor.)

Vidor was named after King Vidor, the movie director who, in 1929, directed *Hallelujah,* the first Hollywood movie with an all-black cast. The entire community was white, except for a handful of families. In 1994, the Department of Housing and Urban Development decided to move three black families into a local housing project. The black families, scared of what awaited them there, moved in only after then–housing secretary Henry Cisneros set aside $3 million to upgrade security. Within days the residents were too frightened to stay. There were death threats. Several Klansmen showed up in white sheets to protest. Michael Lowe was among them.

"The federal government had no right to bring in low-income families into Vidor, a city that didn't have enough jobs anyway," Lowe said. "And they were transferring whites out to bring the blacks in. I didn't think that was right, and I said so."

Blacks and whites from neighboring cities still won't stop in Vidor for gas at night. "People ain't right there," said one. "They may have taken down the sign they had that said 'Nigger, Don't Let the Sun Set on You in Vidor,' but that doesn't mean their attitudes have changed. They've just become harder to track."

While Lowe said most of his members were hardworking white men in their twenties, thirties, forties, and fifties, the truth was the Klan trolled for members chiefly among the newly unemployed in towns with factory closings. In the late 1990s, membership was climbing in the rust belt of Indiana and Michigan, where workers were looking for someone to blame for downsizing and job losses. For similar reasons, the Klan also found support among poor white kids, disaffected uneducated youth not unlike Bill King.

*   *   *

"THE LORD HAS a plan," Reverend Lyons began his sermon on June 21. More than a week had passed since the funeral. "Sometimes we have trouble seeing it, and we wonder whether he has forsaken us, but God has a plan.

"We put people in categories. God doesn't do that. No matter what color your skin, you're still brothers and sisters. It's an unwritten law. Whenever you mistreat a child of God, you may get away but you won't get by. The revenge will be with God. Cain murdered his brother. You know when you've done wrong, even if you don't read the Bible. God has a way of letting us know. God works with your conscience. That's worse than any whipping. Worse than anything man can do.

"The worst person in the world has an unseen connection with God because they have a soul. You might have done something and thought no one saw you. But there's another eye who sees what you do, and God will get his revenge."

Reverend Lyons's cadence that day sounded like that of Martin Luther King Jr., and the congregation heard it and took solace in words from a pastor who, unlike the crowd that had descended on Jasper, was one of their own.

*　　*　　*

THE DAY BEFORE the Klan rally, June 26, intelligence reports from the FBI in Dallas began coming over Alexander's fax machine at the police station. Lowe wasn't going to be alone. The rally was actually the brainchild of Darrell Flinn, imperial wizard of the Knights of the White Kamellia, and he had invited Lowe's group and the imperial wizard of the North Georgia Knights of the KKK, Dan Romine. Romine was worried enough about the rally that he left his second in command, Grand Dragon Jimbo Bennett, in Georgia, just in case he was hurt, according to the FBI report. The group, the sources said, would be armed. All told, the authorities were expecting between forty and seventy-five Klan members.

Romine, in an ominous directive, was told not to bring any women, children, or guns and not to use the N-word at the rally.

There were some things in Jasper that people just knew. If one was in legal trouble, one had to get Joe Tonahill for the defense. Or if one wanted a drink and didn't have a membership card at Casa Ole, the only place to get beer was eight miles up the road at Solley's Liquor and Beer in Newton County. If one had a craving for chicken-fried steak, it was best satisfied on Wednesday nights, when one could get an entire chicken-fried steak dinner with fries for $2.99 from Eliza's Café. One would also think, living in Deep East Texas, just about anyone would be able to recognize the grand dragon of the Knights of the Ku Klux Klan.

Pat and David Stiles owned the Belle-Jim Hotel, a quaint bed-and-breakfast with a sweet smell to it, all cinnamon spray and scented candles. On the shelves were jars of jelly with cotton print fabric tops and heart-shaped pillows stuffed with potpourri. David Stiles left the Belle-Jim on Friday to go to the bank while pockets of journalists set up cameras on Courthouse Square for interviews with Klan members and Black Panther leaders in Jasper ahead of the rally slated for the next day.

Stiles, a former law enforcement officer and navy veteran, walked across the street with a pouch of money from the hotel. He had his eye on the hundreds of reporters set up cheek by jowl and decided that things looked peaceful enough and, as an afterthought, that it looked like rain. He took long strides across the street and ran a checklist of errands through his head as he went into the bank.

His weather forecast was dead-on. Moments later it began to rain, and reporters and cameramen and soundmen began to stream into the Belle-Jim Hotel, the closest refuge. One television reporter brought in Lowe and sat him down at a front table. They needed a sandwich, the reporter told Pat Stiles matter-of-factly. Stiles went back into the kitchen, into a gaggle of waitresses who thought they recognized their latest customer.

"That's Michael Lowe, the Klan guy, isn't it?" one asked another.

They peered around the partition to double-check. It sure looked like Lowe, but he was dressed in a tie and a button-down shirt. Frankly, it could have been someone who only bore a resemblance, they said. Pat Stiles fixed Lowe's sandwich as the women in the kitchen argued among themselves. Then the phone rang.

"If you are going to serve people like that, I will never come into the Belle-Jim again," the voice said. Pat Stiles thought she recognized it. It was another proprietor on Courthouse Square. A white woman. Pat Stiles stammered. She wasn't quite sure what to say.

"Who are you talking about?" she began.

"The Klansman, the head of the Klan; if you serve those kind of people, I won't ever eat at your restaurant again," the voice said. The line went dead.

Pat Stiles was finding it hard to breathe. Everything she and David had was in this hotel. This was their home. They lived here with their children. They had sewn the bedspreads themselves. They had decorated the rooms the way they might have looked in 1910 when the two-story wooden hotel was built. In that moment, she saw everything they had worked for disappearing. She hung up the phone determined to drive Lowe from the restaurant, midbite if necessary. Then her husband returned from the bank, and she began to cry.

David Stiles was as mild-mannered as a man could be. His slow, deliberate ways hid an ability to quickly assess volatile situations. Lowe, he decided in an instant, couldn't be expelled. To do so would give him the headlines he wanted and the Belle-Jim the very publicity it wanted to avoid. He tried to calm his wife.

1

Huff Creek Road had always been a mecca for drunk drivers, partly because such isolated roads allowed anyone who had had a few too many a way to skirt sheriff's cruisers and get home without a DWI. In 1998 it was where James Byrd Jr. was dragged to his death in one of the worst racially motivated killings since the 1955 murder of Emmett Till.

3

ABOVE LEFT: Hours before he was chained to the bumper of a truck and killed by three white supremacists, James Byrd was drinking with friends. "You watch," Byrd told them. "When I go, everyone is going to be calling me Mr. Byrd." This family photograph was taken in 1997, a year before his murder.

ABOVE RIGHT: Jasper County sheriff Billy Rowles was fighting history. For a long time East Texas criminal justice had been ruled by white cops, white grand juries, and white judges. Billy Rowles became the embodiment of all that was right and wrong in the law enforcement that had gone on before him. He is shown here during his first press conference after the murder, June 9, 1998. "Those boys didn't learn how to hate here," Rowles told the assembly.

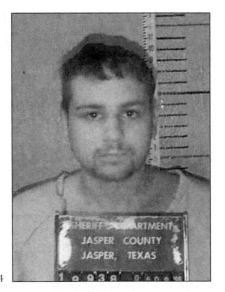

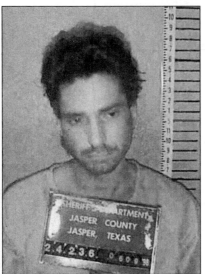
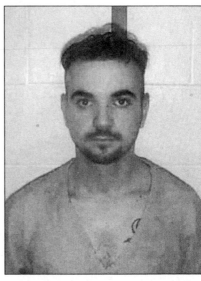

Bill King (TOP) and Russell Brewer (ABOVE LEFT) met in the Beto unit of the Texas Department of Criminal Justice in 1995. Beto was considered a "gladiator" unit, filled to bursting with 3,000 young toughs. Prison inmates survived by making alliances with whomever served them best. Brewer, seven years older than King, knew the ropes of prison life. King, quick and charismatic, impressed Brewer with conversation sprinkled with vocabulary he had never heard before. Shawn Berry (ABOVE RIGHT), a childhood friend of King's, had been in trouble with the law but had managed to avoid prison. The sheriff's office taped these photographs of King, Brewer, and Berry on the front windows of the Jasper County Jail a day after their arrest.

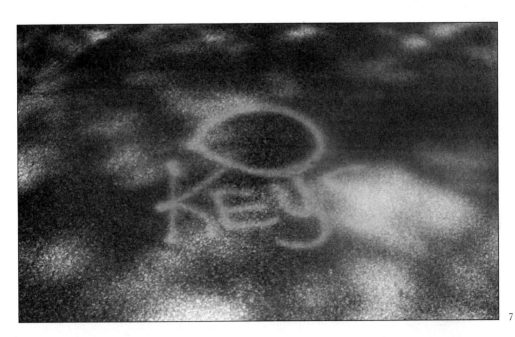

As Sheriff Billy Rowles followed the trail of blood and evidence on foot, he took off his big white hat and placed it next to a set of keys for investigators to mark. Three feet farther up the road he put a tin of Skoal chewing tobacco beside a set of dentures. He saw a wallet, then loose change, puddles of blood, and more than a mile down the way, an arm, and James Byrd's head. When Investigator Curtis Frame handed Rowles a Zippo lighter with the symbol for the KKK on one side and the word "Possum" below it, Rowles's heartbeat began to quicken. "This country boy's in trouble," he thought.

10

A crowd had formed outside the Jasper County Courthouse on the morning of Tuesday, June 9. Residents had heard that the three men accused of the Byrd murder would arrive. No one expected violence as they were led into the courthouse. What they were anticipating was shouted abuse. But when the group caught sight of the accused with their escort of officers, they were struck dumb. King smirked for the cameras. Brewer stared at the ground. Shawn Berry tried to hide his face.

11

12

"I remember when we took Bill to adoption court," Bill King's father, Ronald, said as his son sat blocks away in the county jail, accused of killing James Byrd. "He was nine months old. I remember he had on a pair of red, white, and blue shoes." Family photos show Bill King at age eight and again, in 1998, shortly before the murder, his arms covered in jailhouse tattoos.

One of Jasper's principal gossip dispensaries, the Belle-Jim Hotel had virtually banned the James Byrd murder as a topic of conversation. Jasperites were trying to move on. "I had people call me and ask if it was actually safe to come to Jasper after the murder," said Pat Stiles, one of the owners of the hotel. "It said a lot about how people were seeing us."

ABOVE LEFT: On the days when the routine of quiet country lawyering began to grow old, Joe Tonahill, left, would close his eyes and imagine himself back in Judge Joe Brown's Dallas courtroom, sitting at the defense table with Jack Ruby, center, and co-counsel Melvin Belli, right. As the years went by, the trial became an emotional touchstone for Tonahill and, by extension, for Jasper.

ABOVE RIGHT: Mike Lout was a small-town newsman. In a single day he would attend Chamber of Commerce meetings, accidents, City Council gatherings, and anything else that might be fashioned into a news item for KJAS. The Byrd murder changed the way they covered news in Jasper, Lout said. "It was the difference between daylight and dark. All of a sudden we weren't holding anything back."

"God has a way of doing great things in small towns with ordinary people," Jesse Jackson told more than three hundred people at the Greater New Bethel Baptist Church. "I see a new Jasper. The old Jasper has passed away." Jackson hugs Renee Mullins, James Byrd's daughter, while visiting the Byrd family three days after the murder.

RIGHT: The *Jasper Newsboy* printed a lengthy account of the James Byrd funeral with a list of the politicians and dignitaries who attended. Reverend Jackson announced that basketball star forward Dennis Rodman, a native of Texas, had pledged $30,000 to help pay for funeral expenses. Fight promoter Don King also offered $100,000 to defray the costs of the Byrd children's education.

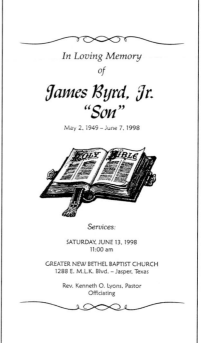

In Loving Memory
of

James Byrd, Jr.
"Son"

May 2, 1949 – June 7, 1998

Services:

SATURDAY, JUNE 13, 1998
11:00 am

GREATER NEW BETHEL BAPTIST CHURCH
1288 E. M.L.K. Blvd. – Jasper, Texas

Rev. Kenneth O. Lyons, Pastor
Officiating

"The Klan" was the first thing that ran through the minds of the black community when they heard about James Byrd's death, said Reverend Kenneth Lyons, pastor at Greater New Bethel Baptist Church. "Our main concern was that whoever it was would strike again."

LEFT: Walter Diggles, the executive director of the Deep East Texas Council of Governments, joined Jesse Jackson and Representatives Sheila Jackson-Lee and Maxine Waters in front of the county jail after the Byrd funeral. RIGHT: Hours later, Quanell X, a Muslim leader from Houston, held a press conference of his own.

Lonnell Chursky, left, leans over the grave of James Byrd Jr., as friends Kendrick Conner, center, and Janell Brown look on, after the Byrd funeral. Less than a month later, vandals stole the metal nameplate marking the grave.

22

23

24

Khallid Mohammad (TOP LEFT), leader of the New Black Panthers, walked the streets of Jasper hours after the Byrd funeral. The black community of Jasper needed protection, he told Sheriff Billy Rowles and Police Chief Harlon Alexander (BELOW LEFT). Both made sure there were more police officers than there were Black Panther members. Across town, Ku Klux Klan members gathered. As the two groups threatened to face off, Rowles pulled the plug on the Klan's public address system. ABOVE: Police and Texas Rangers line up on Courthouse Square to keep the Klan and Panthers apart. BELOW: The KKK's Michael Lowe, left, and Darrell Flinn, meet with Sheriff Billy Rowles.

25

Jasper residents gather outside the Jasper County Courthouse for a prayer vigil on June 15, 1998. More than five hundred people gathered. BELOW: Carzetta Powell, left, and a woman who wished not to be identified sing during the vigil.

Weeks after his first visit to Jasper, Muslim leader Quanell X tries to get past a Jasper police officer as members of the Ku Klux Klan end their own rally. The KKK said they came to Jasper to denounce the dragging death of James Byrd. Later, Michael Lowe, their best recruiter, said the rally was one of their best public relations coups of the year.

As jury selection began in January 1999, King was led into the Jasper County Courthouse in leg-irons and a bullet-proof vest. Lawyers sifted through more than four hundred juror applications and questionnaires. King was the first to be tried because prosecutors, when they are forced to choose, invariably proceed first with their strongest case.

Investigators found blood and skin samples consistent with James Byrd's type on the bottom of Shawn Berry's sidestep truck.

31

Jasper assistant district attorney Pat Hardy displays the chain used to drag James Byrd to his death. The chain, District Attorney Guy James Gray said, was the murder weapon.

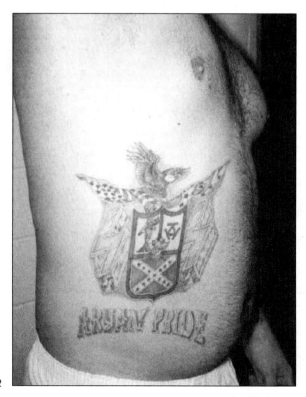

The police search of Bill King's apartment had yielded racist literature, including a book on the Ku Klux Klan and an *Esquire* magazine article about the 1955 case of Emmett Till. Gray focused on King's white supremacist tattoos, including one of a hanging black man and a shield on his side that read ARYAN PRIDE.

32

LEFT: Billy Rowles and Guy James Gray meet reporters in front of the Jasper County Courthouse after a jury finds Bill King guilty of capital murder. BELOW: James Byrd Sr. and his granddaughter Renee Mullins, right, gasped when the verdict was read. Rowles, standing by the judge's bench, blew the family a kiss.

Convicted and sentenced to death, King is escorted from the Jasper County Courthouse to a car waiting to take him to Death Row. His father, Ronald King, said the whole ordeal—his son's arrest, prison stay, and trial—stirred memories of an earlier family trial that thrust his parents into a similar media spotlight nearly sixty years before.

RIGHT: Lawrence Russell Brewer, thirty-two, burst into tears after he was sentenced to death by a jury in Bryan, Texas. "We didn't mean to kill Mr. Byrd," he said, as he wept on the stand. BELOW: His father, Lawrence Russell Brewer Sr., broke down when the judge read the verdict. His son had been in and out of prison since he was nineteen. Prosecutors said he had recruited King into his racist gang.

Shawn Berry, twenty-four, stood as he was sentenced to life in prison by a Jasper jury in November 1999. Berry, who said he was a frightened bystander, was the only one of the trio who was not sentenced to die by lethal injection.

39

James Byrd Sr. had said little publicly during the melee that followed his son's murder. A quiet, gentle man, he seemed overcome by the swirling events. He stepped up to the microphones, however, after the Texas state legislature failed to pass a tougher hate crimes bill.

The Byrd family became national figures. Renee Mullins, James Byrd's daughter, met with President Clinton when he arrived in Austin, Texas, in May 1999. "For me, as a white Southerner, the thought that a man could be murdered because of his race in 1999 is heartbreaking," Clinton said.

Renee Mullins and Jamie Byrd, James Byrd's son, address the Democratic National Convention at the Staples Center in Los Angeles in August 2000.

BELOW: Texas governor Rick Perry, right, prepares to sign into law the James Byrd Jr. Hate Crimes Act in May 2001. In the background are James Byrd's parents, Stella and James Byrd.

The phone rang again. A different voice came on the line.

"Are you-all really feeding that Klansman?" the voice said. News traveled fast in Jasper.

Three more phone calls came in before Lowe actually finished his sandwich and stood up to leave. Pat and David Stiles stood in the back and helplessly watched him go. Cameras encircled him as he stepped off the front porch and into the street. Things had gotten so crazy in Jasper, just feeding a Klansman set tongues wagging and threats flying. The Stileses' experience was only the beginning.

*   *   *

THE MERE RUMOR of a Klan rally was enough to spark a response from black militant groups, who had been chafing at news reports that said the New Black Panthers had been carrying unloaded guns when they patrolled Jasper on the day of the Byrd funeral. They had lost face and wanted to return and challenge the Klan. Police chief Alexander and Sheriff Rowles were worried.

Members of the Mental Freedom Obtains Independence, MFOI, led by Quanell X of Houston, began making ominous public statements about retaliation against white supremacist organizations for the murder of James Byrd. The MFOI was an offshoot of the Nation of Islam black separatist movement led by minister Louis Farrakhan. Quanell X was the former national youth minister for the Nation of Islam and was considered too extreme by some in Farrakhan's circle. That led to the creation of MFOI in Houston. During a joint interview in New York with Darrell Flinn about the Byrd murder shortly after the funeral, Quanell X said that the MFOI would "tear ya'll's ass" if the KKK stepped out of line.

At best, he was an unsavory character. He had been convicted of dealing crack cocaine in 1989 before founding MFOI. He had formed MFOI while working as an aide to Texas state representative Ron Wilson of Houston, and the group's goals included unification of black street gangs. "The Bloods and Crips must become the army of God," Quanell X said. He was a follower of the late hardline Nation of Islam minister Elijah Mohammed. He described white people as devils and the enemy.

The New Black Panther Party had also vowed to return. "The New Black Panther Party did not march with unloaded guns in Jasper, Texas, on June 13th," they said in a press release announcing their intention to march in Jasper on June 27. "Their shotguns were and will be fully loaded in compliance with Texas State law."

The lead story in the *Jasper Newsboy* warned residents to stay away from the square that Saturday. Area businesses were shuttered. David Stiles put a closed sign on the door of the Belle-Jim. "I wasn't going to make the same mistake twice," he said. The Stileses had sent their two children up to Sam Rayburn Reservoir with friends so they wouldn't see the rally and any violence that might ensue.

Jasperites who did show up at the courthouse, where the Klan had established a presence, condemned the spectacle as an unwelcome product of too much media attention. Dozens of journalists, including some from Australia, Portugal, Denmark, France, and England, gathered early Saturday morning to await the demonstrations. At least a dozen television satellite trucks jammed the post office parking lot. The square was full of strangers.

A black man from Houston, who called himself Motapa, vowed to "fast on air for three days" to show his solidarity with James Byrd. His face was painted blue, red, green, and yellow. The cameramen took aim. "The blood of James Byrd is like the sacrament of Jesus Christ. It will spread all over America." The journalists scribbled in their pads. "We're here to denounce the murder of

James Byrd as an unnecessary act of violence that did nothing but cause a lot of problems for a lot of organizations and people in Jasper Country," Michael Lowe said in his trademark lisp from the gazebo in front of the county courthouse. He was wearing a suit and tie. Darrell Flinn was in full Klan regalia: robes and hood. He was carrying a Confederate flag and was surrounded by reporters.

The Knights of the White Kamellia had released a statement about the Byrd murder on their Web site. The incident was a "heinous crime" that had been overblown by the "Zionist Occupational Government" in order to sully the reputations of white supremacists. "Was this murder a hate crime?" the statement read. "You bet it was. But so are the tens of thousands of murders of Whites at the hands of negroes that are being committed without even the slightest recognition by the controlled media. Why are they swept under the rug?"

Now the Knights of the White Kamellia had their moment in the spotlight.

"Can you turn this way? Perfect, perfect," a cameraman coached.

"Do you hate me?" a black reporter asked a young Klansman standing next to Flinn.

The boy, from behind his hood, shook his head.

"Then who do you hate?" another reporter called.

The boy paused, and then blurted out, "Everybody."

It wasn't much of a demonstration, one of the Jasperites muttered aloud.

Black demonstrators had been marching in East Jasper peacefully until just after lunchtime. Then they mobilized. As they marched the handful of blocks to the courthouse on Houston Street, Billy Rowles's voice came over the police radio channels: "We are in deep shit."

The Panthers were chanting "Black power" and "We can take those bastards. We can run over the damn police and take their asses." Quanell X was wearing a burnt orange Armani suit and alligator shoes. He was being filmed by a Klansman who was being filmed by police, all of whom were being filmed by the media. Seven Panthers charged the barricades at Milam and South Main. David Stiles was watching from the window of the Belle-Jim in disbelief. Separated only by drums and plastic mesh, Panthers and Klansmen converged on Courthouse Square in what was sure to be an unpleasant confrontation. "It was like watching all this unfold on a big-screen TV in front of us," David Stiles said later. "All the potential danger we had read about all our lives was fixin' to happen here. They were swarming around like insects, mixing it up and then stepping back and then mixing it up again with every kind of insult," Stiles said. "It looked like a war was fixing to start."

Quanell X and Khalid Mohammed kept challenging the riot-gear-clad officers, shoving and pushing as the officers pushed back. Unable to break through, Mohammed finally spun around and told his followers, "Let's go get the guns." He returned to the rally minutes later to hear Alexander shout an order to remove the Klan from the lawn.

Billy Rowles saw the same thing. While lawmen had formed a cordon around the Klansmen and Texas Rangers had encircled the Panthers, the situation threatened to get out of hand. Rowles told the Klansmen to get out. "You all get your ass out of here," he said, looking at his watch. He had ended their rally fifteen minutes early. Flinn began to protest and then looked back at an angry group of Panthers and reconsidered.

"African-Americans break the law and have their way," Flinn said into the microphone. "If you don't wake up, you'll lose your lives." Then the P.A. system went dead. Rowles had pulled the plug.

The handful of Klansmen hustled to the parking lanes beside the courthouse and climbed into their truck. It wouldn't turn over. Rowles was getting nervous; the Panthers were in hot pursuit. "Just get your ass out of here," he said again.

The chief and other cops had surrounded Khalid Mohammed, isolating him from the crowd. Alexander and Mohammed were eye to eye.

"Am I breaking the law being here?" Mohammed asked Alexander.

"Sir, I'm asking you not to," Alexander responded, standing his ground.

"Don't let them get into the cars like that," Mohammed shouted. "Chief, I'm not armed."

"Neither am I," Alexander said.

Mohammed backed off.

Over Alexander's shoulder Mohammed could see the Klansmen hustling from a truck that would not start to a small Yugo. Six or seven of them piled into the car in a tangled mass of bodies. Some feet were sticking out the front window. Hooded faces were pressed up against the glass. As they drove away, the car bumper was sitting so low under the weight that it dragged along the pavement, shooting up sparks.

Rowles said later that he had ruined a new sixty-five-dollar hat during the rally. "I sweated it down," he said. "I was glad when it was over."

CHAPTER EIGHT

BENEATH THE SURFACE

A MONTH PASSED, and another. The three defendants, King, Brewer, and Berry, sat in their small cells at Jasper County Jail with long hours to lose and little to distract them from the crime they had committed. The jail cells contained only a toilet, a shower stall, a cot, a chair, and a table. It was at the table that King spent most of his waking life; he ate his meals there, wrote letters, and on cheap sheets of ruled paper sent messages to Brewer through a fellow prisoner, known as Spider, in a bid to get their stories straight. ("We'll have to do something for Spidey," King wrote in one of the notes that he folded so intricately that he reduced a half sheet of ruled paper to the size of a dime. "We'll get him some cigarettes when my next care package comes through.")

Bill King's trial, the first of the three, was set to begin in February 1999. The authorities had the murder weapon: the thirty-foot-long logging chain. A day after the arrests Shawn Berry had led them right to it. Berry, a troop of sheriff's officers, and FBI agents traveled by squad car to Tommy Faulk's trailer in the woods, where King and Brewer had paid a visit the day after the murder. With a shackled Berry taking the lead, the group cut across the field and headed for the trees. Berry kicked up a piece of plywood that lay over a hole where the trio had often taken cover during paintball games in the past. The chain lay in the dirt below. The law enforcement officers exchanged glances and led Berry back to the squad car. Curtis Frame tested the chain for any traces of Byrd's DNA, but the trio had hosed off the links at the car wash and the results came back negative. Prosecutors had better luck on other evidence. DNA consistent with Byrd's was on all the defendants' shoes, traces of blood matching Byrd's were found on the underside of Berry's truck, King's DNA was on a cigarette found in a clearing at the top of a dirt road off Huff Creek. Brewer's DNA was on a beer bottle there, too. That, along with an eyewitness placing Byrd in the truck that night, tied most of the evidence together. The grand jury had quickly handed down an indictment.

*   *   *

THE LEAD STORY in the *Jasper Newsboy* in early July said it all: "Grand Jury Indicts Four."

"As expected Monday a Jasper County grand jury handed down four capital murder indictments in two brutal cases, one of which focused international attention on this town," the story began. "That case has been labeled a racial hate crime since the victim was black and three accused in the death are white. No motive has been given for the death other than the victim was black.

"All three men arrested and charged in the June 7 dragging death of James Byrd Jr.,—Shawn Allen Berry, John William King and Lawrence Russell Brewer—were indicted. At least two of the three—King and Brewer—have been reported to have ties to racist or white supremacist organizations."

Then, almost as an afterthought, it read: "Donald Louis Kennebrew was indicted for capital murder in the beating death of Jerry McQueen on May 30 (see related story)."

"According to statements to investigating officers, the three men had picked up Byrd in northeast Jasper in the early morning hours on the pretense of giving him a ride the short distance home," the article continued. "Instead the ride ended several miles away on Huff Creek Road where Byrd was beaten into unconsciousness and, according to investigators, his face sprayed with black paint, Byrd was then chained by the ankles to the back of the truck and dragged to his death.

"When asked if he was going to seek the death penalty for all three men in the Byrd case, the district attorney said he had reached no firm decision on Berry but it was 'pretty likely' on King and Brewer. Gray said there were two options in a capital murder case—death or life without parole.

"Jasper County Sheriff Billy Rowles, who has directed a multi-agency task force in the Byrd case, was asked how difficult it would be to house all the capital murder defendants in the county jail. Rowles told the media and a few citizens that it wasn't really too difficult. 'The only problem is that we have had to isolate them and they're [each] occupying two-man cells.'"

*   *   *

BILL KING WAS getting lonely. He missed Brewer. Since his arrest, King had not been allowed to communicate with his prison buddy, and that, freedom aside, was what King really wanted. He wanted to talk to his friend and see in his eyes the admiration that King didn't get anywhere else. Brewer was the person to whom King was closest at that moment. That was part of the reason why King asked Spider, the trusty, to pass notes to Brewer.

"They are trying to say Bird [sic] was kidnapped in order to make it capital murder," King wrote Brewer in Jasper County Jail. "But my lawyer said they have to prove that he was kiddnapped [sic] and unable to get away at any point in time. I do know that one pair of shoes they took were Shawn's dress boots with blood on 'em as well as his pants with blood on 'em. As far as the clothes I had on, I don't think any blood was on my pants or sweatshirt, but I think my sandles [sic] may have had some dark brown substance on the bottom of 'em . . . if they don't find us guilty of kidnapping but do find us guilty of murder, it will be a simple first-degree murder, bro. No death sentence!"

What King and Brewer could not have known was that their notes did not travel directly from one cell to another. They made a stop instead in Sheriff Billy Rowles's office. Curtis Johnson, or Spider, didn't feel right passing the jailhouse notes, or "kites." He said later that what King and Brewer were accused of doing seemed beyond the pale. Johnson was a black man and saw something sinister and frightening in both King and Brewer. The accused men failed to see the irony in counting on a black man to help them pass notes to concoct a story that could help them wriggle out of a racially motivated murder. Spider took the first note to Mo Johnson, the jailer, and asked her what he should do. She asked him to meet her outside, where they could talk and not be overheard by other employees or trusties.

"Bill King and Russell Brewer were willing to use anyone if it was going to further their cause, and Spider was no different," said the jailer. "Curtis is a good guy, really. He just got himself in some trouble and wound up at the jail. His conscience wouldn't let him carry those notes, so he came to me."

As long as Spider hadn't been asked by any jail employee to bring the notes forward and had done it voluntarily, the kites could be used against King and Brewer in court. The problem was getting the notes open, peeling back the folds without tearing them, Xeroxing them, and then reassembling the folds so the pair inside would never suspect. "You have no idea how hard it was to get those notes refolded back together again," Rowles said later. "We'd spend half an hour getting them refolded just right so they wouldn't know they'd been intercepted."

The patience paid off. King and Brewer all but admitted in the notes to committing the murder. Defense attorneys said later that it was the most damning evidence against their clients. Prosecutor Gray had singled King out as the mastermind behind the killing: he was the most racist, Gray said, and, with a 109 IQ, the smartest of the three men accused in the slaying. The notes bolstered the prosecutor's contention that the murder was a racially motivated one and that Brewer and King were proud of it.

"Reguardless [sic] of the outcome of this, we have made history and shall die proudly remembered if need be. Much Aryan Love, Respect and Honor my brother in arms."

The note was signed "Sieg Heil, Possum."

What King could not have known, as the small note made its way from his cell to the sheriff's office, to the copier, back to Rowles's office, and then to Brewer, was that he had become a father. His girlfriend, Kylie Greeney, eighteen, the same girl whose mother had arrived in Rowles's office with pictures of her daughter and King months before, had just given birth to his illegitimate son, Blayne. He was two months premature.

*   *   *

WEEKS AFTER THE murder, out-of-town journalists continued to arrive as if out of thin air, peeking into dark corners Jasperites thought were better left undisturbed. Residents tried to explain how things worked in Jasper to the newcomers, but they only seemed to make things worse. "When northerners all say 'nigger,' they mean it with hatred," said one white Jasperite, trying to explain. "When we say it, it is just a name, just an expression. It doesn't have all that negative stuff attached to it. Northerners put it there. Hell, niggers even call themselves niggers. So why is it so bad when we all say it? People have just gotten too sensitive about the whole thing, so we end up having to mind our *p*'s and *q*'s and be careful not to say it in case it is misinterpreted, and the truth is we don't mean nothing by it. 'Nigger' is just a word."

"Of course it is," the journalists said, not sounding, exactly, as if they agreed.

After a while, unable to explain how "nigger" was not a pejorative, the white community made an extra effort not to use the word in front of strangers.

Everything had seemed so much simpler just a year before, when the mayoral election had drawn to a close with longtime city councilman R. C. Horn, a black man, emerging as the winner. Certainly the election of Horn meant that Jasper was readying itself for a very different place in history. It had to be proof that Jasper was not one of those backwoods towns with their antique visions of racial justice. Of course, R. C. Horn was no threat to the white community, no more than the other African-Americans in powerful positions in Jasper had been. The leaders of the chamber of commerce, the local council of governments, the hospital, and the school board were black, but they had been handpicked, elevated precisely because they did not preach radical ideas of equality. Whites were happy because their way of life was not threatened, and most blacks were happy with the mere idea of a black mayor, even if he did not fight for their interests. "Name one thing that R. C. Horn has done for the black community that whites didn't approve first," said Unav Wade. "These elections were to make the whites feel better about themselves. This wasn't about giving blacks a voice or an equal place at the table. We knew that and, well, the whites did too."

For a long time, residents in the black community worried about the ability of local law enforcement to protect them. They were edgy about the general atmosphere of racial animosity visited on blacks by whites. They asked Horn about jobs, and training, and streetlights in black neighborhoods. Horn would nod empathetically and promise to bring the concerns up at the next council meeting. Nothing ever came of these small requests. Horn didn't have the power to push the council to take action. Some members of the black community saw the murder as a new opportunity to make their voices heard.

This began in small ways. Christine Carter piped up when white ladies jumped their turn in line. Eddie Land bristled when gas station attendants left him waiting longer than white patrons. Reverend Lyons told his clergy to stand up for themselves. Elmo Jackson started tallying the hundreds of slights he had endured over the years. Leaders in the black community wanted job training programs and a task force to help race relations in the community. Rather predictably, behind closed doors in town, white residents were having the opposite reaction. Those niggers were making too much of this murder. They needed to remember their place. Blacks needed to remember who ran Jasper.

"This was a terrible crime," said Joe Tonahill from behind his massive desk. "But what worries me is how some folks—not every- one mind you, but some folks—will try to take advantage and make this worse than it already is. There are some people in the black community who say this proves that Jasper has race problems, and this murder doesn't prove anything of the sort. It proves that three drunk boys, and one of them wasn't even from Jasper, committed a terrible murder. This wasn't a conspiracy; this was a random act. But some people just don't want to leave it that way. They want to turn it into something more."

Unav Wade watched Jasper's worlds collide from behind the tinted glass of her storefront beauty salon. She did not see a white conspiracy as much as she saw complicity on both sides. The white community had turned a blind eye to the black community's com- plaints for years, and the black community had allowed them to do so. After the murder, with the arrival of outsiders, blacks and whites suddenly had to explain themselves to prove they weren't racist, and to strangers who did not believe that meanness was not behind every slight. It was no longer enough to say it was different here, or that northerners, or foreigners, couldn't understand.

The journalists' questions—probing, slightly impolite—began to change how Jasper viewed itself. As Jasper residents saw them- selves on national newscasts and in front-page stories, they started to see themselves as strangers did. They learned the latest twists and turns of the case not from the *Jasper Newsboy* but from the *Houston Chronicle* and the *Dallas Morning News*.

"The old, ancient cultural and structural inequality, the lega- cies of slavery and legal segregation, the cultural barriers that sepa-

rate races all are pervasive," Jesse Jackson told the *Houston Chronicle.*
Jasper had a "mixed report card," he said.

And as Jasperites read the articles by journalists who had
arrived in town to talk to anyone willing to venture an opinion or
open a front door, they looked beyond themselves and saw a different Jasper. Maybe, just maybe, there was racism there after all, residents said to themselves. Maybe, just maybe, this murder happening
in Jasper was not such an accident after all. Maybe there were racial
problems that needed tending.

Teachers began getting telephone calls from administrators in
late August. They were called back to school early for sensitivity
training in anticipation of tension between black and white students in the classroom. Football players were told to turn the other
cheek if tempers flared on the field. Mayor R. C. Horn and Walter
Diggles called community outreach meetings.

Jasperites filed into the hospital cafeteria and the Jasper High
School gym, and they began to confess, and apologize for, past prejudice. Whites apologized for calling the largely black housing project behind the theater the "hatchery." The gatherings were
awkward and ended with fumbling hugs and uncomfortable smiles.
As citizens walked across the dark parking lots to climb into their
trucks, the unuttered question on everyone's mind was the same:
How long would this last?

In the weeks after the arrests Billy Rowles could feel the pressure building, and so could his wife, Jamie. A petite redhead with an
easy laugh, Jamie Rowles had some idea of the strain her husband
was under. She saw her job as jailer in nearby Orange County as a
duty she could perform with dignity. She had realized long before
that interpersonal skills were key, so she found a way to meld toughness with respect for her inmates. In return, they respected her.

"They don't swear at me, because if they start I just tell them it is inappropriate and I won't stand for it," she said. "When Billy was going through all this, most of the inmates were thanking me, saying Billy was doing right by the black community. There were some negative comments, about whether justice would be served, and I know Billy was worried about that. I talked to the kids. I told them to just give him some space, so they did."

Then at night, when Rowles would come home, Jamie would put dinner on the table and ask gentle questions. "Billy just wanted to talk it all out," she said. "He would talk about the evidence and about the case and about the security they were trying to put together. Thing was, he was convinced if anything went wrong it would be his fault, and it would reflect badly on Jasper. So he wanted to think of everything, and he was racking his brain to make sure nothing was forgotten. It was a very difficult time for him."

Where the sheriff found solace was in his religion. Only several years before, Billy Rowles had become a born-again Christian, and it was a profoundly settling influence on his life. Inspirational passages seemed to put all the meanness the lawman saw around him in perspective. It was in the early weeks after the Byrd murder that Rowles began to find himself reading a passage called Footsteps in the Sand.

"One night a man had a dream," he read. "He dreamed he was walking along the beach with the Lord. Across the sky flashed scenes from his life. For each scene, he noticed two sets of footprints in the sand; one belonging to him, and the other to the Lord. When the last scene of his life flashed before him he looked back, at the footprints in the sand. He noticed that many times along the path of his life there was only one set of footprints. He also noticed that it happened at the very lowest and saddest times of his life. This really bothered him and he questioned the Lord about it. 'Lord, you said that once I decided to follow you, you'd walk with me all the way. But I have noticed that during the most troublesome times of my life there is only one set of footprints. I don't understand why when I needed you most you would leave me.' The Lord replied: 'My son, my precious child, I love you and I would never leave you. During your times of trial and suffering, when you see only one set of foot-prints, it was then that I carried you.'"

The Rowles family reunion had been scheduled for June and was postponed when it became clear Billy Rowles needed to be in Jasper to ensure the Klan rally didn't erupt into something more violent. A month later, Rowleses from all over Texas came to Buna to meet with members of their extended family. Traditionally, the family members brought wrapped presents to the gatherings which they would choose from a table at random. Billy Rowles was the last one to choose. As he peeled back the wrapping paper, he was taken aback. It was a small glass paperweight inscribed with Footsteps in the Sand.

"It wasn't any accident; I knew that God was watching out for me and this would all work out fine," he said.

*   *   *

JASPERITES WERE ALSO trying to move on. The town's princi-pal gossip dispensaries, Texas Charlie's and the Belle-Jim Hotel, virtually banned James Byrd as a topic of conversation. "Every once in a while someone new comes into town and we have to go all over it all over again," said Pat Stiles, who rented all the rooms at the Belle-Jim nearly every night since the killing. "I mean, what a thing to be famous for. I've had people call me and ask if it was actually safe to come to Jasper after the murder. Can you imagine? Is it safe? Of course it was, but it said a lot about how people were seeing us."

While the white community was sure that it wanted to keep any semblance of racial disharmony from the prying eyes of strangers, the black community in Jasper was torn. Diggles and Lyons and other leaders saw an opportunity to even things out. The door to equality had been cracked, and they were trying to decide how to throw it open. Perhaps this was the time for blacks to stop living in their parallel universe, where whites would wave from the other side of the street but would never actually stop to talk.

"The prejudice here is more insidious," said Christine Carter. "It's in all the little things that we see the racist side of whites. Whites, because it doesn't really affect them, can't see what they are doing. They don't see the way they look at us or treat us as prejudice."

"The murder made the white folks around here wake up and act the way they thought they were supposed to," said Unav Wade. "They suddenly were treating us with all this respect because outsiders were watching. Tourism is a big business here; imagine if everybody decided not to come here anymore. . . . That was going to hurt everyone. So being extra polite to black people, well, that seemed like a small price to pay."

Radioman Mike Lout did not think the newfound politesse of the white community would be enough to erase the stigma Jasper had already acquired. "Jasper will be known forever as the place where a black man was dragged to death," he said. "The city leaders don't like it, but we're the new Mississippi, the Old South rising, proof that prejudice is just as bad here, now, as it was in the 1950s. The fact that that's an exaggeration, and that this really was an isolated incident, won't change what people think of us. That was kind of sobering."

*   *   *

WHITES WERE TOO frightened to discuss aloud what might happen if the killers, King, Brewer, and Berry, weren't found guilty and sentenced to death. Never mind all the community programs and task forces and apologies. The trials were still the litmus test for Jasper's black community. That would show more than any white resident waving for them to cross against the light how the races were faring in Jasper.

The risk that somehow the trio wouldn't get the death penalty worried lawyer Joe Tonahill. "I would have run away from these cases as fast as I could," said Tonahill, adding that if he had been appointed to defend one of the trio, he would "have told him to go to the top of the courthouse and dive off, head first. It seems pretty clear they are guilty; what isn't certain is that Guy James will be able to get lethal injection. If he doesn't, that will be almost like losing completely."

Because this was a crime of such magnitude, it piqued the interest of lawmen and lawyers everywhere, particularly those intent on rolling back perceptions of backwoods justice in Deep East Texas. A guilty verdict in Jasper for a hate crime could help cleanse the reputation of the whole region. No one understood that more than Guy James Gray, for whom the whole Byrd episode appeared to be all twister and no Oz. Gray believed the cases needed to be tried in Jasper County. It was the only way, he reckoned, Jasper would ever be able to prove that it wasn't racist. "We had to take care of our own mess," Gray said.

Such a strategy came with both a monetary and a psychological cost. Gray figured each case would cost between $200,000 to $300,000 to try. Even if there were a change of venue, something Gray opposed, Jasper County would still be liable not only for the trial costs but for the housing and travel expenses of everyone involved. The only place Gray saw Jasper getting a break was from the federal government's willingness to pay for forensics, provide investigators to interview witnesses, and commit federal attorneys to help with the prosecution. The federal prosecutors were a backstop if Gray failed to get a conviction in Jasper. Gray hoped he would not need to worry about federal charges.

Already questions about race were swirling. Would the jury have a balance of black and white jurors? How many members of the grand jury that indicted the trio were black? (Two.) Suddenly it was more important to have a black member of a jury than a fair jury. The questions chilled Gray. The trial jury would be selected from a juror pool selected at random by computer from the general county population. If the jury represented the county population, there would likely be three or four blacks sitting on it. This was a double-edged sword for Gray. Blacks tended not to believe in the death penalty and could exclude themselves during the voir dire phase of jury selection. All jurors seated on a capital murder case had to say whether they would be willing to mete out the death penalty. If they were not willing to do so, they were automatically excused. Gray knew that most blacks in the random pool wouldn't make it past voir dire for that reason. "I'm not sure if it is for religious reasons or because they feel the death penalty is given to blacks more than whites," said Gray. "But that was one of the big things I was worried about. You can lose a trial on jury selection." What he didn't say until the trial was over was that he was worried that if an all-white jury acquitted King, all would be lost.

* * *

FOR JASPERITES TRYING to escape the events of the past few months, there was always football. The Jasper High School Bulldogs offered a ready diversion. The Bulldogs were certainly not the winningest high-school football team in Texas history, but the boys made it to the state championships often enough to keep the hopes and dreams of Jasperites alive. Every Friday night from September to December, when the Bulldogs played, the community turned out in droves. It hardly mattered whether citizens had a son on the team or a daughter on the cheerleading squad. What was important was that the fans turned out, and for several hours they forgot whatever else might have been troubling Jasper, be it job losses or a gruesome murder.

Even before the first whistle blew, hundreds of people filled the stands, waving the Bulldog banners. Then the boys, both black and white, galloped onto the field to do battle with the Evandale Rebels or one of the other East Texas teams. Cheerleaders chanted the fight song. Booster mothers dispensed hot dogs and soft drinks. Certainly football was something on which everyone in Jasper could agree. Once the cheering died down, however, and the banner waving became less frequent, one noticed something about the spectators in the stands: whites sat on one side of the benches, and blacks sat on the other.

* * *

GUY JAMES GRAY was aware of hate groups in a general kind of way and had read articles about the Aryan Nation and white supremacist groups, but he had never had the occasion to give them much thought before he began to prepare for the King trial. Gray

knew King had racist tattoos all over his body, but he was still working out how he would connect them with the Byrd murder. He
looked for clues in King's prison record. At first the folder did not
provide much information. There were the usual inmate misbehav-
ior reports—one of the tools guards could use to control inmates.
Guards filled out a form, got a sergeant to sign it, and then sent the
package off to a so-called adjustment committee. Inmates who were
written up faced a number of different punishments, from constant
confinement to revocation of visits. By this measure, King was
hardly a model prisoner. He seemed to take a perverse pleasure in
needling authorities.

As he leafed through the file, Gray saw several references to
"Christian Identity." Given King's rap sheet, Gray saw little evi-
dence of Christianity in the young man, so the reference stuck out.
It was only after Gray had logged onto the Internet and began visit-
ing white supremacist Web sites that he learned about the Christian
Identity movement and how little it had to do with Christianity.

King was a member of the Confederate Knights of America, one
of the eleven major racial gangs or groups that have flourished in the
Texas prison system. The Confederate Knights was an offshoot of a
Ku Klux Klan group out of North Carolina and was one of the least
violent of the prison gangs. Originally organized by a man named
Terry Boyce in the 1970s, the Confederate Knights believed that a race
war was imminent. The Knights got most of their recruits from two
places: prisons and poor towns like Jasper where disaffected youth, like
Bill King, wanted to find someone else to blame for their failures.

The ideological backbone for such groups was, Gray discovered, the benign-sounding Christian Identity movement. A sort of
religion on steroids, Christian Identity followers reinterpreted the
biblical story of creation to come up with a cosmic justification for
modern-day racism. As he clicked through Internet pages, Gray

found out that members of the Christian Identity movement read like a Who's Who of America's antigovernment movement. An off-shoot of the sect first plotted the bombing of the Murrah Building in Oklahoma City in the 1980s. Randy Weaver, whose wife and fourteen-year-old son were killed at Ruby Ridge in a shoot-out with federal agents in 1992, was also linked to the movement. Timothy McVeigh, who was convicted of the Oklahoma City bombing, placed a call to Elohim City, in the Ozark Mountains, where some of the sect's elders have a community, before the fertilizer bomb explosion in 1995.

East Texas, with its inherent economic and racial divisions, was fertile ground for Christian Identity practitioners. By the mid-1990s churches had begun springing up around Jasper, including one in nearby Burkeville, where King's friend Tommy Faulk had his trailer. Christian Identity leaders' strategy had been to look for small autonomous county churches with no debt to set up their parishes. They would bring in new members to pack the congregation, then would fire the pastor, get the tax exempt status, and proselytize in the name of religious and racial purity.

Many practitioners were young, white, working-class kids who were drawn to the movement because it had pat answers for difficult racial questions. Christian Identity was an enticing reach for a quick answer. Fifty years earlier, Christian Identity had fewer than 100 followers. In 2001, they numbered about 50,000. The Christian Identity movement ultimately inflated the self-importance of otherwise unremarkable young men, often with disastrous results. It gave them a way to find someone they hated more than themselves. Asian and African races, for example, were the biblical "beasts of the fields," a lower order than humans.

There might never have been the lethal combination of Bill King and Russell Brewer had both men not failed to convince members of the Aryan Brotherhood, arguably the meanest white supremacist gang in Texas prisons, to admit them to their gang. Both King and Brewer were too small and too scared in prison to make the grade. Both were told they couldn't join the Aryan Brotherhood or the Aryan Nation.

The groups organized themselves like boys pulling together a secret club, with officers and by-laws and initiations. The Brotherhood was organized under a "wheel," or steering committee, which was led by a president. Each wheel member oversaw a different group of prison units. Each prison unit had a captain and a lieutenant. The group's structure was spelled out in an elaborate constitution, which was passed from inmate to inmate. Spin-off groups included the Aryan Reich, the Aryan Circle, and the White Knights. Inmates referred to Aryan Reich as "arf" and the Aryan Circle as the "circle jerks." While the groups were dangerous, there was something very high school about it all. Prison culture was oddly cliquey, and King and Brewer were not allowed to be part of it. So the pair started their own little sect, the Confederate Knights of America.

"I wasn't a gang member; I am just proud of my Aryan heritage," King told Rowles during their conversation minutes before his arrest. Rowles watched King carefully. "By the time I left prison, there were only two of us. It was a protection thing."

"You don't have to be blond to be Aryan," King said. "Some of the Vikings had dark hair and dark eyes."

People outside prison didn't understand the difference between racism and protecting white rights, King said. "By the year 2040, whites will be outnumbered by the combined nonwhite races in this country," he said. "How are we going to get a fair shake then? People just don't get it. We have to protect our race and build it up. You don't have to hate other races to do that. You just need to concentrate on loving your own."

The problem was that violent racists were emboldened by denials of racism and prejudice. They read them to mean they were doing what white leaders secretly want them to do. "Bill King thought everyone really thought like him," said Guy James Gray. "And it was a big surprise to him when that wasn't the case."

*   *   *

KING AND BREWER, both unemployed and indigent, had court-appointed lawyers. Berry's girlfriend, Christie Marcontell, a former Miss Jasper, asked her wealthy grandfather to pay for Shawn Berry's defense. King's attorney was a tall lean man named C. Haden "Sonny" Cribbs, known as one of the best defense attorneys in East Texas and one of the few qualified to represent a defendant in a capital murder case. Cribbs wasn't keen to represent King but figured since the court saw fit to appoint him, he had to take the case. Truth was, he owed Judge Joe Bob Golden a favor.

In 1991, Golden had called Cribbs to defend a man accused of raping and killing a ten-year-old girl from Lake Charles, Louisiana, named Falyssa Van Winkle. The girl had disappeared from a flea market in Beaumont and was found, days later, facedown in a mud puddle beneath a bridge in nearby Newton County. "I told him that with a daughter of my own and all, I just couldn't bring myself to do this one," said Cribbs. "I told the judge to call me next time he had a tough one, and I would do my part. The next time was for Bill King."

Cribbs wore small professorial glasses and had blond hair going to gray that flopped over his forehead. A thick white mustache anchored his face. Everything about him said homespun. He was slow talking and gentlemanly, more Atticus Finch than Perry Mason. His ties were quiet, and his suits were nondescript. His office in Beaumont was ramshackle, stashed away on a part of Calder Avenue that was difficult to navigate. There must have been complaints as prospective clients cruised up and down the main drag in Beaumont unable to find the office, for Cribbs had erected a billboard-size sign in yellow and green in front of it that announced: "Law Offices of C. Haden 'Sonny' Cribbs." The sign gave the impression that he was running for office.

Inside, the decor was early 1970s. The carpeting, green. The chairs, vinyl. There were bars on all the windows, and his secretary sat behind a frosted glass window, like a receptionist in a doctor's office. There was one magazine on the waiting room table: a *Sports Illustrated*. It was more than a year old. Cribbs's inner office carried the same 1970s theme, though it was also decorated with golf mugs and mallard duck prints. The room smelled of wax and defeat. Cribbs always seemed to land the hopeless cases: a man who killed a little girl and left his prints all over the doorknob. Another shot an elderly woman after raping her and would admit to the shooting but denied the validity of the DNA evidence that proved the rape. Bill King was another in an increasingly long list of unwinnable battles Cribbs was assigned to fight.

Cribbs met King for the first time in July 1998 in Livingston prison, and from the start the two men did not get along. "My lawyer thinks I'm guilty, so he won't even help me. You know what he told me on our first interview? The very first time we met? He asked me if I wanted life in prison or the death penalty. He didn't ask if I was innocent." Cribbs remembered the story differently but confirmed its essentials. "I can be a little blunt sometimes," he admitted. "I wouldn't coddle the boy, and he wanted to be coddled." From there, the King-Cribbs relationship went from bad to worse. King insisted on pursuing a "not guilty" verdict, claiming he was dropped off at his apartment and that Byrd was killed later by Berry during a drug-related argument.

Cribbs told him the story didn't hold up, and King got mad. Many times, after Cribbs made the ninety-minute drive from Beaumont to Livingston, King wouldn't come out of his cell to talk to him. Other times King wouldn't sign motion papers. He filed a formal motion in January to have Cribbs dismissed, to no avail. "The kid wanted me to tell him I can get him off, and I just can't; that isn't going to happen," Cribbs said before the trial. "I'm not going to tell him what to say; I won't do that," he said. "I'm not going to tell him how to lie."

In October, King made a public statement on the events of that June night. He had his father type out a seven-page document which he titled "Logical Reasoning." It was meant to be a rescue, a reorganization and retelling of the events that occurred in the wee hours of June 7.

"Emotion and subjectivity ruin facts," King wrote in his own defense. "It is not easy to remove the effect of emotion during an investigation. People who believe strongly in an idea often become so attached to it they bend and twist any facts that cast doubt on the idea. A Federal Bureau of Investigation expert examined the tattoos of Brewer and myself to interpret motive for the offense of murder; motive such as an affiliation to hate crime groups."

By King's reckoning, the blame for James Byrd's murder had been misplaced. The murderer, he said, had to have been Shawn Berry. King said the trio passed a black man walking on Martin Luther King Drive, and Berry picked him up. "He identified him simply as Bird [sic], a man he befriended while in the Jasper County Jail," King wrote. Byrd had supplied Berry with steroids, he added, and Berry was looking to buy more. Byrd climbed into the back of the truck and seated himself behind the cab. "Shawn asked Russell if he could borrow fifty to sixty dollars, because he needed a little extra cash to replenish his juice, or steroid, supply," King's defense continued, adding that Berry dropped him and Brewer off at home before going to make the deal with Byrd.

King said the last time he saw James Byrd he was in the truck with Berry. "What may have occurred afterwards, I cannot justifiably say. Investigators would like to conjure up a credulous [sic] case against Brewer and me, therefore gaining recognition as contributors to the National Honor of a solution to America's racial problems. Russell Brewer and myself are being stereotyped and persecuted due to our difference in appearance, criminal histories and the pride we openly express for our race."

Cribbs was beside himself. The letter, which he had begged King not to send to reporters, gave prosecutors too much information. Even without the letter, Gray felt fairly confident that he had enough to get King just on Berry's statement and the chemical evidence. King's DNA was found on beer bottles and cigarette butts at the murder scene. A pin drop of Byrd's blood was found on King's sandal. There were three pieces of DNA evidence that put King at the scene, though Gray could see how a defense attorney might explain them away: the beer bottle and cigarette butts could have fallen out of the truck, the blood on the sandal could have come from Brewer's or Berry's clothing. After all, the three were staying in the same apartment. Gray also had three airtight pieces of evidence placing Brewer on the logging road. If King and Brewer were together that night, all night, that meant Gray could use six pieces of evidence against both King and Brewer. King's statement, eventually printed in the *Dallas Morning News*, was very helpful indeed.

Cribbs told King straight-out that the letter was "the dumbest thing he ever did. He probably killed himself," he said later. "Until he wrote the letter, they had no one who could put him in the car on the night in question other than the codefendants. They had a couple of pieces of evidence that could have been explained."

Cribbs decided avoiding a death penalty sentence for Bill King wasn't going to come by refuting the prosecution's evidence, which was damning. He figured his only chance was to make an emotional appeal, to try to create a spark of sympathy for King, who was the target of an all-out vendetta by an overzealous government team. "If I can show how much they are ganging up, I have a chance to save this boy's life," said Cribbs.

*   *   *

OCTOBER 10 WAS supposed to be a special day, the annual Jasper Fall Festival on the square. There were booths, mayhaul berry jelly, jams, pies, and decorations for Halloween. The only problem was, this year some uninvited guests were scheduled to arrive: the Ku Klux Klan was planning another rally.

Police chief Harlon Alexander and Sheriff Billy Rowles had known weeks before that Michael Lowe was going to ask for another rally permit. "We'd had time stolen from us during the last rally, and we wanted to make up for that," said Lowe. "We had lost face, had been humiliated, and we needed to make that right."

Radioman Mike Lout had uncovered the Klan's intention when he stumbled on an announcement for the rally while cruising their Web site on the Internet, something he had started doing after the first Klan demonstration back in June. "I called the chamber of commerce for a comment, and they went crazy," said Lout.

Diane Domenech, one of the chamber's members, was aghast that Lout was going to run the story about the Klan rally on the air. "We don't need that on the radio, Mike," she said. "It will ruin our Fall Fest."

Lout laughed. "Well, between you and I, if the Klan shows up on October 10, I think your Fall Fest is going to be ruined anyway," he said. "There are going to be sheets and apple pie on the same day whether I put it on the radio or not."

The Fall Fest was postponed.

CHAPTER NINE

HOOK, LINE, AND SINKER

January 1999

IN MID-JANUARY, Bill King was led into the Jasper County Courthouse in leg-irons and a bulletproof vest. The leg-irons were a testament to the severity of his alleged crime, and the vest was a reminder that if a jury didn't decide to kill him by lethal injection, someone else might be willing to do the job. Around his waist he wore a device that could deliver a 50,000-volt shock to his kidneys—not lethal but enough to stun him—at the touch of a button on one of two remote controls held by his guards. King had entered a not-guilty plea. He wasn't even there in the woods that night, he said. Instead, he and Russell Brewer were at home, asleep.

Judge Golden's courtroom, like the man, was unpretentious. It was plain, with white walls, ceiling fans, and ten rows of pewlike spectator benches. Golden had been on the bench for ten years, felt no need to wear judicial robes, and was known for answering his phone himself since he had no secretary. He had been the first law clerk for Tonahill's friend Joe Fisher, a U.S. district judge. Golden had also once practiced law with Tonahill. There weren't many spectators at these early hearings. The satellite trucks had left long before, and the only reporters who bothered to show up for the pre-trial motions were local.

As King entered Judge Joe Bob Golden's courtroom, he scanned the spectator benches. His eyes stopped on the Byrd family, sitting in various positions of discomfort in the first row. King's father and his girlfriend, Kylie, sat toward the back of the room. There was palpable tension between Bill King and the Byrd family. During one pretrial hearing, King moved his chair to face James Byrd's father directly. Byrd, a small, soft-spoken man, stared back at him with a mixture of hatred and bafflement. King tried to look menacing, but there was nothing electric about him. Despite his tattoos, he still looked more like a high school sophomore than a murderer, too soft around the middle and baby-faced to be lethal. He complained to sheriff's officers about high blood pressure and bloody noses.

King and his lawyer hardly spoke. If Cribbs leaned over to whisper something to him, his client would sit there dumbly, without so much as registering a change in expression. The two men, it was clear from across the room, did not get along.

The statement of probable cause against King, Brewer, and Berry was ten pages long, three pages of which were taken directly from the statement Berry gave police hours after he was taken in for questioning. (Berry might have gotten an immunity deal when we first started out, Gray said, but as his story evolved it became clear he was involved in the beating as much as King and Brewer and he had lied.)

King's trial was scheduled to start in mid-February 1999. In the weeks preceding, Cribbs had tried to get his client to help in the defense. King was truculent. Cribbs filed a motion in December to have the trial moved from the piney woods of Jasper to just about anywhere else in Texas. He had more than a dozen people lined up to testify they had already made up their minds about Bill King as proof that an impartial jury could not be empaneled. However, only two of the people on his list showed up. "He looked stupid up there when no one showed up," King said. Cribbs said people in Jasper, black or white, were reluctant to look like they supported Bill King in any way. Character witnesses evaporated, he said, almost as quickly as they emerged. "I don't know how to defend this kid," he said before the trial. Cribbs's motion for a change of venue was temporarily denied. Judge Golden said he would make a determination on venue prior to choosing the jury.

Weeks later, Cribbs filed another motion to have the judge himself removed from the case because he was a property owner in Jasper. Cribbs's reasoning was that Golden had a conflict of interest because taxes were going up in the county to pay for the trial—and that any Jasper property owner would therefore be prejudiced against King.

As Cribbs prepared his arguments against Golden, a drama was unfolding at the Jasper County Jail. It was beginning to dawn on Bill King, just two weeks before jury selection, that his situation was dire. When Curtis Frame and several deputies came to his cell to take him to a hearing, King refused to go. "He used harsh profanities to describe his lawyer and to display his unhappiness with his situation in general, he flatly refused to be transported to the courthouse," the *Jasper Newsboy* reported. Cribbs was beside himself.

"This boy really doesn't do himself any favors," said Cribbs. "And he's making it damn hard to defend him. He thinks if he doesn't show up or if he drags his feet, the trial won't happen. The trial is going to happen, regardless of how he feels about it." Then Cribbs filed a motion to be removed as King's lawyer. "This is really just for the record, to help in any possible appeal," he said. "My duty is to protect Bill King's rights and see that he gets as fair a trial as possible whether he wants to help me or not."

Cribbs's motions, to remove Golden from the case and to be excused as King's lawyer, were both denied. Golden's portion of the tax increase that would be used to pay for the capital murder trials—$16.41, according to county assessors—wasn't enough to affect his judgment in the trial, 128th District Court judge Pat Clark ruled. Jury selection would go ahead as scheduled.

Jury selection began at the end of January and took more than a month as Cribbs and Gray sifted through more than four hundred juror applications and questionnaires. King was the first in the docket because prosecutors, when they are forced to choose, invariably begin with their strongest case. Gray figured a jury would find nothing to like about a young man covered with racist tattoos.

"Bill King's been planning something like this for some time," Gray told reporters during jury selection, adding that he had proof that the crime was premeditated. "Was he stalking James Byrd? I don't think so. But did he leave the house that night with a racially motivated crime in mind? Absolutely."

*   *   *

A JURY OF seven men and five women, including one black, were seated in February just before Presidents' Day. During the selection process, most prospective jurors were solemn, even frightened, when they took the stand for questioning. One young woman confessed she was nervous. She said she didn't think she could give anybody the death penalty, an automatic reason to be excused in a capital murder case. She wanted to start her jury service with a less critical case. "Give me an easy one," she said, "an insurance case."

"You're a delightful young lady," Golden said. "You're very refreshing. You're also excused."

Cribbs began laying the groundwork for the defense, working on jurors' emotions. At every pretrial hearing and during jury selection, Cribbs referred to King as "this young boy" and cautioned jurors that it was one thing to say they believed in the death penalty but quite another to actually deliver the sentence.

Guy James Gray had other concerns. While the FBI evidence was piling up against the trio, Gray had to find enough jurors willing to put King to death. Gray, who had trouble reconciling the death penalty with his own Catholic beliefs, felt that if there was ever a crime that deserved such a punishment, this was it. "It's a scary thing," he told reporters before the trial opened. "The town and community are depending on you, and the result could have dramatic consequences for Jasper. We're ready, but I don't deny for a minute that I'm nervous about it."

When the jury was finally set, Golden decided not to sequester them. Each day, they would gather at 8:45 A.M. at an undisclosed location, and they would try to break off at 4 P.M. so they could be home before dark, he told them. Golden then walked the jurors through the basics: what is evidence, what is not; the court's definition of "reasonable doubt"; the differences between a murder and a capital murder case. He read the charges and explained that they needed to find King guilty of both kidnapping and murder to merit a capital murder charge.

In choosing a jury, Cribbs and Gray had been trying to find people in Jasper County who hadn't yet made up their minds. The story the black community had pieced together over the intervening months revolved around the Klan. They were certain King and Berry were members, had organized the murder, and had planned others which would have occurred under the cover of darkness by coconspirators and haters of blacks had they not been arrested. Conversely, the white community had decided the whole episode was a drug deal gone awry. Byrd was no angel, and this was no hate crime, they said. He wasn't killed because he was black or because Jasper was a racist town.

"Just shows what alcohol can do," Shawn Berry's mother told reporters.

*   *   *

THE POLICE SEARCH of King's apartment back in June had yielded racist literature, including a book on the Ku Klux Klan and an *Esquire* magazine article about the 1955 case of Emmett Till. The DNA experts found the blood on King's sandal. Gray also planned to focus on King's white supremacist tattoos, including the one depicting the hanging of a black man.

"The thing I need to battle is that if Bill King was sitting on my back porch attending a barbecue, you might just take a shine to him," Gray said. "He can be polite and charming. But the truth is he's a killer and he's mean."

As the evidence against his client mounted, Cribbs's strategy became a counterstrategy. If the three men were on Huff Creek Road and did tie Byrd to the bumper of the truck, then the three men ought to pay equally for it, Cribbs said. Increasingly, King looked like a fall guy, and Cribbs hoped that would spark some sympathy.

By October 1998, the district attorney had filed 3,876 separate pieces of evidence in the case. And with every envelope, with every

DNA test and FBI interview, King's future looked bleaker. Everyone behind bars in Texas who had ever even heard of Bill King was calling the D.A. and the FBI offering a deal. They offered to testify against King if their sentences were reduced, or if they could get some privileges reinstated. "How do you fight that?" Cribbs said.

Gray was planning harrowing testimony. In as much detail as Judge Golden would allow, Gray wanted to show the jurors footage of Huff Creek Road, photographs of Byrd's headless body, the clearing off the dirt road where Byrd had been beaten, the eighty-one circles of Day-Glo paint on the pavement, letters written by King in which he talked about killing "niggers," and photographs of the gallery of tattoos that attested to the hardening of his heart. All together, Gray said, this testimony would help draw a convincing portrait of a racist murderer.

The prosecution had a list of 189 witnesses. One was Ronnie Bryan, who ran the Superior Building Construction Company in Jasper and who had fired King and Berry just a week before the murder. Bryan could describe his discomfort as King used the word "nigger" and other racist epithets when he was working construction in indigent housing projects. ("These blacks were all sitting around drinking beer and ordering us around to fix things around their houses," King said. "I thought they should get their lazy asses up and do it for themselves. When I see something like that, sure, I guess I have to say I'm racist.")

Gray wanted the government's case to unfold like the dark movie of a young man's life gone awry, from the letters he wrote to others about race wars to his references to girls as his "Aryan Princesses." Gray had letters that indicated King had planned some sort of racial crime for July that would ignite a race war in Jasper.

*   *   *

SONNY CRIBBS'S JOB in capital murder cases was to find mitigating circumstances and convince the jury that a defendant's history ought to be reflected in his sentence. Cribbs believed there might have been a kernel of meanness in Bill King's heart before he went to prison, but that his experience there was what made it grow. He thought King might have been abused in prison—either beaten by a black gang or possibly raped by one—and that was what kindled the hatred in his heart. Cribbs, who had been interviewing prisoners all over East Texas for months in a search for clues, had been counting on uncovering some event in Bill King's short life that would somehow explain how he could chain a black man to a truck and drag him to his death. Unfortunately, Cribbs couldn't find any proof.

Cribbs saw less hatred in Bill King than bravado. Some people in Jasper who knew Berry and King said the pair did not fully understand what they were doing when they took a thirty-foot section of chain and bound Byrd's feet and began to pull him down the dirt road in the forest. In the most forgiving of scenarios, they panicked when they realized that they had severed James Byrd's head and arm from his body on a culvert, leaving the pieces a mile up the road like a semicolon at the end of a trail of blood, Cribbs said. That is why they left the body at the side of the road and rushed home without bothering to hide the clues that would lead authorities to their apartment and a pile of racist tracts they had stored there. "This wasn't supposed to end in a killing," Cribbs told reporters. "Things just got out of control."

Bill King, in the face of DNA evidence that placed him at the scene, continued to deny he had any role in the murder. "No family should have to go through what they are going through," he said, when asked about James Byrd. "From what I've read, it was a terrible way to die."

Like many talented criminal-defense attorneys, Cribbs excelled at shifting the focus of his trials from the behavior of his clients to the behavior of the investigators or the police or the other suspects in the case. "There weren't piles of evidence against him until he started conducting his own defense, giving reporters copies of his so-called Logical Reasoning, which said he was with Brewer all night," said Cribbs. Until King had done that, the D.A. couldn't affirmatively place him at the scene, Cribbs said. An eyewitness who had seen Byrd in a truck that looked like Berry's around 2:30 A.M. on the day of the murder said there were "two or three people" in the cab of the truck. There was a sandal footprint on the dirt tram road off Huff Creek Road where the beating had taken place. But all three suspects had the same type of sandals, and the investigators couldn't prove the print belonged to King or say conclusively how the drop of blood got on King's shoe.

With the other evidence they found—King's cigarette lighter, the cigarette butt with his DNA on it, fibers on Byrd that could be tied to King—Cribbs thought he could have planted at least a seed of doubt in a critical juror's mind. King's writings made that more difficult. With King claiming he was with Brewer all night long, he was implicated by association, Cribbs said. Prosecutors could place Brewer at the scene based on forensic evidence and because he injured his toe kicking and beating Byrd. Now they could place King there too.

Two weeks before the trial, King made matters worse. He kicked in the screen of his television and made a knife to attack the jail guards. No one was hurt, but King's frustration came out when he told his captors that with all he was accused of, he had nothing to lose by adding aggravated assault. King started speaking with his lawyer after that. Cribbs said it was too late. "I'd rather be Guy James Gray than me," he said a week before the trial. Unless a one-armed man suddenly appeared and confessed to the murder, he said, he would have a tough time getting a jury to believe that Bill King deserved to live.

Cribbs's determination to find some alternative explanation for the murder came not from any desire to save Bill King but from a deep-seated belief that the death penalty was wrong and that in Texas it had become too quick an answer for the shortcomings of society. "This is going to bother me a long time if Bill King is put to death. If I have to, I'm going to talk a country jury into having some mercy. This is a horrible crime, but I really believe there needs to be, in this case, some mercy."

*　　*　　*

ALMOST TWO MONTHS after King was arrested for murder, his son, Blayne William King, was born. Two months premature, Blayne clung to life in the intensive care unit at a hospital in nearby Newton County. His father's prospects for life appeared equally as fragile. Until jury selection for his trial began in January, King had only seen his son through the glass of the jail visitation room at Jasper County Jail. Blayne was six months old before he was touched by his father for the first time. During a break at the court-house, King was allowed to hold the baby.

As he climbed into the waiting police cruiser at the end of the day, King was asked about his son. "It was great," he beamed. It would be the last time he would ever hold his boy. There were no contact visits for inmates on death row.

"Hug. That's something Bill and I could always do," Ronald King said after he had watched Bill hold his grandson. "Don't ever forget to hug your boy. He's my baby boy." The elder King forever after kept a photo of Bill and Blayne in his breast pocket. He would show it to strangers with such frequency, it was not long before it had curled at the edges.

*   *   *

MEANWHILE, JASPER'S RECONCILIATION committee, which included Mayor Horn, Texas Charlie's owners, the Nicholsons, and Walter Diggles, among others, was trolling for symbols of its own. It found one in the city cemetery, where the fence separating the white and black sections of the graveyard had stood for more than 160 years. "The community is pulling itself back together," said Assistant City Manager David Douglas to the assembled press corps at a ceremony to tear down the fence in early February.

The city's task force had sent tickets to media organizations so they could publicize the dismantling of the fence. "This will never work; they'll never fall for it," Mike Lout told the committee members when they informed him of their plan to invite media and provide a positive story for them to run before the King trial began in earnest. "I was astounded when it did. And it was the perfect photo-op. There was this low-lying fog, and the cemetery looked like something out of Transylvania. It was in papers all over the country, newscasts, everything. The committee got exactly what it wanted."

Across the country the news reports were uniformly positive. "In one particularly noble gesture of good will, black and white residents tore down a fence that had separated black and white grave sites in a local cemetery, a relic of the days of legal segregation," Pulitzer Prize–winning syndicated columnist Clarence Page wrote. "Until now, even while mostly white Jasper elected a black mayor, few had seen the fence as something important enough to worry about. Now in the wake of the hate King displayed as plainly as the racist tattoos on his body, even the most benign forms of segregation have taken on new and ominous weight."

Black Jasperites just shrugged. The fence hadn't taken on any newfound significance since the murder. "The truth is the fence was not separating black graves from white; it was an old cattle fence," said Christine Carter. The whites were buried inside the fence where cattle couldn't get in, and the blacks were buried outside. This was a big deal for the white community. Frankly, we in the black community couldn't have cared less. Just goes to show how sophisticated these people got. They wanted to paint a picture of Jasper as harmonious, and they created a news event to show it was so. And the visiting reporters gobbled it up."

Mike Lout agreed. "Hook, line, and sinker."

CHAPTER TEN

BLOOD IN, BLOOD OUT

February 1999

WHEN THE JASPER County Courthouse was built in 1889, locals scoffed at the unnecessary extravagance of constructing it entirely of brick. County officials had wanted a modern, serious-looking building, so they added every accoutrement to show that Jasper wasn't so country as not to know how to build a proper courthouse. They perched a clock tower with four faces on the roof, as was the fashion for public buildings at the time. Directly behind the main building, they built a jail that residents quickly dubbed the "hanging jail" because a tower at its top housed the old gallows. The last hanging was in 1909. Most of the old jail was demolished in 1936, and a new one was erected in its place behind the courthouse a short time later. The bars from the old building were used in the new. More evidence, city leaders said, of Jasper's thriftiness.

As there was little else to showcase in Jasper, besides pines and bass fishing, Courthouse Square became a pet project. Various community groups took it upon themselves to improve it. They planted pecan trees in the 1960s. The Ladies' Guild raised money for a gazebo in the 1970s. The city, constantly primping and tinkering with the building, decided to paint it all yellow in the 1960s. The act, some locals muttered, made the original expense of brick construction largely beside the point.

Despite the cheerful yellow of the courthouse facade, it couldn't mask the fact that one was seeing the end of something in Jasper. The era when pump jacks dipped up and down in the distance seemed a long time ago, replaced by wind banging on the empty windows of the now-defunct Hancock Drug Store. Gone too was the unspoken understanding that the world was disposed to act in the best interests of Jasper's elite. Outsiders had decided that the James Byrd murder was about as raw a display of atavistic inhumanity as one could imagine, and in their judgment Jasper was something ineffably backward and sad. For Jasperites, the very way they measured time had changed: now events were dated from the murder.

Never had there been so much proof about how much Jasper had changed as came in the days before the King trial when cameras, reporters, and satellite trucks once again descended on Courthouse Square. And never had Jasperites been so united about their courthouse, their town, and the "terrible thing done to James" as when the cameras rolled, the pencils moved across pads, and the tape players recorded. The Jasperites huddled together, clicking their tongues and commenting on how fortunate they were to have a courthouse that belied the hick Texas town stories that the newcomers wanted to tell. How fortunate that Dan Rather anchored his evening newscast from the freshly refinished gazebo out front.

To reach Judge Joe Bob Golden's courtroom on the second floor, one had to pass by the countless cubbyholes of gray-faced county officials: little rooms with practical desks and metal file cabinets for Jasper's assessors, collectors, and adjusters. They sat long hours behind frosted glass doors, with names and titles painted in block black letters with gold trim, waiting to serve. The district attorney had the largest suite of rooms, all thin paneling and nondescript carpets, stashed below the stairs. The whole affair had that familiar government building smell of decaying record books and old damp cement. In a slow town like Jasper, what little foot traffic found its way into the courthouse was usually social in nature. Someone coming by to pick up someone else for lunch at the Belle-Jim. Students wandering in, sure they could find a county clerk or someone on Guy James Gray's staff who could be cajoled into buying a raffle ticket to raise money for the Jasper High School band.

The departure from the familiar, quiet routine made the melee on the first day of Bill King's trial that much more startling. As the impeachment trial of President Clinton moved toward what many felt was certain acquittal in the U.S. Senate, in Jasper knots of cameramen and reporters were rushing anyone who ventured onto the square in the days before the trial. The media frenzy sent members of the Belle-Jim breakfast troupe fleeing to the safety of their cars. The boom mikes floated inches from their faces, camera lenses zoomed in, hoping for an expression that would capture the essence of this Deep East Texas town. Weary Jasperites never got out of their trucks. Instead they just drove slowly around Austin and Milam Streets taking in a scene to which they had grown accustomed ever since the murder. Some made excuses at work, or called in sick, and then waited in the first-floor hallway of the courthouse in hopes of gaining admittance to the courtroom. This was, after all, the most dramatic case in Jasper in thirty years, when Joe Tonahill had successfully defended three local hunters for putting buckshot into a man who had killed their best hunting dog.

As the trial began on February 15, the crowd was an eclectic mix one seldom saw gathered in one place in Jasper. Flamboyantly suspendered white men in cowboy hats and heavy jewelry and big belt buckles stood shoulder to shoulder with black women in traditional African dress. Around them stood the anonymous members of the white and black communities, the ones who held their hands up in front of their faces when the cameras panned the crowd, and who had risen extra early to put on their best button-down shirts and cleanest trousers for the opening arguments. People too poor to own a car stood beside Jasperites who had to choose from three shiny vehicles in the garage. There were the black Jasperites who had arranged rides and carpools or had walked along Highway 96 before the sun had come up to see for themselves if Jasper would find vindication. And there were their white counterparts who had awakened late in their cool houses only minutes from the square. The racially mixed crowd arrived at the courthouse armed with differing suppositions that led, inevitably, to the same conclusion.

Whites were sure the facts would show the problem was with King alone. This killing didn't come from any homegrown local hatred, they told themselves. The crime was the work of a psychopath, an act inextricably linked to a bad throw of the genetic dice. At best it was a bad reaction to a prison system that had turned him into a murderer. Jasper wasn't responsible. The trial would show, after nearly a year of living under a cloud of suspicion, that white Jasper couldn't be held accountable for what had happened. A guilty verdict, a lethal injection, would cleanse the town of this terrible stigma with which it had been branded. The white spectators arrived hoping to see a jury prove they weren't racist by showing Jasperites were willing to kill someone who was.

Members of the black community weren't altogether sure what force had drawn them there. Some thought they just wanted a good look at Bill King, to recognize for themselves whatever it was that had caused him to kill James Byrd the way he had. They were searching for a way to satisfy their sense of meaningful design; certainly this couldn't have been a random killing. The trial was going to show that this was part of a larger plan to return Jasper to the time of "nigger words" and suspicious fires. And they wanted to make sure, for themselves, that the plan had been foiled.

The courtroom was too small to accommodate more than a small number of those who lined up for admittance. The best seats were reserved for the Byrd family, who sat together in two rows on the left-hand side of the room, close to the jury. They were represented by James Byrd's mother and father, Stella and James Sr.; his sisters Clara Taylor and Mary Verrett; two of his three children, Renee Mullins and Jaime Byrd; and his nephew Darrell Verrett. Shawn Berry's lawyer, Joseph "Lum" Hawthorn, sat in the front row on the other side of the room with a yellow legal pad on his lap.

The conversation in the hallway as the spectators filed in was about the technical legal details of a case that only weeks before few could have spoken about with such authority.

". . . capital murder will be harder to prove," one said.

"After what this boy has done, he doesn't have a prayer. He's going to get lethal injection for sure," said another.

"That King boy has as much as admitted he did it; the only question is whether they kill him for it," said a third. "If they don't, there will be trouble sure as I am standing here. Guy James is sitting on a tinderbox. Anything less than lethal injection and it's going to blow; mark my words."

"Someone told me that Stella Byrd told Reverend Lyons that if there wasn't lethal injection, Jasper was going to pay; she was going to talk to the press and blow the lid off this town," the first man said, opening his eyes wider. The two others shushed him as an invisible signal sent the crowd through the courtroom doors upstairs.

Joe Tonahill, from the comfort of his office across the street, had predicted the worst. "The D.A. is trying to pin capital murder charges on that King boy, and if they can't prove Byrd was kidnapped while in the process of the murder, they won't get capital murder and King won't get the death penalty," said Tonahill. "Guy James is smart, but he may have bitten off more than he can chew. If they don't get the death penalty for these three, there will be trouble."

Security at the 110-year-old courthouse was the tightest it had ever been. FBI technicians had installed surveillance cameras inside and outside the courtroom. Police officers stood at the ready around every corner. Visitors had to go through metal detectors for the first time ever. This was a lengthy process, as spectators set off the alarms with great regularity. Oversized belt buckles, boot spurs, fist-sized rings of keys were piled at the end of the conveyor.

In contrast to the high-tech surveillance, Judge Golden's courtroom was simple. It had twenty-foot ceilings, white walls, and lazy ceiling fans. On one side of the room the jury box held a dozen stark black leather swivel chairs. The jurors would be able to look to their left and see the judge's bench and, beside it, the witness's chair. Straight ahead of them was an enormous photographic map of the crime scene—the first exhibit from the prosecution—which Jasperites took in as they tried to find a seat.

The well of the courtroom held three long rectangular tables, two for the prosecution and one for Bill King, Sonny Cribbs, and

Cribbs's partner, attorney Brack Jones. The prosecution was led by Gray and Assistant District Attorney Pat Hardy, a burly Vietnam veteran who shaved his head and was known for carrying a knife in his boot. John Stevens, a federal attorney, sat next to them. Hardy and Stevens made unlikely seat mates; one was in a bolo tie and cowboy boots, and the other, in his blue suit and standard-issue haircut, looked as if he had flown in from Washington, D.C., not Austin.

Ronald King had hoped a late arrival to the courthouse would allow him to dodge the assembled press corps. It didn't. They surrounded his car like hyenas, shoving cameras in his face, shouting questions. It made it hard to breathe. Some of the sheriff's deputies moved the mob away from the old man and helped him into a wheelchair. They wedged his oxygen canister between the armrest and his leg and wheeled him over to the elevator. King looked as if he had aged twenty years in just nine months. Sonny Cribbs was counting on some sympathy for the elder King from the jury; maybe a devastated father would help save the life of a son.

Inside the courthouse, a large contingent of reporters had already stationed themselves in the hallway, awaiting the younger King's arrival. More than twenty members of the international press corps had arrived to record the proceedings. They were badged and X-rayed and sent to sit two rows behind the Byrd family, close enough to see their reaction but too far away to harass them. The rest of the seats went to Jasperites. The fidgeting of bodies and the murmur of voices as spectators found their seats gave the proceedings an almost festive air.

For many of the reporters, the local faces in the courtroom were now familiar. Arriving days before the trial began, the newspeople had filled the hours by interviewing any Jasperite they could find. The questions betrayed the headlines to come. "Do you think of yourself as prejudiced?" or "Do you have any black friends?" Or, if the subject was black, "Do you have many white friends?" They interviewed Cedric Green and had him photographed next to where he had found James Byrd's body months before. ("They never paid me for that," Green said later. "Shouldn't I be getting royalties or something? That's what my friends say; I should have gotten some money.") They talked to Mayor Horn, who assured them that there was no racism in Jasper. They called on Billy Rowles, who had been interviewed so many times he knew the answers to questions even before they were asked. And they sat down with Guy James Gray, who narrowed his eyes when he talked and worried aloud that Bill King's boyish good looks could charm one juror enough to save his life.

*　　*　　*

THE SOLEMNITY OF what lay ahead became clear to Bill King only after he stepped out of the jail van and saw the crush of people running toward him. There were newspeople of every variation: reporters for wire services and daily newspapers; photographers and documentary filmmakers; representatives from cable television, network television, local television, radiomen, and Jasper's own Mike Lout in his trademark baseball cap.

There might have been fifty reporters altogether, a huge press throng for a trial in this small town. Jasper citizens crowded against the roped-off area where King would be led into the courthouse. The reporters, while they were awaiting King's arrival, had already logged the local reaction. They roved through the crowd asking people what, in their opinion, should be done to Bill King for committing such a crime. Never mind that King had yet to be tried, much less found guilty. That had become a foregone conclusion.

One woman from the Huff Creek community was blunt: "I think they should just turn Bill King loose in Jasper. He wouldn't get two blocks before someone would rip him limb from limb, and then we'd drag his body for three miles behind a truck. Lethal injection, hell, that's too good for him."

Bill King emerged from the police truck dressed like a college student. He wore an ordinary plaid button-down shirt specifically chosen to make him look too average to be a killer. Long sleeves covered his tattoos. ("He was going to have those tattoos covered even if I had to paint shirt sleeves on him," said Cribbs.) Journalists trained their mikes and cameras and tape recorders on King, shooting sidelong glances at the crowd, from whom they anticipated shouted abuse. But when the group caught sight of King, it fell silent, as if for a moment everyone remembered that Bill King was a man who just months before could have been standing behind them to buy a pack of cigarettes at Wal-Mart.

A visiting journalist broke the silence: "How did it feel to drag a black man, Bill? How did it feel?"

Billy Rowles and a deputy hustled King up a set of side stairs into the courthouse. The last thing the cameras caught was the metal side door he slipped through slamming shut.

Cribbs, already seated inside, had come to the conclusion weeks before that he could do little more for Bill King than to be present at his departure. The sheer volume of evidence, which was bagged in brown paper sacks and stacked around the perimeter of the room, was a visual reminder of just how difficult this case would be to win.

Once seated at the defense table, King affected a courtroom attitude that was both uninterested and disinterested; he clamped one hand over his mouth and hardly moved it from that position for the next week.

*   *   *

TYPICALLY, THE BELLE-JIM'S two dining rooms were empty by 10 A.M., a lull that gave Pat Stiles the opportunity to smoke a cigarette, read a chapter in the latest paperback she had picked up at the used bookstore, and prepare cheddar-pimento sandwiches for the lunch rush. Since the jury selection had started weeks before, though, she and David never had the chance to catch their breath. They were overrun with locals and out-of-towners who sipped, whispered, and fanned as they scooted their chairs around to face the windows that opened out onto the courthouse. They wanted to ensure that if something happened they wouldn't miss it. Around Courthouse Square, the eagle-eyed Jasperites among them noticed something else they had never seen before: the town had installed meters at every parking spot. Locals smirked. All those newcomers to Jasper would be paying into the town's coffers, even if it was just twenty-five cents at a time.

"Explain something to me," said a police officer guarding the back door of the courthouse. "Why are all these people making such a fuss about James Byrd? Don't they know what kind of man he was? He was the town drunk, and everyone is getting all bowed up. Here's the question I have: how come no one is making this kind of fuss about Jerry McQueen? A nigger beat him to death with a pipe, and it is as if it never happened."

*   *   *

GUY JAMES GRAY wanted to present his entire case in two days. "I want to go to the jury for guilt or innocence by Friday," Gray told a group of reporters before the trial began. "The proof is going to be that this was more than Saturday night drunks in a fight. I expect the community and the jury to be astonished as the evidence unfolds."

Gray began his opening statement with a narrative. The story was a familiar one to anyone who had ever lived in East Texas or had found themselves looking for something to do on a Saturday night. Bill King, Shawn Berry, and Russell Brewer were riding along back roads in Berry's truck with a cooler of beer, killing time. There had been a party up at Sam Rayburn Reservoir earlier in the day and a casual invitation by some girls they barely knew to come to another party that night. Bad directions were exchanged, phone numbers misplaced, and before they knew it King, Berry, and Brewer had given up on finding the girls or the party. Instead, quite by accident, they turned onto Martin Luther King Boulevard in Berry's gray sidestep truck and decided to pick up a hitchhiker named James Byrd Jr.

The trio and Byrd stopped at a convenience store just outside of town to make a phone call and that's when, Gray surmised, King, Berry, and Brewer decided to take Byrd into the woods and beat him up. "Shawn Berry said that King and Brewer wanted to scare the hell out of James Byrd. They wanted to kick his ass," Gray said. So, with Byrd in the back of the truck, they drove up to Huff Creek Road, turned up one of the logging paths, and stopped the car. That's when the three men pulled Byrd out of the truck, and for no other reason than that he was black and it was easy, they began to beat him up. Even if James Byrd hadn't been drunk, it wouldn't have been a fair fight. King stomped him, and Brewer began kicking him on the head. Brewer kicked Byrd so hard that he broke a toe. At one point, as Byrd lay on the ground, Brewer got a can of black spray paint out of the back of the truck and spray-painted Byrd's face. Byrd didn't resist.

It could have been that passivity that emboldened them to do more. King and Brewer took a thirty-foot logging chain out of the back of the truck and fastened it around Byrd's ankles. Drinking bottles of Budweiser and smoking cigarettes, they tried to find a way to secure the heavy chain around Byrd's feet. They pulled down Byrd's pants to anchor the metal and get it to hold. Then they began to drag him through the soft dirt of the tram road. Byrd came loose, and, according to Berry's statement, King put the truck in reverse and actually backed up over him and then had to pull forward. King reattached the black man.

"The three of them were having a good ole time," Gray said. "And then they turned onto the pavement of Huff Creek Road."

Brewer looked back and was laughing, saying, "Look, he's rolling" or "He's bouncing around all over the place," according to Berry's statement. Then the truck careened around a bend, the body swung off the road and struck a culvert. Byrd was decapitated. The trio kept on driving. They drove another mile before King stopped the truck, got out, and untied the body. Then the three of them drove away.

Gray used a wooden stick to point out blown-up photographs on a giant aerial map of the crime scene before him. There were photos of cigarette butts, beer bottles, a socket wrench with Berry's name engraved on the side. Then Gray handed the jury a book of more than a dozen color photographs of Byrd's corpse.

One woman's cheeks reddened as if she had been slapped, and a few of the jurors, after taking the first distressing glance, had no heart for the task. After more than eight months of hearing about the Byrd murder, they were now forced to see exactly what had happened on Huff Creek Road in all its grisly detail. They flipped through pages that showed what dragging a man three miles along rough road actually did to his body. They saw elbows and heels ground to the bone. The raw flesh on a cheek. It made them angry. It was supposed to.

"He was using his elbows and his body in every manner that he could to keep his head and shoulders away from the pavement," Gray said. "James Byrd was kidnapped; James Byrd did not want to be there."

Before that day, Byrd's family had taken solace in the belief that Byrd had passed out before the dragging began. As Gray moved from one visual aid to the next to outline the events of that night, the jury and spectators watched in rapt attention. Until that moment, Jasperites in the gallery were still torn about what had actually happened. But now they found themselves craning for a better view as Gray walked them through the very thing they, until now, hadn't wanted to know.

Next Gray focused on the defendant. He described what the jurors couldn't see under King's long sleeves and college-student clothing: a body covered in white supremacist tattoos, including one depicting the hanging of a black man. King had attacked Byrd because he was black, Gray said. A search of King's apartment had yielded racist tracts, including a book on the Ku Klux Klan and bylaws for a hate group King had intended to start in Jasper. DNA experts would testify that Byrd's blood was found on King's and Brewer's sandals and shoes.

"Bill King had laid out his intention to form a hate group in Jasper, Texas," Gray said as he wound up his fifteen-minute opening statement. "And he needed to do something dramatic to attract media attention in order to gain, in their warped world, respect for this newly formed gang."

When Gray was finished, the spectators in the courtroom were holding their breath. Blacks listened as Gray confirmed all their worst fears. Whites were incredulous. Certainly, they thought to themselves, this conspiracy theory was all for effect. Byrd's death was the work of three drunk boys who got out of control. Jasper didn't countenance hate groups.

They had barely time enough to digest those thoughts when Cribbs cleared his throat and drew himself to full height above the defense table. They waited for the defense attorney to refute Gray's terrible tale. A hate group in Jasper? It couldn't happen here.

"We have no opening statement at this time, Your Honor."

Cribbs sat down. A fidget of feet and the low hum of whispers filled the courtroom.

"What was I going to say?" Cribbs said later. "You use an opening statement to tell the jury what you are going to prove, and what was I going to prove?"

King, meanwhile, slumped in his seat. He seemed bored and indifferent, more like a student struggling to stay awake in math class than a man fighting for his life. The state summoned its first witness.

"Common sense dictates a lot of what we observe as police officers," investigator Curtis Frame began from the stand. He was wearing a brown sheriff's uniform, having transferred to Rowles's office only a month before. Harlon Alexander had retired from the police department, and Frame had run for the top job in the department. He lost to another man, Stanley Christopher. There was bad blood between the two as a result, so Frame had gone to the sheriff for a job. Rowles was happy to have him. The prosecution didn't bother to explain the job change. Frame was a key witness. Assistant District Attorney Pat Hardy was asking the questions. Hardy was wearing his trademark bolo tie and a suit jacket that was so tight across the shoulders he looked ready to burst out of it.

"Why all these paper bags and not plastic?" he asked Frame, warming to his subject. "In the movies and on television they always use plastic."

"Well," said Frame, pushing his glasses back on his face and speaking to the jury. "I like the paper sack. They allow items to dry and they are easier to write on. Plastic can develop condensation and that can ruin evidence."

"So what you're saying is that we might be country, but we're a thinking town," said Hardy in an exaggerated drawl, awaiting a laugh. The courtroom obliged and erupted into church-quiet giggles.

*   *   *

"BEFORE WE, WHO assume the role of Confederate Knights, can hope to reach our full potential, it is important to understand exactly who we are . . . what we hope to accomplish," King wrote in a recruitment letter in his boyish cursive. King and his followers were "a race of individuals who have found themselves existing on humanity's evolutionary plateau. Born with the genetic capacity for great power, leadership and knowledge; we have chosen the added burden of responsibility to defend those who have not the power nor the resources to protect themselves."

And the race that needed protecting, according to King, was the white race. "At times this will mean coming to the aid of our fellow kindred, providing a defense against those races who feel their powers allow them to dominate others. Just as often, we will be called on to safeguard our Aryan race against those individuals and organizations who fear and hate them simply because we are different. All to [sic] often, we will defend Aryans against their own kind—as the unfortunate quest for supremacy continues." That defense, presumably, included murdering non-Aryans.

King laid out rules and codes of conduct for his rebel soldiers. For example: "The possession of any contraband or consumption of any illegal drugs and/or alcohol at organizational functions is strictly prohibited." Another rule told rebel soldiers to "love, protect, reproduce and advance your folk." "No leader will ever ask you to break the law," King wrote. "It has been my fervent wish, long before the formation of the Texas Rebel Soldiers, that hostilities be avoided at all cost, be it race vs. race or kind vs. kind. In recent years, however, I have become painfully aware that a war is being waged across the planet earth—and that we [the Aryan race] are the first, quite possibly the final, line of defense."

Gray read several passages aloud. "We'd like to admit this into evidence, Your Honor."

Judge Golden nodded. The courtroom shifted uncomfortably. Cribbs didn't object.

*   *   *

THE NUMBER OF spectators in the courtroom fell off by the fourth day of the trial. They had heard more than they ever wanted to know about how the officers handled the evidence, gang life in prison, and racist tattoos. Guy James Gray sensed the jury was getting bored, too.

"The state calls Norm Townsend," Hardy said from his chair in the well of the courtroom. Townsend was a special agent with the FBI. He had been in and out of Jasper since the murder to help with the investigation. On June 8, the day after the murder, he had met with Billy Rowles in Houston, and he was one of a handful of officers who drove out to Tommy Faulk's house in the woods with Shawn Berry in tow.

Tommy Faulk was a twenty-five-year-old beekeeper who had the look of one of those bespectacled children who was always bullied on the playground. He had known Bill King since grade school and saw him as a bit of a "blowhard." King's toughness, Faulk had come to know, existed solely in situations where he unarguably had the upper hand. The last time Faulk had seen King was on June 7, the day of the murder. King and Brewer let themselves in through the back door of Faulk's trailer around 6 P.M. that night and were talking to Faulk about nothing in particular when the phone rang. Faulk picked up the call. When he hung up, King and Brewer were gone. The next day, law enforcement officers, including Townsend, arrived and disappeared into the forest at Shawn Berry's direction. Berry went directly to a ditch between the trees, kicked up a piece of plywood, and revealed the logging chain that lay beneath, Townsend said.

Pat Hardy and Guy James Gray got up and together, with great fanfare, lifted a cardboard box onto the prosecution table. Everyone in the courtroom could hear the sound of metal clicking on metal. Hardy reached into the box and pulled out one end of the chain and raised it above his head. Townsend stepped down from the witness stand and helped feed it out of the box as Hardy walked the end across the front of the courtroom. The spectators gasped. The chain was big and heavy. The kind loggers tied to the hitches on their trucks to pull up stumps.

"Is this the chain you found?" Hardy asked, knowing the answer. Townsend nodded.

"That's all for this witness, Your Honor."

King showed no emotion. He sat with his elbow on the table, his chin in his hand.

"I read a book years ago that said there were two ways to put a thought into a juror's head," Gray said after the trial. "Repetition and drama. If you mention an elephant, you can't remove the thought of that elephant through some sort of negative message. The more you say, 'Don't remember the elephant,' the more they will remember the elephant. You get a jury to focus on something else with positive instruction, something I call a giraffe. You always have to save several pieces of evidence as giraffes. The chain was a giraffe."

Matthew Hoover was a giraffe too. Hoover, a pockmarked, thin twenty-something with greasy hair, had met King in 1996 in prison. Hoover had been serving time for burglary and was a member of the Aryan Brotherhood, he told the jury. King, on the other hand, was a member of the Confederate Knights of America.

"We talked about how you would start a race war," Hoover said as Gray questioned him. One idea "was to blow up the projects, which would incite a riot. You know, kind of like Rodney King."

"Would dragging a black man behind a pickup be considered a way to start a race war?" said Gray from the table.

"I guess, if that's what you want to accomplish," Hoover said. "But I don't particularly want a war started in my own hometown."

"What does 'Blood in, Blood out' mean?" Gray asked.

Some gangs require members to kill someone while in prison, Hoover said, but when prisons started isolating known gang members, the practice changed. Instead of killing fellow inmates, members began waiting until they were released and then killed someone on the outside.

Gray handed Hoover a copy of his prison scrapbook, a kind of yearbook for inmates. He asked Hoover to read an entry written by Bill King.

"And don't forget, a huge Wood gathering, B.B.Q., and bashing on July 4, 1998," King wrote.

"What's a bashing?" Gray asked.

"Beating on someone or killing someone," Hoover answered.

"A black person?"

"Yes, beating or killing a black person."

*   *   *

THERE WERE FISTFIGHTS at Jasper Middle School that winter. It all started during jury selection for the King trial and Jasper residents began wondering aloud what would happen if King weren't convicted. Fuses had grown so short in town, it didn't take much to make tempers flare. With that in mind, school administrators were particularly torn about Josh Letney, a fourteen-year-old middle school student who wore a Confederate flag on his belt buckle. Amid all this talk of hate crimes and gangs and Klan, Letney became the center of attention when school administrators suspended him in late January for "being an ongoing disruption."

The Letney boy came from a difficult family. His father was an avowed supremacist. He flew the Confederate flag on a twenty-foot flagpole in the middle of his yard and, neighbors complained, had a habit of shooting his rifles over the roofs of the subdivision at odd hours of the night. When administrators suspended Letney, his father called on a force he was sure would get the school's attention: the Ku Klux Klan.

Grand Wizard Darrell Flinn arrived in Jasper in the midst of the King trial threatening to hold a Klan demonstration at Jasper Middle School if officials didn't allow Letney to return to class with the flag on his buckle. The principal wouldn't relent. Letney allegedly drew a Confederate flag in the sand at school and made racist remarks, according to school records. He was told four days in a row to keep the Confederate buckle at home "because of what was going on in our community," but he refused. He would, the principal said, remain suspended until the belt buckle was left at home. Flinn thought better of a Klan demonstration at a school full of children, and the matter disappeared. A week later, Letney showed up at school without the buckle.

*   *   *

"I CAN'T WAIT until this is all over," said Sheriff Rowles three days into the trial. "I think we've been through enough and we need a rest."

Rowles, in particular, could have used a break.

"You could tell something was wrong," said his wife, Jamie. "He was just really emotional. I told the children to be careful because he was under so much strain. He'd come home and eat his dinner and just talk about all the preparations they were making, how worried everyone was that there would be trouble. If anything at all went wrong, Billy felt he'd be to blame. It was a lot of pressure to put on himself."

Rowles tried to keep to his regular routine. He was at work by 8 A.M. and tried to get home to have dinner with his high school–aged children every night. The menu was always the same: a rib-eye steak and a potato.

"Billy is one of those people who needs to talk when he's upset; he doesn't just close up," Jamie Rowles said. "So at dinner we'd sit down, and I'd ask him innocent questions and he would just start talking. That was his only release."

Rowles remembers it as a tough time. "I don't cry often, but you know I just felt like I was on the verge of bawling that whole time. I guess I was just real stressed out. But the whole thing upset me so much. I felt like a sissy. This wasn't anything that had ever happened to me before. Sometimes things affect you more than you think they will."

*   *   *

FOUR DAYS AFTER they began, prosecutors rested their case with a dramatic presentation aimed at showing the horror of James

Byrd's death. They began with an hour of testimony from the pathologist who had performed the autopsy on Byrd and ended with an eleven-minute videotape that followed the three-mile streak of dried blood that had been left by Byrd's body on the blacktop of Huff Creek Road. The video began at the end of the half-mile dirt logging road and ended at the gates of the cemetery.

Half of Byrd's thirteen family members left the courtroom during the pathologist's testimony. Most of Byrd's relations appeared stunned as jurors looked at the fourteen photographs of Byrd's head and body. Renee Mullins, his daughter, wept and went outside to throw up during a break. Jurors watched the video grim-faced, and one kept looking over at Bill King.

Jefferson County pathologist Tommy Brown described Byrd's suffering in great detail. He said Byrd's wounds showed how he twisted and turned his body, grinding his elbows, heels, and but-tocks to the bone, as he tried to hold himself off the pavement.

"It's my opinion, while being dragged, Mr. Byrd was conscious and was attempting to relieve the pain and injuries he was receiv-ing," Brown told jurors.

"I think we all know how brush burn abrasions, like if you fall and slide on a surface with your hands, are very painful, and this would have been very painful to him. He would probably swap one portion of his body for the other, trying to get relief as he was being dragged."

The fact that Byrd was still alive while he was being dragged was key to Gray's case, because in order to get a death sentence the prosecution needed to prove that Byrd was kidnapped and was held against his will before being murdered.

All of Byrd's ribs were broken on his right side, as well as eight on his left. His ankles were cut to the bone by what appeared to be a metal chain, Gray said. The brown swath of blood showed that Byrd's body had been slammed repeatedly from one side of the road to the other. After about a mile he was slung into the culvert that tore his head and right arm from his naked torso.

"He was alive until he hit the culvert," Brown said. "He would have been very tired, very worn out trying to do what he could to keep the pain from being so severe."

CHAPTER ELEVEN

"MY LITTLE TOWN STOOD UP"

EVERY NIGHT AFTER court, defense attorneys Cribbs and Jones retired to a rented trailer house nineteen miles outside of Jasper where they thought the media wouldn't find them. The two middle-aged men had known each other since their years together at Baylor University Law School, and they had learned to work around each other's eccentricities. Cribbs would be up until 4 or 5 A.M. preparing for the next day's trial proceedings, and Jones would fall asleep in the back of the trailer sometime around midnight. They ate their meals together quietly.

Between King's jailhouse notes to Brewer and the DNA evidence Gray and the FBI had amassed, Cribbs was convinced King was guilty. More important, he was unsure he could convince any jury otherwise. In the months before the trial Cribbs and Jones had called every high-profile expert in the nation who might have been of help. "I ran out of things to do," said Cribbs. He called the psychiatrist who had worked with Patty Hearst, the lawyers who had handled Timothy McVeigh's defense, and even Barry Scheck from the O. J. Simpson defense team. "They had a lot of ideas, but none of them were any better than what we had come up with," said Cribbs. "Sometimes the facts are just so bad that there ain't a thing you can do."

Cribbs and his experts had to find a way to humanize Bill King, to uncover some explanation for why he had gone from small-time scofflaw to a murdering racist. Cribbs had to find a way to convince jurors that under Bill King's surface bluster and cruelty there was something ineffably sad, something that would somehow mitigate the dragging of a black man three miles down a country road. While Cribbs was sure he couldn't prove that King was innocent, he thought he might be able to move at least one juror's heart by putting the Texas prison system on trial and blaming it for the hardness of young King's heart.

Cribbs had some basic facts working in his favor. In 1998 the Texas prison system was the only one in the nation still under federal oversight, because of a rash of rapes, murders, and injuries. As Cribbs pulled together the threads of his argument in his Beaumont offices and later in the trailer outside of town, he began to focus on incarceration. The best punishment humankind had been able to devise had itself became a social problem, and one of its unintended results was the growth of a brutal prison culture, a Lord of the Flies existence in which prisoner was pitted against prisoner for simple survival. Cribbs had come to the conclusion that if King's old prison buddy Brewer had not arrived in Jasper that weekend, the James Byrd murder would never have happened.

Brewer's abusiveness seemed to enable King's; they became, when together, a twin star of unspeakable meanness and cruelty that neither was when alone. While that was not likely to win King an acquittal, Cribbs thought it might be just enough to save his life.

Bill's birth mother, a Pentecostal in Louisiana, refused to testify. "She was real religious," Ronald King said later. "I understand her church counselor advised against it. And that was that."

The two defense attorneys hit similar roadblocks when trying to find anyone to take the stand in King's defense. The local people did not want to be involved. Six witnesses from the penitentiary at first agreed to testify but later reneged for fear of retaliation. "What do you think it would be like for a black inmate who testifies for this guy? What do you think is going to happen to anybody who testifies for him?" Cribbs said.

William "Big Mo" Mosley, the white man who had put all those tattoos on King while in prison, was the first witness for the defense. Mosley was still serving a sentence at Huntsville prison when Cribbs arranged to have him driven to Jasper for the trial, secretly, because he was in danger of retaliation from other inmates. Fear of such a backlash was the reason that Cribbs made sure Mosley was not publicly identified before he took the stand. Mosley's entrance into the courtroom was dramatic. Still in his orange prison garb, he was forced to take halting steps as he crossed the room to avoid tripping over leg-irons that clanked as he walked. He winked at Bill King, and King smiled wanly in return. Of all the prisoners Cribbs tried to persuade to testify for King, Mosley was the only one who actually came through.

As Mosley passed before the spectators, though, the reaction from the assembly was almost Darwinian. Those in the front of the room instinctively drew back. At the back of the room, the group that sat at a safe distance from the inmate craned for a better look.

When Mosley took the stand, the deputies removed his handcuffs and stepped only an arm's length away, as if Mosley were liable to make a break for it at any moment. The spectators in the front seemed unable to relax, ready to spring out of Mosley's path should he overpower the deputies and leap into the crowd. Getting the better of the deputies was a distinct possibility. Mosley was an enormous man with paw-like hands.

Mosley was, in a very real way, an expert witness, though not of the variety the prosecution had presented. Mosley, serving ten- and fifteen-year terms for burglary and sexual assault, was the personification of everything that was wrong and frightening about the Texas prison system. If he and King had been seated side by side, the two men would not have looked more different: Mosley looked lethal; King, almost collegiate. It was a distinction Cribbs hoped would not be lost on the jury.

Once seated, Mosley was tough and matter-of-fact. In prison, he said, a white inmate had three choices: he could stand up for himself, get raped, or buy off his tormentors with "Mama's money." A white boy the size of King, he added, would not stand a chance. For whatever reason, however, Mosley liked King and showed his friendship by providing King with "skin art." Most of the designs, he said, were found in tattoo magazines and didn't mean much beyond making anyone who sported them look tough.

"In prison, there ain't too many people going to ask for butterflies and roses. That sounds kinda gay, don't it?" His response was supposed to bolster the defense's contention that King's many tattoos were not meant to be great inky galleries of racism, but rather were intended to make the baby-faced King appear more intimidating and therefore less vulnerable to rapes or beatings in the unit. "The double *S* means you're a 'wood,' you stand up for what's yours," Mosley said, interpreting the drawings like a professor deconstructing literature. "The ram's head, well that's not Satanic, it just looks cool. That's all. It's not a goat's head. Bill King was just an ink freak; that's the term we'd use. He thought all these tattoos looked cool."

While Mosley was obviously seeking to help a friend who was on trial, he wasn't making an ideal impression on the jury, who, like the spectators before them, were unconsciously drawing back from him. Mosley's arms were covered with blue tattoos, and his speech patterns were rapid and violent. He seemed on the verge of detonation. By contrast, he said King was kind of a laid-back guy who found it pretty easy to make friends in prison. Brewer was "kind of a flaky individual, if you ask me," he said.

"Was Bill King a racist?" Cribbs asked, looking up from the yellow legal pad on his table.

Mosley nodded. "Prison has a tendency to do that to white boys."

"Is he proud of his race?" Cribbs continued.

Mosley eyed him suspiciously. "Shouldn't we all be?"

*   *   *

THE SECOND WITNESS for the defense was Dennis Michael Symmack. A contractor with long shapeless hair and a drooping mustache, Symmack had hired King to work construction for several months after he was released from prison. Symmack seemed to have taken a genuine liking to King and appeared mildly surprised to be testifying against one of his employees in a murder trial. Symmack said he had a feeling King was racist, or at least was a white supremacist, but he didn't worry about it much because the young man kept his opinions to himself. He kept his tattooed arms covered when working the job, Symmack said, "and I kind of felt he did that out of respect for me. You know, it would be hot as blazes out there sometimes, and he'd keep his sleeves rolled down to cover up his tattoos."

His tattoos were bound to offend, since Symmack's crew was working in neighborhoods where residents were mostly black and mostly indigent. King didn't have a car, so Symmack picked him up and drove him to the job sites and the two talked. "He didn't seem to mind talking about his time in prison, so we talked about that," he said. "He was proud of his tattoos, so he talked about those too. Symmack said King told him that he was scared when he first got to prison and that "he shaved his head, and when he got tattoos, it was for self-protection."

King's boss also heard a great deal about Aryan history, he said. "I can tell you that he was very educated, very educated about Aryans and the Klan. He knew a lot about it," said Symmack. "I didn't even know these people existed."

Eventually the two parted company when King and Symmack disagreed over how best to do some roofing work. Symmack fired him on the spot, and King, who didn't have a ride home, simply waited for Symmack by his truck until quitting time. "There were no hard feelings; he was really polite about it all, really," said Symmack.

There was a pause as the courtroom audience awaited some surprise witness, some person who would come forward and dispel all their worst fears about Bill King and white supremacists in their midst. Sonny Cribbs stood up.

"The defense rests, Your Honor," he said. His entire case had taken less than an hour.

*　　*　　*

PROSECUTORS WRAPPED UP their case by asking jurors to be mindful of two key facts: James Byrd was alive when his ankles were chained to Shawn Berry's pickup, and he had been kidnapped before he was dragged to death. He didn't want to be there, they said. In closing arguments, prosecutor Pat Hardy compared King to Adolf Hitler and urged the jury to ignore the defense's contention that King's tattoos could be anything other than racist.

"Aryan Pride," he said, referring to the large tattoo on King's side. "Ladies and gentlemen, that's Adolf Hitler. These symbols have always had a meaning."

Hardy ended his argument by showing the jury a drawing found in King's apartment: three hooded figures riding horses were superimposed on the pointed star of a baphomet. "This shows exactly what was in the mind of John William King and his cohorts that night. This picture amounts to three robed riders coming straight out of hell, and that's exactly what they were that night. Instead of a rope, they used a chain, and instead of horses, they used a pickup truck," said Hardy. "After they dragged this poor man and tore his body to pieces, they dropped him right in front of a church and cemetery to show their defiance of God, to show their defiance of Christianity and everything that most people in this county stood for."

"What makes a person hate so bad to do something like this to a person they don't even know?" said Hardy. "Well, we've shown you why: the writings of Mr. King, the defendant, told a story. He hated blacks."

In one of his jail messages to Brewer, King bragged about the crime, saying that regardless of the outcome, they had "made history." He signed that note, "Much Aryan Love, Respect and Honor . . . Sieg Heil."

"Honor?" Hardy said. "These were strong men in their twenties, and it took three of them to bring down a forty-nine-year-old, half-intoxicated, disabled man. Where is the honor in that? You need to find this defendant guilty."

Guy James Gray rose from the table. He looked tired, and his shoulders stooped as he walked to the jury box. Bill King had been planning this murder for more than a year, he began. Bill King wanted to attract recruits to his chapter of the Confederate Knights of America in Jasper. The Byrd murder was an initiation rite, and Shawn Berry was going to be the Texas Rebel Soldiers' first recruit. King had only a drop of blood on his sandal because Berry, whose shirt, jeans, and boot were splattered with Byrd's blood, was undergoing an initiation that King was supervising. King's genetic blueprint was on a cigarette butt found in the woods near the crime scene alongside some other DNA that was consistent with Byrd's. (Gray didn't mention that it was a clue the size of a molecule.) Why? asked Gray. Because Bill King was sharing a last cigarette with the man he was about to condemn. A last smoke. King as much as admitted he killed Byrd in letters to Brewer, Gray reminded the jury, and finally, he asked them to think about what a Beaumont police detective found scratched into the paint in King's cell at the Jasper County Jail: "Shawn Berry is a snitch-ass traitor."

*   *   *

IN HIS CLOSING, Brack Jones moved from the defense table to sit on the witness stand, as if he were testifying instead of pleading his client's case. He focused on the kidnapping charge, saying that chaining Byrd's ankles to the pickup was the method of death, not a kidnapping. The jurors needed to believe that King killed Byrd while committing a felony in order to find him guilty of a capital murder charge, he said. "It was a terrible, terrible, brutal, horrendous and painful death," said Jones. "The question is, was Mr. Byrd kidnapped? No. The chain was the murder weapon."

When Jones was finished, Cribbs looked at the jury and summed up the case from the defense table. He reminded the panel that King's white supremacist beliefs didn't prove he was guilty. "You have a right to be racist," he said. "You have a right to be a Satanist. Right or wrong, that is his right." The physical evidence in the case didn't unequivocally place his client at the scene. The cigarette and the lighter could have fallen from the truck without King having been there. The drop of blood on King's sandal could have come from Berry or Brewer's clothing because they all shared an apartment. And the idea that King would share a last cigarette with Byrd was preposterous, Cribbs said. "If the man is such a severe racist, he's not going to share a cigarette with a black man," he said. More likely, he said, King smoked the cigarette earlier in the day and put it in the truck's ashtray and Byrd later found it.

Cribbs paused. He shifted uncomfortably while looking at the yellow pad before him. "Having a hanging black man on your arm doesn't mean you go out and kill a black man," Cribbs began. "He was a normal kid from Jasper and this boy had something happen to him in the penitentiary and he became a racist. He became a hater. The bad part about it, that's his right. That doesn't make him a killer."

The jury deliberated for just two and a half hours. Fifteen minutes before announcing their verdict they asked to see just one piece of evidence: King's "kite" to Brewer. At the bottom he signed his jailhouse nickname of Possum, with each *s* drawn as Nazi storm trooper symbols. Beneath it, he had drawn a symbol of three *K*'s joined to form a triangle, symbolizing the Ku Klux Klan. And beneath that, two words: "Sieg Heil" (Hail Victory).

King looked directly at the jury, eleven whites and one African-American, as they filed in and took their seats, avoiding his gaze. One of the jurors looked like she had been crying. A dozen law enforcement officers lined the walls. The one black juror, a twenty-four-year-old prison guard who had attended middle school with King, handed a small note to the bailiff. "The jury finds John William King guilty of capital murder," Judge Golden read without emotion. There was spontaneous applause in the courtroom, and Golden rapped his gavel for silence. Billy Rowles, standing by the judge with knees locked, blew the Byrd family a kiss.

"The sentencing phase will begin tomorrow morning," Judge Golden said, bringing down his gavel again.

Bill King showed no emotion. His father, Ronald, sitting only three feet away from him, began weeping openly. His tears began to soak the front of his shirt as reporters rushed outside to cover the prosecution's press conference.

"We hate that it happened here," Guy James Gray said from the steps of the gazebo. "But my little town stood up."

*   *   *

THE NEXT DAY, February 24, Ronald King was wheeled into the front of the courtroom and turned to face the jury. His face was ashen, and his gray hair was plastered down on his head. Tubes ran from an oxygen tank on his lap into his nose. He wheezed just sitting still. The younger King had asked to leave, and deputies led him out of the courtroom to an anteroom where he could watch his father on closed-circuit televison.

The penalty phase of the trial required the jury to decide three things, Golden had explained: Did Bill King intend for Byrd to die?

Will King pose a future threat of violence? Are there any mitigating circumstances that should keep him from being given the death penalty?

The jury looked uncomfortable as Ronald King started to beg for his son's life.

"I love him," the older man rasped. "You don't love everything they do. We've invested a lot of love in that boy, and I'd hate to think we're going to lose him."

Cribbs asked Ronald King if he wanted the jury to sentence his son to life in prison. "Anything is better than losing him," the father said haltingly.

Jurors began to tear up.

King said his son had started to get into trouble when his mother died of cancer. Her death was quick and unexpected; it took only three months from diagnosis to death. King was sixteen at the time. His son had never said anything racist before going to prison in 1995. "I would hate to think we're going to lose him," he said.

Cribbs then called Walter Quijano, a former Texas prison system psychologist. There would be little likelihood that King would be violent in the future if he was kept in prison until he was at least sixty-four, his first opportunity for parole, he said. Quijano noted that King had a history of burglary, not violence. "A burglar need not become a murderer," he said.

"But one became one in this case?" federal prosecutor John Stevens asked from his seat next to Assistant District Attorney Paul Hardy.

"Yes," Quijano said. He added that King had shown no remorse about the death of James Byrd.

Edward Gripon, a Beaumont psychiatrist, testified that King was dangerous. His racist tattoos showed that he would present a continuous threat of violence to society. The letters he wrote in jail, Gripon said, showed King had no regrets and that he was a racist. "That kind of ideology is not going to go away."

"Bill King is a young man, but he is old in spirit," said Sonny Cribbs, getting up from the defense table. "You have to ask yourselves, what happened to Bill King in prison? I don't know. What I do know is he wasn't a racist when he went in. He was when he came out. Please don't kill this young man. We've all got to quit hating. We all have to quit being racist. Do we believe in an eye for an eye or a tooth for a tooth? The first chapter in the Bible, in Genesis, Cain killed Abel and Cain was banished. God chose in that chapter not to do the death penalty—and so should you."

Guy James Gray rose to address the jury. "The option here is do you let that man kill again or do you take his life?" Gray began. "He's going to send emissaries to do this again. The question is, do you allow him to hurt another victim in the future? He anticipated the death of James Byrd. There is no mitigating factor to the crime he committed. None."

*　　*　　*

ON FEBRUARY 25, a jury sentenced John William King to die. The crowded courtroom was hushed. "Mr. King," the judge said. "I hereby sentence you to death by lethal injection." There was some spontaneous applause and then silence. Inmate number 999295 would become number 452 on death row and the only white man on death row in Texas for the murder of a black man.

Golden asked King and his lawyers and the sheriff to approach the bench. The group huddled together—the judge, the lawyers, Billy Rowles, and Bill King—with their heads almost touching. From the well of the courtroom it looked as if they were a group of adults calmly discussing a car accident or a truant child. King nodded several times. He looked pale.

"Mr. Sheriff," Golden said, when the group parted, "you may take him to the Texas Department of Criminal Justice to await execution there."

Moments later, King was ushered from the courtroom through a side door, ending the first of three planned death penalty trials for the Byrd murder. As he was being led in body armor a short distance across the courthouse lawn to a waiting sedan, a reporter hollered out a question. "What do you have to say to the Byrd family, Bill? What do you say to them?"

Instead of answering the question, King offered a comment to the waiting journalists who had sought to get a rise out of him for months.

"Suck my dick," he said, ducking into the car.

*   *   *

CRIBBS RELEASED A statement from Bill King minutes after the police cruisers left the courthouse with the condemned man in the back seat.

"Though I remain adamant about my innocence, it's been obvious from the beginning that this community would get what they desire; so I'll close with the words of Francis Yockey. 'The promise of success is with the man who is determined to die proudly when it is no longer possible to live proudly.'"

The note was signed: John William King.

"I think Bill King is a very intelligent man, and I think it is a very, very sad day that someone like him had to be sentenced— bluntly—like he was today," said Laquita Flowers, a forty-one-year-old schoolteacher who had been a member of the jury that sentenced King to death. "I think Mr. King had the potential to be a leader, and I think it's unfortunate that his circumstances and his short life directed him in such a horrendous path."

Joe Collins, a corrections officer from Newton, was the jury's foreman and its only black member. He had gone to middle school with King in Jasper, and he thought, during jury selection, that the racist labels that had been used to describe King might have been wrong. That wasn't the Bill King he had remembered.

"I kind of looked at him and smiled," Collins said. "And he didn't look like he had any hate in him. In fact, he smiled back."

The evidence changed Collins's mind. It wasn't just the physical evidence that convinced him that King had killed Byrd; it was his racist writings before the killing and the intercepted jailhouse correspondences with Russell Brewer following their arrest that led Collins to ask for the death penalty, he said. Flowers agreed. "The writings were very compelling for me," she said. "I felt like he didn't show any remorse for his actions after the deed was done. We looked for redeeming qualities, but we would read those letters and they were not there. We looked for ways to not have to do what we did today, and they were not there."

Flowers looked composed as she thought about her decision to put someone to death, someone from Jasper. "Who would've ever predicted something like this would've occurred in the first place? Who would have thought any kind of hate could exist like that in someone among us?" she said.

That was the one thing everyone in the white community was willing to agree on: Bill King was an aberration. It was easier to think of Bill King as being clouded by some outside malevolent force than to think what he had become had something to do with Jasper.

*   *   *

RONALD KING STOOD outside the courthouse as the crowd began to disperse and said the whole ordeal—his son's arrest, prison stay, and trial—stirred memories of an earlier family trial that had thrust his parents into a media spotlight nearly sixty years before. It was 1939, and he was ten years old. His older brother and another young man, both marines, were charged with killing a traveling salesman in Norfolk, Virginia, by bashing in his skull. Like Bill King's victim, the salesman was disabled and forty-nine. As in Jasper, the defendants were tied to the crime by FBI lab work; incriminating fingerprints were found on beer bottles left at the crime scene.

F. Teague Jennings, a member of a prominent Georgia family, arrived in Norfolk on a business trip on July 24, 1939, and checked into a hotel. Around 11 P.M. that night, a bellboy heard moans comings from Jennings's room and, when he went to investigate, found the Georgia man sprawled across a bloody bed with a crushed skull. He died a few hours later. Witnesses testified they had seen two marines accompany Jennings to his room. Investigators found broken beer bottles in the room, and the fingerprints led them to Lawrence King and Wallace E. Miller, two marines stationed on the aircraft carrier USS *Ranger*. Eventually a marine's khaki shirt, stained with blood, was also found, pulled from the Elizabeth River.

The way the two marines told the story, Jennings had tried to force himself on them once they had joined him in his hotel room for some beers. Jennings "put his hand on the Marine's leg," according to trial testimony, and a fight ensued. The trial made front-page headlines and drew large crowds of spectators. The popular view was that King and his fellow marine were victims, not murderers. Ronald King's brother and the codefendant said they'd had to kill the man because he had made a pass at them and then attacked them for resisting. It was, though the term was not known then, a gay bashing. Never mind that the victim's brother, a doctor, testified that the victim's cataracts and disabled right arm would have made it unlikely that he could defend himself against the two much younger men. The jury acquitted King's brother and his friend in just twenty-nine minutes. Townspeople lined the court-house lawn to congratulate the men after the verdict, according to Norfolk newspapers.

For the elder King the memories came back in snapshots. He remembered seeing a photograph of his much older brother going into the courthouse and snapshots of his parents sitting in the court-room in support. "It was so strange. When I saw all the pictures of me going into the courthouse for Bill, that old man looked like my daddy. Just like those pictures from the newspapers. It was a hate crime, too. Course, they didn't have that word for it back then."

Ronald King's brother had died years before. He wondered whether his son Bill had ever known about the family history. "Some of my other children knew about the earlier trial. I don't think Bill ever heard," King said. "I think about that trial a lot. I think about how my parents felt. Bill's trial would never have turned out like that one. That was a different time."

Ronald King said he sat through as much of his son's trial as he could, to send a message, if nothing else. "I'm not sure Bill real-ized what this had done to the rest of us. It seemed that his only concern was for his own feelings. He's just been thinking about Bill.

"I was hoping I could find out something that would be an explanation, that this is heredity or something like that," he said. "I couldn't find anything."

King mused about his son's extreme mood swings and his temper. "I'm the only person in the world that wasn't afraid of him somehow," he said after the trial. "But none of that can explain this, explain what happened. How can all this have happened without my knowing about it? I should have known something."

Ronald King said he knew that as part of the case the FBI had interviewed some of his coworkers at a Jasper lumber mill, and some of them told agents that he had frequently used racist slurs as a younger man and bragged of once belonging to a Ku Klux Klan group. "Everybody wants to know where all this hatred came from, and they think it came from me," he said. "But it didn't. I don't know how all this happened. I don't have answers, just questions. The world don't work like we want it to sometimes."

At least he could be grateful that his wife had died and never saw all the trouble her son had gotten himself into. "She's so lucky to be dead," King said. "Sometimes I wish I could just go."

*　　*　　*

"I DON'T THINK Mr. King believed Bill did it until about a week before the trial," said Sonny Cribbs months later. "Sometimes you don't have to be a racist to end up raising one. That was hard for everyone, not just Mr. King, to admit."

Cribbs was heartbroken after the verdict. "I don't believe in the death penalty. I just plain do not believe in it. Nobody is all horrible. No matter what the world sees, this man is loved. He loves. And he is a human being. His father's testimony really upset him. He's not as tough as everyone thinks he is."

King essentially wrote himself to death, Guy James Gray said. The physical evidence tying him directly to the crime was narrow. It was King's intense racism that gave prosecutors a way to tie all the events together. His extensive writings on the Texas Rebel Soldiers gave them the motive they needed to show he had planned to kill James Byrd. King's notes to Brewer in Jasper County Jail showed enough inside knowledge of the murder to implicate all three of the suspects.

Cribbs agreed. If King's writings had not surfaced, he said, and if the state hadn't called in federal investigators, his client might have avoided the death penalty. "Smartest thing Billy Rowles ever did," he said. "It would have been impossible for the Jasper people to do it themselves. Guy James's office never could have talked to all those people and prepared all those witnesses. Probably the only other person whose case involved this many people is Timothy McVeigh," he said, referring to the convicted Oklahoma City bomber. Guy James could "pick up the phone and call anyone for help. I couldn't."

*   *   *

ON THE MORNING of February 26, a day after the verdict, there was an electricity in the Jasper High School gymnasium as the students filed in. Bill King had been sentenced to death for the murder of James Byrd, and now, in one of those odd twists of the calendar, students were attending a regularly scheduled assembly to celebrate Martin Luther King Day and black history month. The irony was lost on no one. Nor was the way the students seated themselves. As if by design, the black students sat on the left side of the gym, and whites peeled off from the lines and shuffled across the wooden floor to sit on the right. The students didn't sit by class rank, as most high school students do; they sat by race. And the self-segregation was complete. Not one white face sat on the left side, and not one black face sat on the right. Teachers exchanged worried glances.

Students generally sat with their friends, and racial mixing occurred in pockets around the gym. Never before had the segregation been this pronounced. A documentary film crew had been admitted to film the assembly in the wake of the King trial. Administrators were rethinking the decision. Walter Diggles, the guest speaker, was aghast.

"I wasn't expecting things to be so polarized," Diggles said. "This was an assembly of students sending a message about the King trial and racism in Jasper. We still have a long way to go."

CHAPTER TWELVE

DEATH TOWN, U.S.A.

Render unto Caesar what is Caesar's.
—MATTHEW 22:22

ON HIGHWAY 59, a low-profile four-car caravan sped its way toward Huntsville prison. There were no flashing lights. No sirens. Just a determined, high-speed drive meant to take Bill King out of Jasper for the last time. A Texas Ranger was driving the lead car, and jailer Mo Johnson, a woman who had known King since he was a small child, sat next to him in the back seat of a second. King was handcuffed and in the same bullet-proof vest he had been wearing when he emerged from the courthouse. The trip had been a direct one—the motorcade turned left on Austin Street then right on 59 and drove straight through all the little towns that lay between the piney woods and Huntsville some 180 miles away.

King hardly said a word. Instead of making conversation, he chose to contemplate the scenery outside for the last time: the What-A-Burger on the corner and Bo Jackson's Quality Meats, where King had dropped off his first deer as a boy. "He was really quiet the whole way," Johnson said. "That's different for him. He is usually pretty talkative, and he's known me for years. So it wasn't like he was being shy. Truth was, I think he was shocked. What had just happened finally hit him when he got into the car."

King's death sentence had essentially pronounced him incapable of change, irredeemable, and ultimately, unfit to live. His image would soon be reduced to those photos the media had taken during the trial and the sheriff's office's mug shot, in which he looked dazed and like someone had broken his nose. He would be seen forever as the twenty-four-year-old who gathered energy enough to smirk at journalists and their cameras as he ducked into the car for the drive to death row.

Huntsville prison, a maximum-security unit two hours west of Jasper, encompassed two square blocks of downtown Huntsville and was home to the busiest death chamber in the world. Built in 1849 as consolation to the city of Huntsville when Austin was chosen as the state capital, the prison was almost a city unto itself. Its walls were an eruption of brick rising thirty feet into the air. At night, when the prison was dimly lit, it looked very much like the Forbidden City in Beijing. The difference, of course, was that the high walls in China were meant to keep the masses away from the emperor and his court. In this case, the walls were designed to keep the residents in.

Huntsville had been home to a number of notorious gunslingers. John Wesley Hardin, who claimed to have killed forty-four men, was known as the "meanest man that ever lived" and once, allegedly, shot a man for snoring. Hardin was captured in 1877 and was sentenced to twenty-five years at Huntsville. He served only fifteen years, was given a pardon by the governor, and eventually opened a law office in El Paso, Texas. Jessie Evans, Billy the Kid's partner in crime, served just a year of a thirty-year sentence in Huntsville before he escaped in 1882. He was never recaptured. By 1999, Huntsville was the death row processing center. From there prisoners went on to Livingston's Terrell Unit to await an execution date. They returned to the Walls the day of their execution.

The prison was vital to the economy of Huntsville, and over the years residents had come to take a perverse pride in the place. They printed prison tour guides and quizzed one another and visitors on Huntsville prison trivia. (The first woman inmate was convicted in 1854 and was sentenced to one year for infanticide. The youngest inmate was a nine-year-old boy who was sentenced in 1884 for robbery. The youngest girl behind its bars was eleven years old, locked up in 1884 for administering poison. The most unusual occupation listed by an inmate: gentleman loafer. One man was incarcerated for worthlessness.) The town's intense focus on the prison was in large part motivated by the fact that almost everyone in Huntsville either was employed by the Texas Department of Criminal Justice or had been at one time. Students emerged from the local school system with expectations of working for the TDC. Sam Houston University, sitting just blocks from Huntsville, or "the Walls" unit, used its close proximity to develop one of the best criminal justice study programs in the country. Sam Houston students appeared unruffled by the menacing presence of the Walls, and their carefree collegiate lives went on much as one might expect, with the obligatory keg parties, loud music, the frivolity occurring only steps away from where prison officials put men to death.

Bill King arrived at the Walls without incident and moved from the unmarked cruiser into the James Byrd diagnostic unit for processing. He stopped momentarily at the unit's entrance, read the sign, and turned to Johnson: "This is a joke, right?"

She didn't respond. Life did sometimes provide certain symmetries, she thought to herself. Of course the James Byrd for whom the unit was named was not the man King had killed; he was a former warden at Huntsville. But the sign did provide a moment of poetic justice; perhaps it was God sending King a message, Johnson thought. Everything beyond the momentary pause to read the sign, however, was tightly scripted for the newcomer. King stripped, showered, sat quietly for a close haircut, and then received the white cotton uniform death row inmates were required to wear.

Outside the room, prison guards were ribbing death row captain Robert Burse. A large black man with square hands and a gentle voice, Burse was in charge of giving King his induction interview. The questions and routine were always the same: Burse asked King about his family, any health problems, and the last time he had been to a doctor. He asked about his crime and whether there was anyone at all with whom he did not want to be housed. The last question was moot, of course, since King would be in solitary confinement for the rest of his days.

"How did that go? How was it talking to the biggest racist in this country?" the guards asked Burse when he emerged after an hour.

Burse shook his head. "He was real polite," Burse said. "He was all 'yes, sir' and 'no, sir.' No big deal, just routine."

Bill King was the first man ever to have spent the night in the James Byrd diagnostic unit. Billy Rowles was in such a rush to get King out of Jasper he accidentally left his paperwork in the county jail. It took a day for the paperwork to catch up.

* * *

THE SMALL BRICK building tucked away in the northeast corner of the Huntsville prison compound had been ground zero for so many executions over the years—40 percent of America's executions had occurred there between 1995 and 2000, more than one hundred prisoners—that people in Huntsville had almost stopped paying attention. Just as shuttle launches in the United States had become so commonplace people were shocked when the Challenger exploded, so too, in Huntsville, the only time residents took notice of an execution was when it went wrong. Otherwise, the deaths were routine. The only outward sign that Huntsville residents distanced themselves from the condemned came in the nickname they had given the death row inmates. Those who would have the lethal Texas cocktail injected into their veins were known as "the patients."

On execution days Warden Jim Willett woke a little before 5 A.M. and immediately thought about whether the man who would be put to death after 6 P.M. that evening would resist. A soft-spoken man with gentle eyes and an easy smile, Willett was the warden at the Walls unit from 1998 to 2001. In the year 2000 alone, forty people were given lethal injection in the unit's small green death chamber. It was Willett's job to stand at the head of each prisoner and cue the executioner. All told, Willett had taken off his glasses, his signal to begin the injection, eighty-five times during his career.

"You know, it's odd, but for all the training they put us through in the Department of Corrections, there is no training for this," he said, shortly before announcing his retirement at the age of fifty-one. "I don't think people really realize how much this affects us. I don't like doing what I'm doing. I'm not sure I could be on a jury and sentence someone to die."

Those execution mornings, Willett typically didn't talk about the day's activities with his wife, Janice. He would simply tell her that he would be coming home late, and she knew enough not to ask.

The case of Cruthers Alexander, a man sentenced to death for the 1981 rape and murder of a Texas waitress, was typical. The first person put to death in Texas after former Texas governor George W. Bush became president in 2001, Cruthers Alexander was an example of a man who had been in the system so long he had given up any idea of resistance. He didn't want a last meal, or a phone call, or for his family to attend his execution. Alexander, who had been on death row for nineteen years, just wanted to die.

"All he asked for is clothes to wear for the execution," said Willett.

Inmates have a choice of being put to death in their white prison pajamas or in rough-hewn clothing made by their fellow prisoners. The garment factory was the crown jewel of the Texas death row. It began as an experiment in 1981 and was the only prison program in the nation where the entire workforce was under a death sentence. Shirts from the factory came in only two colors: blue or brown. Alexander wanted to be killed in brown.

Originally from Georgia, Jim Willett had begun his career as a corrections officer with the Texas Department of Criminal Justice twenty-nine years earlier and had worked his way up to warden. When he talked about prisoners who had been put to death on his watch, his voice dropped and his cadence slowed. "I consider myself a happy man, generally, and I don't think doing this has fundamentally changed me," he said. "But I have had enough."

The death penalty opponents who demonstrated outside the Walls during the executions with their placards and petitions often focused their ire on Willett, who saw their anger as misplaced. Willett was not a death penalty proponent; he was a man who had an unpleasant job to do.

Under Willett's charge, Huntsville's execution system had become so efficient that Florida and other states were seeking to emulate it. From 1976 to 2001, the death house had accounted for 206 of the country's 610 executions. But for Willett, the effort to duplicate Huntsville's impressive productivity offered no satisfaction. The law enforcement officials who said the death penalty was a deterrent to crime, the juries who meted out the sentence, the governor who signed the execution order, the prison officials who arrived with notebooks to study what he had done—all were comparatively removed from the grisly process he lived with every day. They never saw, nor fully understood, what it was that Willett had had to do nearly once a week for three years.

"If a jury member ever had to watch an execution, I'm not sure they would vote for the death penalty," said Willett. "There are some things in life you really don't need to experience firsthand. Things that you never really get over. And this is one of them. If you see an execution, it never leaves you."

The van holding Cruthers Alexander arrived from Livingston, Texas, forty miles east of Huntsville, around 2 P.M. on January 29, 2001. The drill was always the same. The vans from the death rows around the state drove around the back of the prison through a succession of electrified fences to the small brick death house at the edge of the compound. Years ago, offenders on death row were kept in one of the eight small cells only steps away from the death chamber. The cells were identical slivers of rooms, seven feet by five feet, furnished with a bunk, a toilet, a basin, and fluorescent lighting overhead. One cell, the one closest to the death chamber door, had only a stool and a toilet inside, and the bars were covered with black wire mesh. There were no windows in any of the cells.

When the ranks of the condemned swelled beyond Huntsville's capacity, death row was eventually moved to Livingston. Prisoners returned to Huntsville only hours before they were put to death. Willett saw the change as a good thing. The Livingston unit was more modern, and with the prisoners out of sight until the day of their death, the dozen or so people who were needed to ensure an execution went smoothly didn't get to know the inmates beforehand.

"Things are hard enough without getting to know them personally," Willett said. The task of getting to know an offender in the final hours before his death fell to Chaplain Jim Brazzil. He ministered to the condemned. "The prisoners hear all kinds of rumors," said Brazzil. "They hear there is disrespect paid to the body after it's all over. You'd be surprised how many of them are scared of needles. I do what I can to assuage those fears. I'm going in as a minister. It doesn't matter to me if he did it or what he did. That gets in my way. I'm not driving them for a confession. I want them to get their lives right."

Brazzil was short and bespectacled and spoke with the characteristic calm of a man of God. He and Willett and the offender were the only three people in the death chamber when the lethal injection began. Willett stood at the prisoner's head, and Brazzil stationed himself at the foot of the gurney, usually grasping the condemned man below the knee during those final minutes "so he knows I'm here."

Brazzil likened what he did to ministering to terminal patients in a hospital. "If someone was dying of cancer, I would hold his hand until he died."

Cruthers Alexander, a small sturdy man, was taken from the prison van in shackles and handcuffs. The short walk from the van's double doors to the death house was the last time he, or any other prisoner on his way to the gurney, saw sunlight. "For all the prisoners it's the last time to be outside," said Larry Fitzgerald, spokesman for the prison. "Funny thing, though. I have seen so many people walk from the van to the death house, and not one of them has looked up."

When a prisoner arrived from Livingston, he was taken to a chair along the wall by the death house cells and asked to kneel while officers unchained him. Most moved wordlessly from the chair to the awaiting cell.

Brazzil was always there when prisoners arrived at the death house. His small congregation, a Who's Who of Texas murderers, was in constant flux. Just as he got to know an inmate, the man would be led to the gurney and put to death. It wore Brazzil down. He ministered to pickax murderer Karla Faye Tucker, who became, in 1997, the first woman to be put to death in Texas since 1863, and to Gary Graham, who may have been best known not for his crime (he was convicted of the 1981 murder of Bobby Gray Lambert outside a Houston Safeway) but for refusing to leave his cell when the time came for his execution in 1999. Members of the extraction team had to put on their face shields and their armor and forcibly drag him along the ten feet of slick floor to the death chamber. It was only the third time that such an extraction had ever been necessary at Huntsville.

"We've had people who tell us beforehand that they are going to resist," said Fitzgerald. "I had one guy tell me, 'You know it's my nature to fight to the end, so I'm going to fight you. I'm not going to hurt you; I'm just going to fight you,' and that's what he did."

It was Karla Faye Tucker who began a kind of yearbook signing on death row. Shortly before she was put to death, Tucker asked Brazzil if she could borrow his Bible. Days later, as Brazzil was flipping through the endleaves of the book, he found a note from Tucker. "It was like a ton of bricks hit me," he said. Tucker had written her words in the loopy handwriting of a schoolgirl: "Chaplain Jim," it began, "Thank you for bringing love and the fellowship of Jesus to me as I was prepared to be face to face with him. You, my precious brother, are hand-picked by God because of the compassion in your heart, to minister to those who have to walk this road."

A week after Tucker's execution another inmate asked Brazzil, "I wonder what Karla Faye was thinking?" Brazzil handed him the Bible and showed him the note. Now many of the condemned ask Brazzil if they can leave their own final message in the pages of his book. "I never read the notes until they're gone," Brazzil said.

Execution days at Huntsville tended to be precisely scheduled. Inmates arrived from Livingston in the early afternoon, were allowed a phone call at 2 P.M., and met with their spiritual advisers from 3:30 P.M. until they were led to the gurney. The last meal began at 4:30 P.M. Fried chicken and cheeseburgers were the two top picks for last meals, fajitas a distant third. The condemned usually finished the meals.

When Willett arrived at the office on the day of an execution, he began by making more than a dozen phone calls. He would call the attorney general's office and the governor's office to make sure no appeals were pending. He dialed up members of the execution team to tell them everything was going ahead as scheduled. Most of his morning was spent on the phone setting up the execution.

Willett met every inmate before he was killed to pose a series of questions: What did the inmate want for his last meal? What would be done with the body? Did he have a will? Willett already knew the answers to those questions. What he really was trying to gauge was whether the execution would be tough. Would the condemned man be defiant or resigned?

Chaplain Brazzil stayed with the prisoner and tried to calm him. He usually shared the last meal. "No one likes to eat alone," he explained. The officers brought Cruthers Alexander tacos, even though he hadn't ordered a last meal. Brazzil ate one of the tacos, and Alexander ate three.

Willett usually put on his coat at 5:55 P.M. and began his walk over to the death house. "It was such a nervous time. You could see it on their faces. They knew that in just a few minutes they would be dead."

By then, two phone calls had to come in—one from the governor and another from the state attorney general—saying the execution could go ahead. When the warden came into the death house, he would call the inmate by his first name and ask him to walk with him into the green room. "There are no handcuffs then," Willett said.

Four men made up the tiedown team: one each for the right and left arm and another two for the legs. Within twenty to thirty seconds they had the prisoner strapped onto a silver gurney. The straps looked like the broad leather belts weight lifters wear, with thick leather and shiny buckles. At 6:05 P.M. the medical team came into the execution chamber and put IV tubes into each of the inmate's arms. Typically, the prisoner was all hooked up in less than three minutes. The left arm was the one through which the chemicals flowed. The right arm was a backup in case anything went wrong. Once the prisoner was hooked up and the medical team had left, the witnesses were led into the two small rooms that adjoined the death chamber. The state of Texas allowed five witnesses from the victim's side, five from the side of the condemned, and five members of the media. The victim's family and the prisoner's family never met while at the prison. Officials were very careful to keep them apart.

Three feet above the prisoner there was a microphone meant to transmit last words before the chemicals flowed. Willett was never absolutely certain what would happen then. One man started singing "Silent Night." "He didn't get to 'round yon virgin, mother and child' before he had expired." Willett said. "It kind of ruined the song for me, frankly."

Willett removed his glasses and the chemicals began to flow into Cruthers Alexander at 6:12 P.M. The order and the amount of chemicals were always the same. The first drug alone was enough to kill half the inmates in Huntsville. The combination began with sodium pentathol to put the condemned to sleep. Another chemical flowed in to relax the muscles. Then potassium chloride was injected to stop the heart. The microphone was still in place when witnesses heard the last gasp. It sounded like the air running out of a balloon.

Two days after Cruthers Alexander was put to death, Chaplain Brazzil opened his Bible to see what the condemned man had written: "Brother Jim," Alexander wrote in his small perfect cursive, "I want to thank you for being here with me. You do make a difference. May God bless you for your kindness to me and all the others. Much love, Cruthers."

Two blocks from the Walls, two curators from Huntsville's Prison Museum gave guided tours. The museum featured macabre displays of prisoners and death. There was an exhibit about Frank Jones, a former inmate and one of America's best-known primitive artists. The display card was a reminder that this was still the South: "He was, to the Guards, just an old nigger who drew in the yard." One showcase titled "Contraband" featured the makeshift knives and weapons taken from prisoners. "A boot worn by inmate Charles Harrelson before being transferred to a federal prison," said one display card. "A secret pocket for carrying drugs was found in the heel. He was convicted of killing a judge in San Antonio. His son plays the bartender on *Cheers*."

The highlight, the thing most people came to see, was "Old Sparky," the solid oak electric chair in which 337 inmates were put to death. Old Sparky was built by a death row inmate in 1924. For his work in crafting the chair, he was spared from having to sit in it. His sentence was commuted to life.

Like many Huntsville residents, the museum's two curators, Betty Wilkinson and Mary McClain, used to work for the corrections department. "He didn't do what other wardens did," Wilkinson said about Warden Willett. "He's the only warden we had ever seen wash his own car. Usually the trusties from the prison do that."

McClain piped up. "His wife, Janice, says he does that when he's unhappy. It's therapy for him."

"His car has been really clean lately," said Wilkinson.

*   *   *

WHEN BILL KING arrived at Livingston's Terrell unit on February 26, 1999, he was greeted with jeers and catcalls as guards escorted him along the old corridors and iron stairwells. The hallways snaked around, joining the various buildings, and at the beginning and end of each, and sometimes even in the middle, there was a locked gate. The blocks were loud because there was nothing but concrete and metal, which amplified the sounds, and nothing but thin mattresses and inmates' bodies to absorb the noise. There was a cacophony of radios, walkie-talkies, swearing, and bar rattling in the regular units.

On death row, though, what was most eerie was the quiet, a silence that reigned day after day as men spent their time awaiting death in their identical cells. King's only diversions were the few books distributed on the library cart and, if he abided by prison rules, a single radio.

King's five-by-nine-foot cell on the second story of the prison overlooked one of the facility's recreation yards. Peeking through the wire mesh that covered his slit of a window, King could see the parking lot and watch visitors' nervous displacement actions— stretches, adjustment of clothes, deep breaths—before passing through the solid metal doors into the prison.

"I met him on the first day he hit," said Larry Fitzgerald, who by 2001 had witnessed 145 executions and was responsible for the reporters who came to Huntsville. "Bill King came in on a Friday and was transferred to death row on Saturday, and I drove over to meet him because he was one of those celebrity cases; everyone knew about him, and I wanted to see him eyeball to eyeball. Every time someone comes on death row that's a celebrity, they get a rashing, and Bill King wasn't any different."

King was in danger. Aryan Brotherhood groups were after him for pretending to be one of them. He wasn't tough enough to be one of them; he sullied their reputation, they said. The Bloods and the Crips had their own reasons for wanting to hurt him. He had, after all, committed the worst crime against a black man in more than forty years, and that deserved some sort of revenge if the opportunity presented itself. "The cells at Huntsville had old-style open bars in front, and it was plain that he was scared to death what might happen to him there," said Fitzgerald.

Fitzgerald met up with King in the visitor's room on February 27, 1999, to lay out the rules: there would be no media interviews for thirty to sixty days, and until the prison officials knew what kind of inmate he would be, his movements would be restricted. King had control over whether this would be a tough sentence or an easier one. "We operate on a carrot-and-stick theory here," said Fitzgerald. "If they are cussing and throw liquids at the guards, then, well, things get harder for them."

King had been in prison before, and he already knew what lay ahead. If he followed prison rules, he could expect visits from his friends and family once a month. If he remained in Level One Administrative Segregation, or Ad Seg, he could get a radio, books from the library cart, and unlimited newspapers. Problems with guards, however, could strip him of the few rights he had. Ag Seg

Level 3 could whittle down his recreation time to as few as three hours a week. "It's your choice," Fitzgerald said.

During the discussion, King was uncommonly polite, Fitzgerald said. "I kind of walked away thinking, 'How the hell did he get involved in that?' Then the real King stood up. A couple of months later, he started getting verbally abusive, and he thought he was smarter than everybody else and cussed out guards and was always complaining about no medical treatment or the food or anything. I was itching to say, 'Hey, pal, you're here because you made a career choice, and now you have to live with it.'"

There was no air-conditioning on the row and no exercise equipment. The men were responsible for cleaning their own cells. Bill King was issued clean pants and a shirt every three days. The prison provided clean underwear, socks, and a towel each day. King got a shower every day, often the ten-minute highlight of his quotidian existence.

Sammy Felder sat on death row in the cell beside Bill King. A murderer from Fort Worth, Felder had been waiting with resignation for the lethal injection that would finally end his life behind bars. He and King were among the tiny number of human beings to know in advance the day and time of their deaths. Felder, though he was black, had no problems with Bill King. "I don't want to speak to any reporters about living next to Bill King," he told Fitzgerald as reporters asked for interviews. "King doesn't bother me none. He's fine."

*   *   *

KING WROTE LETTERS protesting his conviction. A Web site went up, pulled together by a man in California who had never met King but had decided to turn him into some sort of political prisoner. King contended he hadn't had a fair trial.

According to King, the "political correctness" in Jasper made it impossible to empanel an unbiased jury, so a change of venue should have been granted. One of the jurors knew King and had a predisposition against him, he said. The heaviest salvo was reserved for Sonny Cribbs and Brack Jones, his defense attorneys. No real defense had been prepared, he said, and as a result his conviction was effectively a collusion between the defense and the prosecution. The underlying implication was that because of community pressure, Cribbs and Jones had somehow neglected their duties. ("This is all par for the course; this is what convicted people do on appeal," said Cribbs. "It doesn't bother me a bit.") Worst of all, King said Cribbs never investigated his alibi.

For capital cases in Texas, the median elapsed time between sentencing and execution was usually about six years. Most of those convicted and sentenced to die in Texas thought they would be executed right away. Few understood that there would be years of waiting. Even fewer understood how they were assigned an execution date. The variance depended on both luck and a backlog in the courts. Yet because the conviction and appeals processes appeared to be arbitrary, there was a lot of superstition that swirled about the order of executions. Many men thought their death row prisoner number was related to an execution order—the lower the number, the more likely one would be killed. Another rumor was that if someone with a number near another prisoner's got a date, then that inmate was likely to be on the gurney next. To prisoners with little understanding of their cases or the political environment outside, the whole system appeared to work with the capriciousness of the old army draft system. In reality, the system of appeals was meant to be fixed in favor of criminals. It began in state courts, wound its way through federal courts, and could reach the U.S. Supreme Court. King, however, was unlikely to find any sympathy from any judge, his attorney said. "What court in the land would step in to help him?" Cribbs said.

Billy Rowles, like the majority of American law enforcement officials, was certain capital punishment acted as a deterrent to violent crime. Guy James Gray wasn't so sure, as a Catholic, that capital punishment was what God intended. "If it was ever earned, though, this was a case that deserved it," he said.

Just up the hill from the Walls, behind Sam Houston University, in a field surrounded by pines, there are rows of concrete crosses. A trailer park sits on one side of the road. A car wash sits on the other. Eighteen hundred inmates, left at the prison after their death, lie in the Captain Joe Byrd Cemetery. (Joe Byrd was the man who used to pull the switch on Old Sparky.) The scene looks like Arlington Cemetery just outside of Washington, D.C.

The twenty-two acres that make up the cemetery were deeded to the prison in 1885. Back then, prisoners were taken up the hill in pine boxes for burial, and their graves were hacked into the tangled underbrush. The graves were eventually swallowed up by vegetation. As a result, no one is quite sure how many prisoners are actually buried up there. Of the 1,800 known graves, more than 200 belong to offenders put to death by the executioner. A few were slain by guards during escape attempts; others were killed by fellow inmates. Some died of natural causes. One out of every five prisoners who die in the Texas prison system today are left to be buried by corrections officials. There are nearly five hundred deaths a year in Texas prisons. Those who are without families willing to bury them are lowered into the red clay in cheap blue coffins. Graves of death row inmates can be recognized by walking along the rows of concrete crosses. Crosses with just a prisoner number, and not a name, mark graves of those who were executed.

CHAPTER THIRTEEN

THE MORE THINGS CHANGE

*You've got very badly to want to get rid of the
old before anything new will appear.*
—D. H. LAWRENCE, *WOMEN IN LOVE*

JURY SELECTION IN Russell Brewer's trial began in late August
1999, more than fourteen months after James Byrd had been laid to
rest. Brewer's lawyers had successfully convinced a judge that
people in Jasper knew too much about the crime to give Brewer a
fair trial. So after nearly thirty Texas counties were considered,
Bryan, Texas, home of the Texas A & M Aggies, emerged as the
venue, largely because they did not loudly object. Whether Brewer
would live or die depended on a jury seated 150 miles southwest of
his hometown of Sulphur Springs.

Russell Brewer's friends were as shocked as anyone when they
read in the newspapers that one of their own was accused of the
murder of James Byrd. Brewer had been a petty thief, targeting his

own family or the families of friends by snatching stereo speakers or loose bills, but he was not a murderer. His friends insisted the letters and tattoos and racist talk were only prison posturing. Brewer was doing what he had to to survive in the penitentiary. The Russell Brewer they knew was from a good Christian family, and entertained his girlfriend's children by making them special meals. The Brewer they knew had appeared at a hearing that spring flashing a message he had scrawled on an envelope: Happy Mother's Day to moms everywhere.

Brewer said he had not done it. Yes, he was there, the evidence said as much. But he didn't kill James Byrd, he said. Shawn Berry did. It was District Attorney Guy James Gray's intention to dismantle Brewer's lies.

Gray's opening statement lasted only fifteen minutes, and his narrative was a simple one: Brewer and Bill King had met in prison, and the older man was King's mentor and hate teacher. Brewer approached King in the Beto I unit and asked him to join the Confederate Knights of America. "He schooled the young man," Gray said. "This guy was the mentor. He took Bill King under his wing and taught him about the structure of the organization."

Brewer's attorneys, like King's lawyers, declined to give an opening statement. In many ways, the second trial was a reprise of the King proceedings six months earlier. Gray called nearly fifty witnesses, many of whom described Brewer as a committed racist who had risen in the ranks of the Confederate Knights and signed a blood oath to the Klan in 1995. By the time he met Bill King at Beto I, Brewer was the top CKA officer at the prison, the "exalted cyclops." The D.A. didn't say how big the gang was, or what an exalted cyclops did behind bars—that was beside the point. He only needed to prove Brewer was a racist and had been part of the killing trio. Gray introduced more than one hundred pieces of evidence, including a cigarette butt and beer bottle found at the crime scene with Brewer's DNA. Byrd's blood was on Brewer's shoe. Gray had little trouble placing Brewer at the clearing at the top of the tram road.

Brewer's intercepted jailhouse notes were even more incriminating than King's had been. "I am the God-damned hero of the day!" he bragged to Bill King in an eight-page letter. He wrote about a conversation he had had with another inmate while serving time for burglary and parole violations at the Beto I unit. That prisoner had spoken of "rolling a tire," Brewer said. That was prison slang for assaulting a black person. "Well, I did it; and no longer am I a virgin," Brewer wrote. "It was a rush and I'm still lickin' my lips for more." Gray introduced the letter as a virtual confession to the murder. Brewer's lawyers said the letter referred to Brewer having sex.

Gray called Jesus Moran, a prison inmate who had met Brewer at Huntsville's diagnostic unit after his arrest for the Byrd murder. Moran testified that Brewer had confessed to the murder and said if he had to do it all over again, he would make sure he got away with it. "If it was up to them, they would like to take the whole black population and shoot them behind the head—men, women, and children," Moran said.

Brewer testified. He spent more than four hours on the stand; occasionally breaking into sobs. He tried to convince the jury that although he kicked James Byrd and spray-painted his face black, he did not kill him. "I don't want to look at those pictures," Brewer cried, turning away when the lawyer approached the stand with photos of James Byrd's body. Shawn Berry offered Byrd the ride as he walked down Martin Luther King Boulevard in Jasper in June, Brewer said. It was Shawn Berry who had killed Byrd by slashing his throat with a knife, stripping him, and dragging him three miles behind his truck. "Then I heard Shawn's knife pop open, and Shawn, I guess he cut his throat," Brewer told jurors, his voice breaking. "He slid down the side of the truck, I got inside the truck and I smoked a cigarette."

Brewer said he heard the chain clatter as it was pulled out of the bed of the truck, and he tried to talk Berry out of dragging Byrd. "I was in a state of shock," Brewer told jurors. "We never meant to hurt Mr. Byrd. We didn't mean to kill Mr. Byrd." He sobbed again, saying he was sorry he was unsuccessful in persuading Berry to let Byrd go. Throughout his testimony, Brewer refused to repeat any swear words or racial slurs, saying, "I can't say any cuss words to these people."

Brewer said he had joined the Confederate Knights of America for protection while he was in prison. To join the group, he had hidden the fact that he was then married to a Hispanic woman and had a child with her. He had hidden his membership with the Knights from his black cellmate, he said. He had covered his CKA tattoo on his arm. "I didn't want him to sneak up on me and kill me," Brewer said as he burst into tears.

"The Brewer trial was sickening," said Mike Lout later. "He was blubbering like a sissy, like a girl. He talked in this high-pitched whiny voice and was just pathetic. Whatever you think of Bill King, at least he took it like a man. Brewer was all 'Mr. Byrd' this and 'Mr. Byrd' that. It made me want to throw up."

Jasper assistant district attorney Pat Hardy appeared to be thinking the same thing. "That's your big Aryan warrior story?" he shouted at Brewer on cross-examination. "You couldn't handle little-bitty Shawn Berry?" He asked Brewer how the blood got on his shoe. "That's a very good question," Brewer said. He couldn't explain why, in his notes to King, he had written that he was worried about investigators finding his fingerprints on the logging chain if he had never touched it.

Assistant U.S. attorney John Stevens, clad in his Brooks Brothers suit, asked Brewer about a letter he had written to his former wife while he was in prison in 1993. She had been seeing another man. "I feel as though I've been drug 120 miles chained by the feet to the bumper of a Corvette doing 90 miles an hour," Brewer wrote. Stevens asked Brewer about the similarities between his letter and the way Byrd was killed. It was, Brewer said, "a most unusual coincidence."

During closing arguments, Gray reminded jurors that the Byrd autopsy showed there was no evidence of a knife wound. "He was alive and he was conscious, and Shawn Berry didn't cut his throat," the D.A. told the jury. If Berry had slit his throat, Byrd's undershirt would have been soaked with blood. It wasn't. Brewer had concocted his story to convince a jury that he was only minimally involved in the murder. "Russell Brewer crafted his story to stay just short of a capital offense," Gray said. "He's not afraid of the penitentiary. Out here on the street, he can't hold a job. He can't do much of anything. But in that penitentiary, he's an officer. He's a big shot. He's the exalted cyclops of a prison." The jury deliberated for four hours before finding Brewer guilty of capital murder on September 20.

"I'm relieved," Guy James Gray told reporters gathered outside the Bryan courthouse. "When Jasper returned the case against Bill King, some people would say they were just trying to protect themselves. When you move it halfway across the state of Texas, and another jury returns a guilty verdict, it kind of broadens the scope. The message is we're long past those days that we were embarrassed by. Race relations have improved a whole lot, and we don't want to see them slide backwards."

It took the Bryan jury a little longer, more than fourteen hours, to agree that Brewer deserved to die. Tension was mounting in Jasper when the deliberations stretched into a second day. It had taken Jasper jurors just two and a half hours to deliver the death penalty in the King trial. "Everyone was so relieved when we heard Brewer had been sentenced to death," said David Stiles, who had been at the Belle-Jim when the news came. "This has taken so much out of Jasper. It is like the whole town has been beaten up. We're exhausted. This is almost done, and then things can settle down again."

*   *   *

THE LAST TRIAL, Shawn Berry's, began in early November. Berry's lawyer fought to keep the proceedings in Jasper, and that worried Billy Rowles. "I thought there was a real chance that Shawn wouldn't get the death penalty, and I was worried people would get bowed up about that, so we took some extra precautions."

Those precautions included plastic barriers, instead of the thin ropes that protected King. The big plastic wall led to the side door of the courthouse so people would not be able to rush officers escorting Berry to and from the courtroom. Rowles set up metal detectors at the courthouse door and created a press room in the basement. Further complicating his job was an interview Berry did with Dan Rather for *60 Minutes II*. The three-hour interview in Jasper County Jail was meant to provide Berry's version of events, a recounting that minimized his role in the killing. Only eighteen minutes of the interview aired, but it ran just weeks before the trial began and many Jasperites saw it. The show stirred up issues residents had hoped would be laid to rest when King was sentenced to death. They wondered aloud how the world would see them if Berry dodged the death penalty. "I was just hanging out with a bad crowd," Berry told Rather tearfully. "The Bible says you aren't supposed to hate people, but I really hate Bill and Russell for what they did."

Guy James Gray had always known it would be difficult to get a Jasper jury to sentence Shawn Berry to death. Too many people knew him as the affable manager at the Twin Cinemas. Gray decided to focus on Berry's role in the events of that steamy June night. Berry may not have been as big a racist as Brewer and King, but he was driving the truck that dragged James Byrd to his death. Hardy had always believed Berry was driving the truck. "It was his truck, his chain, and he's the one that got the man in the vehicle," Hardy said. "Everything in common sense points that he was the one driving."

"If you're satisfied that it's his hand on the steering wheel, weaving down the road, and his foot is on the pedal, I don't think you have any option but to find him guilty," Gray said in his opening statement. "Maybe he was living with them and their beliefs rubbed off on him. Maybe he was just a thrill seeker. Maybe he wanted to play with a rattlesnake and see what happened."

Joseph "Lum" Hawthorne, Berry's attorney, told the jury that nothing Berry had ever done or said indicated that he was the kind of person who could commit such a racist crime. Prosecutors were trying to "weave a tale of guilt by association," he said. "Shawn knew they talked the racist talk, but there was no reason for him to believe that they were violent people," he told the all-white seven-woman, five-man jury. Berry had tried to stop King and Brewer as they beat and stripped Byrd, he said. After King threatened him, Berry backed off. "He was scared," Hawthorne said. "He was so afraid that he wet his pants."

Berry admitted during the trial that he had invited Byrd into his truck and that he had driven Byrd, King, and Brewer up to Huff Creek Road, but he denied participating in the crime.

"You know, I wanted to believe Shawn Berry," Billy Rowles testified at the Berry trial. "His uncle and I are good friends. We had worked together in the Highway Patrol. I felt sorry for this kid." That changed, Rowles said, when the evidence began to pile up against Berry. "He kept changing his story," Rowles said, "to fit whatever new evidence we had. Instead of believing him, now he had this big question mark over him."

Hours after Rowles testified, Shawn Berry was on the stand.

"Let's go on to another lie," the prosecutor began. "When you picked up James Byrd, and Bill King told you, 'Let's go kick his ass,' and then Mr. Byrd asked you, 'Man, where are we going?' what did you tell him was going to happen? What happened was you stopped and killed James Byrd, didn't you?"

"What happened was that I stopped, and Bill King and Russell Brewer killed James Byrd," said Berry. "I am very sorry for what happened to Mr. Byrd and I've said that from day one. And I would do anything in the world if I could do it over."

The prosecutor paused. "Does that include going home and going to sleep after dragging James Byrd down the road?" he began. "In forty years, if this jury spares your life and you get out of prison, do you think a black man would feel safe walking down Martin Luther King Boulevard?"

Berry was quiet. "I don't know."

It took jurors more than ten hours to deliver a guilty verdict, and less than two hours later they spared Berry's life, sentencing him to life imprisonment instead of death.

"The Shawn Berry case was the hardest one for me," said Guy James Gray, months after the verdict. "I always knew it would be hard to get death for Shawn. I feel okay about this. Two death penalties and a capital conviction and a life sentence is a satisfactory result."

There were shouts when Berry emerged from the courthouse. "May you rot in hell, Shawn Berry," one woman screamed as he climbed into the car.

*   *   *

DEATH MAY MAKE slow people hurry and force them to see things as they are instead of the way they want them to be. What it doesn't do is keep things that way. Black Jasperites first noticed that old patterns had begun to reappear in the weeks after Bill King's conviction. After ten months of living day in and day out with the murder and the media attention it brought, everyone's senses began to numb. The small courtesies, the racial hypersensitivity that emerged right after the murder, began to fade. Once again, black customers at the variety store had to wait longer than whites, just as they had for decades. All the talk about job opportunities, industrial parks, and training centers began to dry up. Whites figured the black community got what they wanted—a death sentence for Bill King—so this bending over backward to be polite did not seem as necessary as it had in the weeks after the murder.

"The blacks really took advantage of us," said a prominent white citizen from one of the rocking chairs on the porch of the Belle-Jim Hotel. "They knew we felt bad about what had happened, so they tried to convince us that we had somehow done them wrong. They got uppity, demanding things like jobs and special treatment. The real world doesn't work that way. The real world doesn't give anyone special treatment."

Blacks were aware in a vague way how the whites felt after King was sentenced. The return to the old ways, to no longer treating them "as people," put everything that had come before—the prayer vigils and community meetings—in a bad light. Those meetings were not meant to change things, they decided, but rather were to placate the black community and divert the visiting media.

"It was so there could be this big collective sigh of white guilt, and then everybody could go home and say they had changed," said Unav Wade. "The saddest thing was that for a while we actually thought this would stick, that Jasper would suddenly rush into the twenty-first century. Then it stopped."

Reverend Lyons was more philosophical. "I really think the white community thought there would be some overnight transformation. They would be racist in the morning and then suddenly not racist by evening," he said. "You don't become a better person overnight. It is something you have to work at, little by little. Just because this was hard for them and they had to admit to being racist, that doesn't wipe the slate clean or let them off the hook. A dragging murder happened in Jasper; the Lord is trying to tell us something, isn't he? Now the question is: Are we listening?"

Jasperites weren't the only ones who had been hopeful that the town had changed. Journalists had wanted to see the end of something too. After months of headlines about a young president and his affair with an intern, Jasper's response to Byrd's murder offered a welcome change of pace. Whites and blacks were working together, seeming to embody the end of a time when America left racism unanswered. Jasper appeared to provide proof that the nation was learning to recognize prejudice and handle it better. "Jasper has shown the rest of us the right way to respond to a racial tragedy," syndicated columnist Clarence Page wrote shortly after the King trial. "Most citizens think of themselves as too busy to hate, until a crisis in their town exposes the hornets' nest of prejudices and misperceptions that swarms just beneath the surface of their city."

If one asked the black community in Jasper whether they had became a model for dealing with racial hatred, however, they were less sure. "The great irony of this entire thing was that Jasper's white community was saved by Jasper's black community. We sat next to them on podiums and took turns at the microphones and said this wasn't a racist town," said Unav Wade. The black community had done that in hopes of giving the idea of equality in Jasper a good sharp nudge. But once the media had left, it didn't work out that way. "We should have known better," said Wade. "Public dialogue is never really dialogue. Nobody will admit to anything in a crowd, so all those public meetings, well, they were for show."

Vander Carter and his wife, Christine, said most of the changes, such as they were, had faded, and the old familiar patterns that defined black life and white life in Jasper had returned. The community meetings about healing were sparsely attended. There was a ground-breaking for a training center, but it stood half finished within eyeshot of the high school. Blacks doubted it would ever be completed.

"Now the dirty work is just under cover," said Christine. "You can take a fence down in a graveyard that separated black graves from white ones, but until there's a black person buried in the front row, I'm not going to believe things are any different. We integrate in Jasper when people are watching. Now that the story is over, a year has gone by, we segregate, just like we was."

*   *   *

ONE DAY IN December, Billy Rowles put on his cowboy hat and pushed through the double glass doors of the Aubrey Cole Law Enforcement Center into the sunlight. Across the parking lot he could see a young black mother and her toddler son walking along the road toward downtown. The pair looked over at the sheriff; the mother smiled thinly and nodded. Rowles gave them a wave and started to climb into his truck. And then he stopped. Suddenly waving didn't seem to be enough.

After everything that had happened over the past nine months, hailing the two from the lot seemed wrong. Rowles began walking toward them. The boy's eyes grew wide as the tall, lanky sheriff approached. Rowles stopped about ten feet from them and sat down on the curb. The mother slowed. Rowles smiled and held his arms open for the boy. The mother dropped her son's hand and nudged him. He crab-walked over to the sheriff and sat next to him by the side of the road.

"What's your name, partner?" Rowles began gently.

The boy smiled shyly, and his mother answered for him and then added, "Thank you, Sheriff, for what you've done."

"It was hard to explain what happened to me right then," said Rowles. "I guess I had never thought of myself as being prejudiced, I thought of myself as color-blind. But at the same time I think I decided, just at that moment, that it wasn't enough to just think I wasn't prejudiced. I had to make more of an effort than that. If we were going to put all this behind us, people couldn't just expect it would go away; we had to work at it."

In the end, Billy Rowles appeared to be one of the few people in Jasper who understood that. Though Rowles hardly expected to have such an awakening, he behaved well when he was caught by circumstances, and in a small way that made him a hero. Weeks after the Berry trial bumper stickers began to appear on trucks around town. They were pasted below union stickers and Chevy decals, and they read: "Thank you Billy Rowles, for being our sheriff."

*   *   *

THE HALL AT the Los Angeles Convention Center shook as Democrats gathered to give Al Gore the nomination for their party in August 2000. Rarely had anyone seen the vice president in such fine form. The music was deafening, and the crowd began to chant and wave their placards as Gore entered the hall from one of the side doors. He gave delegates high-fives and handshakes as he made his way down the ramp and stepped up to the podium. The party was about to invest its hopes for the future in this Tennessean.

In the first balcony, surrounded by politicians and party luminaries, including vice presidential nominee Joseph Lieberman, James and Stella Byrd awaited their moment. Democratic Party operatives had invited the Byrds to the convention to prove that under Gore's administration hate crimes legislation would be a top priority.

". . . and I would like to thank the Byrd family for being here tonight," Gore said as the klieg lights found James and Stella Byrd in their special seats. The pair sat up straight and nodded to the presidential nominee. They looked uncomfortable as the cameras zoomed in and the giant screens transmitted their picture around the world. The whole appearance, after the flights and arrangements and carefully chosen wardrobe, lasted no more than fifteen seconds before the nominee had moved on to another campaign pledge.

Two months later the Byrd murder would come up in the presidential debates. "All three of the men responsible for the Byrd murder will pay the ultimate price, they will pay with their lives," Texas governor George W. Bush told the audience during the second debate, trying to deflect vice president Gore's question on why Bush had not signed a hate crimes law in Texas. As the credits began to roll on the second debate, Bush operatives had rushed out to the press room. They needed to amend the candidate's statement, they said; only two of the killers had been sentenced to death, not all three. What they didn't mention was that slightly more than two years after James Byrd was dragged three miles down a country road in one of the nation's most infamous killings, the governor of the state of Texas couldn't remember, exactly, what had happened to the killers. Already, memories were beginning to fade.

*   *   *

BILL KING'S BIRTH mother was twenty years old when she added him in 1975 to the three other children she had already borne. She was barely enough mother to go around, Ronald King said later, and his house offered the infant boy four mothers—two daughters in their high teens, Jean King, and her mother. In the end that might have had something to do with Bill King's undoing. With four doting women in his life, he was rarely held accountable for anything, his former teachers and friends said.

"Do I wish I had been harder on him? Sure I do," Ronald King said months after his son's conviction. "You keep going back to things you might have done differently, but it is a little late for that. My wife's death could have been a big factor. It wasn't but months from diagnosis to death for her, and that hit him pretty hard."

As if to prove that Bill King hadn't been a racist all his life, his father began singling out black childhood friends his son had had. Christopher Thomas, a black contemporary of the younger King's, was a teenage role model. He could have done anything he wanted to, his father owned his own logging company, and he and Bill got along famously. They had sleepovers. "Just like normal boys," Ronald King said. He remembered a time when Thomas had lent

Bill King a camera to take photographs of his mother's birthday celebration. But when it came time to have someone testify on Bill King's behalf, Thomas didn't want any part of it. "I can't blame him," Ronald King said.

King wouldn't talk about his son's guilt or innocence. The trial was unfair, he was sure about that, but he wouldn't say whether he believed a jury would render a different verdict, given the evidence, if they were called upon to do so again. What Ronald King did do, with dutiful regularity, was go see his son in prison. ("The guards pick on him, and sometimes he gets in trouble and he's not allowed to have visitors," the father explained. "The guards made one of his visitors wait two hours to see Bill, and Bill mouthed off about it and the guards beat him up. They bloodied his nose. He's got a toothache, real bad, can't even eat, and they won't take him to the dentist. They are really treating him bad out there.")

King was too feeble to make the drive to Livingston on his own, so he had worked out an agreement with a "lady friend," who drove him out to the prison, dropped him off, and then went shopping for a couple of hours. Sometimes there were visits, if Bill King behaved himself, with his family. Ronald King would arrange to arrive with Bill King's girlfriend, Kylie Greeney, and his son, Blayne. Those were the visits that made the elder King happiest. "Blayne is just the spitting image of his daddy at that age," he said. "It is so great to see them all together."

King seemed to forget that bullet-proof glass stood between everyone involved and that Blayne had been held only once by his father in his young life. The entire situation was one that lent itself to such lapses. One had to wonder if it was a good idea to bring a toddler into a prison where his father sat on death row. King said he had thought about that and decided the visits were fine. "Odds are that Bill will probably be executed before Blayne really has a memory of him," he said. "I think my boy has two or three years to live. By the time he's in kindergarten, Blayne won't even have this much with his daddy anymore."

*   *   *

IT WAS EASTER Sunday 2000, two years after the murder. The press had long since finished its stories pegged to the first anniversary of the murder. "Jasper had tried hard to prove to the world— and to itself—that what happened to Byrd on June 7, 1998, was an aberration, but no one seemed to be listening," the *Dallas Morning News* reported. "Reporters, some from out of state and a few from abroad, kept returning to Jasper looking for the truth behind America's most heinous hate crime in decades. . . . Like Dallas after Kennedy, Memphis after King and Birmingham after Bull Connor's attack dogs, Jasper was a place etched into the national conscience like a bad tattoo."

The Byrd family had hoped that dedicating a small park to their son would change some of that. When they gathered that Easter morning, only one local news crew showed up. After all the talk of rebuilding the Lone Star Youth Center and naming it after the dead man and the rumors of statutes erected in his memory, Jasper citizens quietly decided that James Byrd hadn't been the type of man anyone ought to look up to, even if he did die in a dreadful way. At first the Byrd family protested, but when it became clear that the only ones supporting a memorial for James were the white people who hardly knew him, even his family gave up.

What they decided on instead was modest: a basketball park, a single half court of pavement with a hoop and stand. The elevated lot, just down the street from the Byrd house, was overgrown with weeds. All it supported were twelve parking spaces, a couple of pic-nic tables, grills, and small cinder-block restrooms. There was something forlorn about the whole affair. Only a handful of people showed up for the dedication. The sign, commemorating the area, calling it James Byrd Jr. Park, was outsized for the strip of green it identified. The park dedication was the second-to-last story on the local evening news.

Meanwhile, out on Huff Creek Road, the black community still jumped at the sound of scraping feet on gravel and still thought that back in the woods, where no one could see them, lethal white men were waiting for an opportunity to drive the blacks out of Huff Creek and return them to a time when just being black was enough of a reason to worry about being murdered. The eighty-one circles of Day-Glow paint that had once marked the undoing of James Byrd had faded. Two years of traffic on the road—from the locals to the documentary filmmakers to the curious journalists—had erased the visual reminders of the murder. Of course locals could still see the marks in their mind's eye. They would walk along the pavement and look for them, seeing the faint smoky shadows in those specific spots where they knew the marks had been. And, on lonely nights, the cracking of branches in the forest and the sough-ing of wind in the pines still made them jump.

In the South, wrote William Faulkner, the past isn't dead; it's not even past. No one knew that better than the people of Jasper. It was a place that knowingly and willingly doomed itself to repeat history. If there were to be a recovery in Jasper, residents seemed resigned to the fact that it would be short-lived. Two years after the murder of James Byrd, Wayne Martindale was found dead on his property outside of town. One of his employees, a white man named John Herrin, had shot him and then dragged him for more

265

than a mile behind his truck. The murder wasn't racially motivated, but the echoes of the Byrd murder weren't lost on anyone.

"No matter how much we try to put it behind us, the Byrd murder is always there," said Mike Lout. "People who think it will go away are kidding themselves. It is our scarlet letter."

In 2000, a reconciliation committee started raising money for a $100,000 sculpture called *Circle of Peace*. Created by Utah sculptor Gary Price, the sculpture depicts a broken circle of seven children of different ethnicities. The circle can only be completed when a person enters the circle and joins hands with the children. Support for the fund-raising drive was mixed. "I could think of some other uses for the money," Reverend Lyons said.

Sculptures aside, little had fundamentally changed in Jasper. Among themselves, white Jasperites said the problem of race relations in Jasper in 2001 was mostly in the minds of the black community. Blacks said that whites shrugged off their concerns because they could forget about race when they went home; blacks could not. The whiff of racial condescension, Christine Carter said, will always be present in Jasper. The Byrd murder could not and did not change that. To think otherwise would be naïve. "When anyone is watching, well, they will make the effort again," she said of the white community. "But only as long as they need to."

EPILOGUE

BILL KING was delivered to death row in Livingston, Texas, in February 1999. The remainder of his existence, until he is put to death in Huntsville, will revolve around three meals a day, showers, short exercise periods, and waiting. Two years after the murder, on June 7, 2000, the Byrd family filed a wrongful death lawsuit against King, Brewer, and Berry. King answered the suit by saying that he was innocent, despite the evidence against him. At the same time he wrote a letter to the Jasper County district clerk's office asking the court to waive his automatic appeals.

"I've come to the realization that I cannot do everything myself with regards to legal matters no matter how much diligence, effort or time I devote to my plight," King wrote. "And it's become

---

increasingly obvious that court appointed lawyers in this state only give a damn about themselves and saving face with the courts. To put it mildly, I simply don't care to pursue these cases any longer." King's letter was somewhat academic. Texas law mandates that death sentence appeals continue regardless of a prisoner's wishes.

Several months later, on October 18, 2000, the Texas Court of Criminal Appeals upheld his death sentence. In a unanimous opinion, the nine-member court rejected all the challenges to his conviction. King's lawyers had argued there was insufficient evidence to prove that Byrd had been kidnapped on that June night. King said the evidence proved he was a racist, not a kidnapper or murderer. The court disagreed. It concluded that King's guilt was supported by DNA evidence. What's more, it said, there was "extensive evidence of [King's] hatred for African-Americans." King's letters to the media and his "kites" to Russell Brewer could have been construed by the jury as an admission of guilt, the court said. Guy James Gray was right; King had written himself to death.

In December 2000, a Bill King Web site appeared on the Internet. Posted with a link to the Lamp of Hope Project, a non-profit organization that provides a forum for death row inmates to post their writings, seek money, and find pen pals, the Web site outraged Jasperites. The Web page solicited donations to the John King Defense Fund at the First National Bank in Jasper. Ronald King said he did not know how much money was in the account, but he sent his son money from the bank when he needed it.

As of mid-2001, a date of execution has yet to be set.

*   *   *

RUSSELL BREWER was to spend the rest of his days on Livingston's death row as well. He and King resided in different wings of the prison. And while it was unlikely that the pair would have had much of an opportunity to communicate, prison officials said they could have been sending kites to one another. No kites had been intercepted to date. Brewer's case was also on automatic appeal, and by May 2001 he had yet to have an execution date assigned.

*   *   *

SHAWN BERRY was kept in isolation at Livingston prison as he began serving his life sentence. He would be eligible for parole in 2039. His four-year-old son, Montana, was not permitted by prison officials to touch his father. Montana lived with his mother and grandparents in Newton County, Texas. In April 2001, an appeals court began deliberations on whether to grant Berry a new trial. His lawyers argued the case before the Ninth Court of Appeals in Beaumont, Texas, saying Berry should never have been tried in Jasper. Their eighteen-point request for an appeal was filed more than two years after the murder, in August 2000. They argued that all the media coverage made it impossible for Berry to receive a fair trial in Jasper.

*   *   *

KENNETH LYONS remained pastor at Greater New Bethel Baptist Church. Relations with the Byrd family had grown strained in the aftermath of James Byrd's funeral. The issue was money. The sheer number of people who attended the service meant that Greater New Bethel had to rent a tent and cater food. The bill came to eight hundred dollars, and with all the donations coming in to the Byrd family, Lyons assumed they would pay back the church. They didn't. "The church elders eventually told me just to let it go, so I did," said Lyons. In the months after the King trial, the Byrd family began to return to Greater New Bethel for Sunday worship. James Byrd Sr. returned to his post as deacon. Stella Byrd, James's mother, was teaching at the Sunday school. While the church was still barely getting by financially, what it lacked in money it made up for in spirit, Lyons said.

*   *   *

CHARLENE ADAMS, the East Jasper resident who had lost her granddaughter, moved, with her two remaining grandchildren, from East Jasper to a small house behind the Twin Cinemas downtown. Adams didn't have money enough to pay for a marker on the grave of her granddaughter. One of her employers, a school-teacher at the high school, bought a headstone which marks the grave in the city cemetery today.

*   *   *

VANDER CARTER and his wife, Christine, are both retired. Vander hurt his back at the John Hart Lumber Company where he was working and then contracted pneumonia. He decided to take early retirement rather than kill himself working, he said. Despite a lifetime of timber work, Vander Carter still had all ten of his fingers. His brother, James Carter, was Jasper's first black deputy and worked for Sheriff Billy Rowles.

*   *   *

HARLON ALEXANDER, Jasper's former police chief and the man who stared down Black Panther Khalid Mohammed in the streets of Jasper, left the police force in December 1998. He became, instead, a full-time cowboy. He and his brother broke horses and trained them for cattlemen. He still lived in the double-wide trailer near the railway tracks, a stone's throw from the creosote plant. From his front yard he could watch the workers put creosote on telephone poles in the hot Texas sun.

*   *   *

UNAV WADE saw business drop off at Unav's Salon off Courthouse Square. No one came in for wigs anymore, and the pink overhead hair dryers stood in their rows gathering dust. Her granddaughter, a well-spoken girl who made good grades at Jasper Middle School, was the subject of ridicule, Wade said, because she spoke properly, as her grandmother had trained her to do. "This is the kind of town in which if you speak like you should, with good diction and a proper vocabulary, you are accused of putting on airs," said Wade. "The black children say she is trying to be white by speaking so proper. Poor thing, she can't win."

*   *   *

WALTER DIGGLES, in mid-2001, was considering writing a book about his role in Jasper's struggle for redemption. He continued to work for the Texas Council of Governments, doling out grants to the deserving. He won Jasper's Citizen of the Year award in 1999. White Jasperites were quick to point out the award had gone to a black man. It was, they said, more evidence of how enlightened they were. It was proof, they said, that they weren't racist.

*   *   *

KHALID ABDUL MOHAMMED, the former Nation of Islam activist and personal assistant to Louis Farrakhan who led the New Black Panther rallies in Jasper, died at the age of fifty-three of a brain hemorrhage in February 2001.

*   *   *

DARRELL FLINN, the grand wizard of the Knights of the White Kamellia, disappeared without a trace or explanation in 1999. Klan officials, including Michael Lowe, said there had been money missing from the organization's treasury. Flinn was suspected, they added. Others said, privately, that Flinn was found to be living with a black woman and was, as a result, stripped of his Klan membership. Neither law enforcement officials nor the Southern Poverty Law Center, which tracks Klansmen and their whereabouts, have been able to find Flinn.

*   *   *

MICHAEL LOWE, the Klan's best recruiter in Texas, continued his day job as a master carpenter in Waco, Texas. In his spare time he continued his Klan recruitment efforts, attended cross lightings, and did his part to cleanse the white race.

*   *   *

WARDEN JIM WILLETT retired from the Texas Department of Criminal Justice in March 2001, leaving it to someone else to preside over the Huntsville death chamber. The job, he said weeks before his retirement, had come to wear too much on him. He, his wife, and their children continued to live in Huntsville, Texas, not far from the Walls unit.

*   *   *

WILLIAM "BIG MO" MOSLEY, the inmate who testified on Bill King's behalf in February 1999, returned to prison. There were reprisals for his support of King. Inmates attacked him weeks after the King trial and broke both his hands by putting them into the prison shop's bench vice. Mosley's tattoo inking prowess was irreparably damaged as a result.

*   *   *

MICHAEL LOUT, the reluctant newsman and owner of KJAS-Jasper, won the Texas Radioman of the Year award in 1999 for his coverage of the events in Jasper. In 2001, he continued to air his weekend crime reports and community bulletins from his house on the hill. "Jasper won't ever get over what's happened," he said. "When people think of us, they'll think of the dragging. People remember bad things that happen better than good things that do. That's Jasper's curse, I guess."

*   *   *

JOE TONAHILL, pushing ninety years old in 2001, was still running one of the best-known law firms in East Texas. After the King trial it was more obvious than ever that he is at the faded edge of the continuum that was Jasper, Texas. He was a man who had been eclipsed by a heinous crime and spectacular trial in which he played no part. Tonahill's popularity in Jasper no longer stemmed from the power he possessed but rather from his longevity. Now it was his history in Jasper that gave weight to almost everything he said. After years of loneliness in the wake of Violett's death, Tonahill surprised everyone in 2000 by finding a girlfriend. His latest purchase surprised them all too: a bright yellow Hummer truck, the only Hummer in Jasper.

*   *   *

RONALD KING, turning seventy in 2001, and crumpled by a lifetime of adversity, became an anti–death penalty advocate, traveling around with volunteers from the Lamp of Hope Project to preach about the problems in the nation's judicial system. He was certain, more than two years after his son's conviction, that Bill King was railroaded by an overeager district attorney and Federal Bureau of Investigation. King continued to live in his ramshackle house a quarter of a mile from Vander and Christine Carter. On bad days he spent hours hooked up to his oxygen tank to quell emphysema attacks. He visited his son in Livingston once a month, sometimes bringing his grandson Blayne with him. "The whole thing," he said, "breaks my heart."

*   *   *

After winning all three cases, District Attorney GUY JAMES GRAY was angling for a federal appointment. Jasper had come to wear on him. "Every house I see, every corner I pass, I think of some crime that happened there," Gray said. "It has just become too hard." Gray was on President George W. Bush's shortlist for a number of top civil rights jobs, but as a lifelong Democrat, he decided it was unlikely he would ever get the job he wanted. Instead he began a speaking tour and gave presentations, often with Billy Rowles, on how law enforcement departments could work together.

*   *   *

Two years after Senate allies of Texas governor George W. Bush suppressed hate crimes legislation because it included protection for gays, Texas governor RICK PERRY signed the James Byrd Jr. Hate Crimes Act on May 11, 2001. The measure strengthened the penalties for offenses against racial minorities, gays, and others.

*   *   *

SHERIFF BILLY ROWLES will likely be allowed to remain in office as long as he cares to hold it. "This is the job I've always wanted," he said. "And if the people of the county will have me, I'll be sheriff forever. I think this is what the Lord meant for me to do."

NOTES ON SOURCES

I ARRIVED IN Jasper, Texas, several months after the murder of James Byrd Jr. with only a newspaper clipping and curiosity. I had read about the way the white community in Jasper had been bending over backward to make amends for the murder, and something about the story gave me pause. I bought a plane ticket and went to Jasper to see for myself.

One of the nicest things for journalists visiting small towns is that everyone, from school board members to the mayor, is listed in the phonebook. I picked up the phone and began calling anyone mentioned in the article. Within hours I was sitting on District Attorney Guy James Gray's back deck talking about the Christian Identity movement and prison gangs and speaking with Sheriff

Billy Rowles about the events that had transpired the morning of the murder.

It was when I met Bill King's father, Ronald, however, that I decided that this book needed to be written. I phoned Ronald King from a pay phone outside the Wal-Mart in Jasper with barely an hour left before I had to catch a plane back to Washington, D.C. The elder King insisted he didn't want to give any interviews but did say that he had a statement from Bill, which he had just finished typing and was willing to fax to me. I told him I was in Jasper, and he was so surprised he offered to meet me at the Holiday Inn Express on Highway 96—about a hundred yards from where his son, Brewer, and Berry had picked up James Byrd that June night— and give the papers to me personally.

Jasper was struggling with 15 percent unemployment in 1998, and in the weeks after the murder even the bass fishermen who used to stop in town on the way to Sam Rayburn Reservoir decided against the overnight in Jasper. The town had already started to develop a sinister reputation. Evidence enough was the parking lot at the Holiday Inn Express. It was empty, except for my car. When Ronald King drove in, he circled the entire vacant parking lot before stopping before my car and cautiously rolling down his window a crack.

"You the reporter from Washington?" he asked.

I nodded and walked over to his car. He pushed the papers through the window and said he didn't want to give any interviews. I said I understood and added that I would be back and maybe we could help each other down the road. I wasn't expecting what happened next: Ronald King burst into tears. He began to try to explain why the son he loved so much couldn't possibly have committed the crime he was accused of.

When Ronald King cried, he shed tears in such volume that his shirt was soaked. He spoke and wept for forty-five minutes, never taking his foot off the brake pedal and never taking the car out of drive, as if at any moment he would need to make a quick getaway. As he spoke I noticed his hands, the nubs where fingers had been, and an oxygen canister, to which he was connected, in the front seat. He finally drove away, and I realized at that moment that the story of Jasper had yet to be told. As it turned out, the actual story—a tale of how an entire town dealt with tragedy and tried to convince skeptics that the age-old matter of race in the South had been largely resolved—had yet to unfold. In the fall of 1998, no one was sure whether a Jasper jury would sentence a white man to death for killing a black one. No one was sure whether the racial sensitivity whites exhibited in the days after the murder would last. No one understood what motivated Bill King, Russell Brewer, and Shawn Berry to take James Byrd Jr. into the woods and kill him. Those stories had yet to reveal themselves, in all their complexity. In late 1998, Jasper had not yet found a sympathetic witness, an outsider, who would record the turn of events. I tried to be that person.

This is a work of nonfiction; all the characters are real, as are their names and the details of their lives. Where I used dialogue, it was based on the recollection of at least one participant or was uttered in my presence. Some of the best commentary I found came from jokes, asides, and incidents that occurred unexpectedly, not from interviews or my own analysis. One member of the black community asked me, quite frankly, after several hours of conversation, whether whites in Jasper called blacks "niggers" behind their backs. I was torn. I wanted to say they did not, to do my part to heal the rift between the races, but instead was honest and confirmed that they did. Without missing a beat, my companion laughed and said, "Isn't it amazing they don't slip up in front of us?"

Spending so much time with the subjects of the story meant that I generally failed to keep the necessary journalistic distance. I found myself wanting to intervene, most unjournalistically, in their lives. I made a point of visiting Charlene Adams whenever I came to Jasper and spent long hours on the front porch of the Belle-Jim talking about nothing at all. At first I was seen as a "journalist" and was viewed with suspicion. As the months passed, though, most Jasperites I spoke with came to believe that I was trying to get the story right. I was not one of those reporters out to get a quick story, but instead I was trying to understand. The conclusions I came to about Jasper are my own, and the people who helped me over the three years I spent writing this book bear no responsibility for them.

Much of the reporting and research for this book was done contemporaneously. Residents of Jasper, from the start, were gracious, particularly in trying to help a northerner understand their town's difficult past. Southerners generally tend to hang on to their histories, and people in Jasper were no different. There was always someone who knew someone who had been in the center of whatever took place in town. Though it is a relatively small town, Jasper has a first-class historical commission and researchers with long institutional memories and a flair for storytelling. I spent long afternoons leafing through photographs of downtown Jasper from the early 1900s to the present while being regaled with stories by Bertie Bryant and the ladies at the commission.

Research came from the most unexpected places. When I started the book I was the White House correspondent for *Bloomberg Business News*, and the White House historian was none other than William Seale, a direct descendant of one of Jasper's oldest families. A friend of mine had interviewed Seale about White House restoration, spied a Jasper address on his business card, and made the subsequent introductions. Seale was the first to tell me that Violett Tonahill's letters existed and the first to suggest they might provide a way to see Jasper as it had been and as it evolved over thirty years.

Prologue:

The book is full of Texas expressions from "death making slow people hurry" to people describing the murder in terms "of the way James was done." I tried to capture that language as best I could. Details about the morning after the murder came from interviews with everyone involved, including Sheriff Billy Rowles, District Attorney Guy James Gray, Deputy Joe Sterling, investigator Curtis Frame, parishioners at the Greater New Bethel Baptist Church, morticians Dorie Coleman and Billy Ray Robinson, Jasper Cemetery Club president Tommy Adams, George Coleman, Margaret Tukes, and Cedric Green. Friends of James Byrd's who had been with him at Willie Mays's party the night of the murder—including James Brown and Arthur Lee Parks—provided some background on Byrd. And Shawn Berry's statement to the police and trial transcripts helped piece together what happened before the trio offered James Byrd a ride. Interviews with James Byrd's friends in East Jasper helped complete a portrait of a man whose character had been kept under wraps during the initial media rush following the murder. The Byrd family declined to provide any help with this book and signed an exclusivity agreement with a documentary filmmaker before my work was completed. Under that agreement, they were not permitted to talk to me. The details about James Byrd's relationship with his parents came from Reverend Kenneth Lyons and a handful of James Byrd's friends, including James Brown and Arthur Lee Parks.

The history of Jasper's black community came from various sources, including Nida Marshall, who provided vignettes of Jasper history for KJAS radio. She later published the ever-helpful *Jasper Journal* (Austin, Tex.: Nortex Press, 1993).

Chapter One: Dante's Inferno

Cedric Green's account of discovering James Byrd's body came from several front-porch interviews. I cross-referenced his story with sheriff's office records, police records, and Shawn Berry's subsequent statement to the sheriff's office about the trio's activities after the murder. Trial testimony by Louis Berry and Tommy Faulk, friends of King's, also substantiated their whereabouts. Exclusive interviews with Bill King in Jasper County Jail also supported and added to some of law enforcement's rendition of events.

The basis for saying Carolyn McQueen wanted Kennebrew to plead guilty in order to avoid a trial came from Sheriff Rowles, District Attorney Guy James Gray, and several investigating officers who declined to be further identified. Details regarding the McQueen murder came from police reports, interviews with Joe Sterling, Rowles, and former police chief Harlon Alexander. McQueen's widow declined to be interviewed. Sterling and Rowles and Alexander provided the chronology of events.

The history of Jasper's KJAS grew out of interviews with residents and Mike Lout's own recollection of events. Interviews with Gloria Mays and Lout helped me piece together the early reports of the discovery of James Byrd's body. Articles from the *Dallas Morning News* and the *Beaumont Enterprise* in the days after the murder were also immensely helpful in sorting out the various players. Rowles, Curtis Frame, Dorie Coleman of Coleman's Mortuary, and Detective Phil Denny were also helpful in reconstructing the events of that first morning.

Chapter Two: Jasper, Texas

Detailed accounts of East Texas history came from a number of sources, including William Seale's *Texas Riverman: The Life and Times of Captain Andrew Smyth* (Austin, Tex.: University of Texas Press, 1966). Members of the Jasper community who drifted in and out of Joe Tonahill's law office—from District Attorney Guy James Gray to Judge Joe Bob Golden to Pat Adams, Jasper's most prominent real estate tycoon—all helped provide more insight into Jasper's oldest families. William Seale, related to Tonahill by marriage, was also very helpful in providing anecdotes about the venerable lawyer. I also interviewed Tonahill more than half a dozen times over the course of three years, checking and rechecking details about his history, Jasper history, and his reaction to the Bill King trial.

In addition to dozens of interviews with timbermen both past and present, including Eddie Land, Elmo Jackson, Ronald King, Vander Carter, and workers at Temple-Inland and Louisiana-Pacific I met during mill tours, I relied on several books to provide historical balance to the oral accounts. The story of Thomas Lewis Latane Temple stepping off the train in Angelina County in 1893 and the history of the timber industry more generally in Deep East Texas came from Robert Maxwell's *Whistle in the Piney Woods: Paul Bremond and the Houston, East and West Railway* (Denton, Tex.: East Texas Historical Society and University of North Texas Press, 1998) and his *Sawdust Empire*, written with Bob Baker, which is considered the definitive work on Texas forest history; *East Texas: Mill Towns and Ghost Towns*, volume 2, by W. T. Block (Lufkin, Tex.: Pineywoods Foundation, 1995) and *Backwoodsmen: Stockmen and Hunters along a Big Thicket River Valley*, by Thad Sitton (Norman: University of Oklahoma Press, 1995).

The staff at the Texas Forestry Association in Lufkin, Texas, was invaluable in explaining the machinations of the timber industry. They allowed me to attend the weeklong Teachers Conservation Institute, sponsored by the TFA, in the Angelina Forest to learn about logging from start to finish. My colleagues there, funny and patient East Texas middle and high school teachers, were also very helpful in providing some perspective on how the rest of East Texas viewed Jasper, the murder, and its economic prospects given its reliance on timber. Local OSHA representatives in Dallas and Houston, who declined to be quoted on the record, explained how safety issues forced the industry to modernize.

The anecdotes about Sheriff Billy Rowles, from the discovery of the sex doll to the telephone conversations with distraught parents, were heard firsthand. Interviews with Rowles and Kylie Greeney's mother provided details on the initial discussions about the graphic photos of Kylie with Bill King. Interviews with Jamie Rowles, Dorothy Bagesse, Durwood and Mildred Cox, and Rowles himself provided the fodder for the section on Rowles's family history.

The definitive work on the Loyal Garner case is the prize-winning *Dallas Morning News* journalist Howard Swindle's *Deliberate Indifference* (New York: Viking, 1993). The book follows the events from when Garner was stopped by Hemphill's white police chief near the Louisiana border, taken to jail, and beaten to death with a lead-filled blackjack through the subsequent trials. "As if the 70-foot-tall pines were an impenetrable social barrier," Swindle writes, "Deep East Texas lies stagnant in a civil rights time warp, more forties and fifties than eighties and nineties." While it was not in dispute that Garner suffered a beating in the Hemphill jail, officers were acquitted of violating his civil rights on July 15, 1988. Two years later, in 1990, with the legal muscle of the Southern Poverty Law Center in Atlanta, Hemphill police chief Thomas Ladner and two county deputies, Billy Ray Horton and James M. Hyden, were eventually convicted on state murder charges. Horton's conviction was later overturned.

The story was well known in Jasper, and in East Texas more generally. In addition to Swindle's book, I relied on newspaper accounts of the 1987 killing, recollections by KJAS radioman Mike Lout, who was working in the town of Hemphill at the time, and coverage from the *New York Times* (May 4, 1990, and May 11, 1990), which provided details on the convictions of policemen in Garner's beating. Other history was collected by members of the sheriff's office, Rowles, former police chief Alexander, and from records at the Jasper County Historical Commission and interviews with members of the Jasper community such as Vander and Christine Carter. There were no records of the beating of black citizens at the hands of former sheriffs, but prominent members of both the black and the white communities—including District Attorney Gray, Rowles, Police Chief Alexander, Reverend Lyons, Elmo Jackson, and Eddie Land—confirmed the problem existed. Alton Wright died of diabetes in 1998 and never commented on the accusations of beating black motorists. The story, however, was corroborated by so many different sources that I am confident of its validity. Wright's widow, Willie May Wright, and his daughter, Linda Wright Powell, said that the former chief "could have" beaten blacks while they were handcuffed. They said that he was a "tough man" and that that was "a different time."

Officer Sterling, Rowles, and Police Chief Alexander, and District Attorney Gray provided details on Rowles's first run for Jasper County sheriff. Jasper citizens confirmed that they felt Roscoe Davis had become too distant and difficult to contact during his tenure as sheriff, and that is one of the reasons they voted for Billy Rowles when he ran a second time against Davis.

Rowles provided the skeleton of the story of his two shootings, and the subsequent inquires into the shootings supported his version of events. Details on cases brought against Rowles were found in court papers and Texas Highway Patrol files. Rayford Clinton Armstrong brought the civil rights case against Rowles and had been convicted of murder. He was in prison when he filed the civil rights case against the sheriff. Rowles requested that the name of the young man whom he shot to death be kept confidential to spare the dead man's family.

Chapter Three: "Ain't Nothing We Can Do"

Details of life in East Jasper came from a number of door-to-door interviews over the course of three years, including discussions with school superintendent Herman Wright, Councilman Clyde Williams, Reverend Jerry Lewis, Reverend Kenneth Lyons, Walter Diggles, Council Member Nancy Nicholson, Becky and Tim Berryman, Jonathan Berryman, radioman Mike Lout, Steve Scott, Unav Wade, Keisha Atkins, Christie Marcontell, Curtis Frame, Assistant District Attorney Pat Hardy, Officer Rich Ford, Deputy James Carter, Bill King, Tommy Faulk, Johnny (Abdul) Rashid, Louis Berry, jailer Mo Johnson, Bill King defense team Brack Jones and C. Haden "Sonny" Cribbs, Belle-Jim owners Pat and David Stiles, Joe Tonahill, William Seale, Father Ron Fosich, Jamie Gunner, Gloria Mays, the Southern Poverty Law Center's Mark Potok, Tommy Adams, mortician Dorie Coleman, George Coleman, Officer Larry Pullman, Joe Sterling, Judge Joe Bob Golden, restaurateur Patrick Lam, Police Chief Stanley Christopher, Lilly Scott, Wilma Dougherty, historian Bertie Bryant, and Booker T. Hunter, founder of the Jasper chapter of the National Association for the

Advancement of Colored People. Those interviews also provided details about the death of Ray Peacock.

East Jasper's Charlene Adams was particularly helpful, telling me a great deal not only about her family and her battle with cancer but also about life in East Jasper generally. Where possible, dates were checked against hospital records and neighbor and employer recollections of what occurred during her illness and at the time of her granddaughter's accident.

The story of Ray Peacock grew out of interviews with family members and friends, discussions with Booker T. Hunter at the National Association for the Advancement of Colored People, and police reports. The story of J. H. Rowe came from newspaper clippings from the time, interviews with his former pupils, including Christine Carter, Reverend Lyons, and Eddie Land, and accounts in Marshall's *Jasper Journal*.

Chapter Four: Young Men, Go Home

The chronology of events that led to Brewer's arrival in Jasper was derived from interviews with Bill King and where possible were cross-checked with FBI and Jasper County investigations. Firsthand observation and discussions with King neighbors who had contact with Brewer, interviews with people in Sulphur Springs who knew Brewer growing up, and trial testimony helped in piecing together a picture of him. A combination of newspaper articles from the *Dallas Morning News*, the *Beaumont Enterprise*, the *Houston Chronicle*, police records and several one-on-one interviews with Bill King were the basis of the description of the Brewer-King relationship. Numerous published reports said that King and Brewer were cellmates; according to Texas Department of Criminal Justice records and

King's own account, they never shared a cell. Brewer's account of his early days in prison are part of his trial record.

King's rendition of life in prison and his education about the Aryan movement was derived from a series of one-on-one interviews with King in Jasper County Jail. The portrait of Ronald King evolved over the course of many interviews with him and discussions with members of both the black and the white communities in Jasper, including Bill King, Vander and Christine Carter, Mo Johnson, Father Ron Fosich, C. Haden "Sonny" Cribbs, Rowles, and Guy James Gray. Whenever possible, I tried to cross-check Ronald King's stories about his son with childhood friends of Bill's, teachers, and neighbors, including Pat Behator, Tommy Faulk, Louis Berry, Mike Lout, Vander and Christine Carter, and Tommy Adams.

Reverend Kenneth Lyons's recounting of his genealogy was buttressed by William Seale's own version of events, and Seale provided details about "Uncle Dick," whom he has researched for his own scholarly work.

The Beaumont riot accounts were taken from newspaper articles published at the time and interviews with Dorothy Bagesse and Durwood Cox, who were in Beaumont when the violence broke out. Bagesse and Cox provided details on their activities that evening and said that if anyone had been outside their back door when they rushed outside with rifles drawn, they would have been shot. V. J. Withers, who had known Billy Rowles's father, died twenty years ago.

The reenactment of the early hours of the investigation grew out of interviews with Rowles, investigator Frame, District Attorney Gray, Phil Denny, Police Chief Alexander, and funeral home director Dorie Coleman. Steven Scott told Rowles that he had decided not to give James Byrd a ride when he saw him staggering down the road. James Brown said in an interview that he had offered Byrd a ride from Willie Mays's party. My account of events that led to the arrest of King, Brewer, and Berry for the murder was pulled together from interviews with Rowles, Gray, Bill King, and officers Curtis Frame and Joe Sterling.

Chapter Five: Joe Tonahill's Texas

Nearly everyone in Jasper had a story about Joe Tonahill, and the anecdotes that appear in the book have been verified by at least two sources and, when possible, by members of both the black and the white communities, including Tim and Becky Berryman, William Seale, Reverend Kenneth Lyons, Walter Diggles, District Attorney Gray, Rowles, historian Bertie Bryant, David and Pat Stiles, Elmo Jackson, Vander Carter, and Unav Wade. Details from the Ruby trial were pulled together from newspaper accounts and interviews with Tonahill.

Violett Tonahill's letters, which describe her visit with her husband to the Ruby trial, are collected in two four-inch leather-bound volumes that, until now, have only been seen by the family. I spent several afternoons in 1998 in William Seale's Alexandria office reading the letters and getting to know a woman whom I had never met. Joe Tonahill graciously allowed me to excerpt some passages from the more than 1,000 pages of letters. Joe Tonahill subsequently gave me permission to print some excerpts.

Members of the black community, who declined to be named, said they had voted against Gray when he ran for reelection in 1998 in order to protest what they saw as a pattern of prosecuting small-time black pushers rather than white kingpins. Gray said he had heard that criticism and that it was ridiculous. White and black drug dealers had been arrested without any connection to race. Guy James Gray's history came from the district attorney himself, interviews with his contemporaries in Jasper and at law school, and interviews with Joe Tonahill.

Harlon Alexander, Gray, and Rowles provided details on Shawn Berry's family history. His mother had been in and out of prison and in 2001 was out on a blue warrant for violating her parole and turned herself in to Billy Rowles. Interviews with Billy Rowles, Guy James Gray, Mo Johnson, Curtis Frame, and Bill King provided details on the early morning interrogation of Shawn Berry.

The Emmett Till murder in Money, Mississippi, has been documented in numerous articles and history books. J. W. Milam publicly confessed to the murder not long after he was acquitted, and there are many newspaper and historical accounts saying as much. The Till murder was a galvanizing event for the blossoming civil rights movement. Till's mother had his body flown up to Chicago, Illinois, and had an open-casket funeral, which was widely attended. *Ebony* magazine put a picture of the open casket on its cover, and many historians say it helped give Martin Luther King Jr. the ammunition he needed to start to demand equal rights in earnest. There is a particularly good article by Bebe Moore Campbell in *Time* magazine (March 8, 1999) that outlines the similarities between the Till and the Byrd murders. Campbell is the author of *Your Blues Ain't Like Mine* (New York: Ballantine Books, 1995), a novel based on the Emmett Till killing.

Chapter Six: Small Conspiracies

Rowles said he had been reading from a script prepared by the FBI during the press conference outside Jasper County Jail. "It was a mistake," he said later. "I was stumbling over their words and it wasn't the way I talked. It was the last time I read something that they had written word for word like that. It made me look stupid, like I couldn't talk."

The Nicholsons did not acknowledge that the clientele at Texas Charlie's was nearly all white, and they tended to preach racial harmony whenever asked (Mrs. Nicholson was a member of the city council). That said, after many dozens of visits to Texas Charlie's I could count on one hand the number of times I saw black customers sitting in its booths. Reverend Lyons confirmed my impression when he came to see me for an interview at Texas Charlie's. After we had finished our meal I asked if he had ever eaten there before. He shrugged and said "not often," adding that it was a "white people's place."

The closeness that grew up between the black and the white communities in Jasper was widely reported in the weeks and months after the murder in both local and national newspapers, including the *Beaumont Enterprise*, the *Jasper Newsboy*, the *Houston Chronicle*, the *Dallas Morning News*, and the *Wall Street Journal*. When journalists grew weary of the story, however, the black community noticed the white community made less of an effort and returned to their old ways of treating blacks.

Stories about Reverend Billy Ray Robinson came from first-hand accounts by either police officers, sheriff department officials, Dorie Coleman, or Billy Ray Robinson himself. Robinson provided the details on James Byrd's embalming and funeral arrangements during an interview at the funeral home in 2000. Members of the Byrd family, bound by an exclusivity agreement, would not comment on why they used Robinson for the funeral. Robinson did say that James Byrd owed him money for bonds he had posted when Byrd did not have the cash to get himself out of jail.

The account of the interplay between Diggles and Jesse Jackson came from three sources who were in the room at the time, including sheriff's officers, Diggles, and Reverend Lyons. Jackson aides said they were not aware members of the Jasper community didn't want them to come to Jasper.

Walter Diggles, Harlon Alexander, and other Jasper police officers provided accounts of the rally negotiations. Khalid Mohammed also confirmed the details of the discussions.

Details about the funeral, which was closed to the public, came from interviews with half a dozen Jasperites who attended the service, including Reverend Lyons, Margaret Tukes, and Rowles, and from newspaper accounts of what was said inside and press conferences held afterward. The Byrds did not acknowledge that they had settled on a regimen of tough love or that James was not welcome at their house. Interviews with Reverend Lyons, the Carters, Arthur Parks, and James Brown, among others, confirmed that James Byrd had a distant relationship with his parents.

Chapter Seven: Outsiders Come to Jasper

Ronald King, Belle-Jim owners David and Pat Stiles, Reverend Lyons, Rowles, Police Chief Alexander, Bill King, reporters Michael Journee and Mike Lout, and Klansman Michael Lowe described the reaction of Jasperites in the days after the funeral. Reverend Lyons provided cassette tapes of his sermons in the weeks leading up to and after the Byrd murder, and excerpts appear in the book by permission.

The account of the Klan rally grew out of police reports and more than a dozen interviews with Klansmen, Jasper citizens, law enforcement officials, including Darrell Flinn, Michael Lowe, Pat and David Stiles, Janie Sheffield, Rowles, Police Chief Alexander, investigator Frame, Tim and Becky Berryman, and Joe Tonahill. Lowe confirmed that he had served in prison for possession of an explosive device in his "younger days." The conviction, according to FBI intelligence reports, earned him the epithet "Mad Bomber" among lawmen. Lowe spoke matter-of-factly about the practical obstacles involved in cross lightings, during a lunch interview in Waco, Texas, in July 2000.

Details on Russell Brewer's home life, from living with Tammy Perritt and her young children, were gleaned from trial reports and published accounts. Brewer was said to have told his father that the only person who had ever loved him was Bill King. The comment came during an argument between the two.

Quanell X had been convicted of dealing crack cocaine in May 1989, and his comments about white people being devils and the enemy were widely reported in numerous newspapers and in FBI intelligence files. The Southern Poverty Law Center has a Web site that can bring anyone up to speed on the hate movement in the United States. A quick Internet search shows the Christian Identity movement's growth in the past couple of years.

Chapter Eight: Beneath the Surface

All the letters from Bill King and his kites to Brewer became part of the trial record. Exclusive interviews with Bill King over the course of more than a year provided some insight into his feelings about Brewer, his longing to talk to him while in jail, and the way he spent his days in prison. My account of the worries the black community held came from interviews with many Jasper residents, including Herman Wright, councilman Clyde Williams, Reverend Jerry Lewis, Reverend Kenneth Lyons, Walter Diggles, Unav Wade, deputy James Carter, Gloria Mays, Tommy Adams, mortician Dorie Coleman, George Coleman, Lilly Scott, and Booker T. Hunter, founder of the NAACP Jasper chapter, and newspaper articles from the *Jasper Newsboy* and the *Beaumont Enterprise*. The chapter also drew on interviews with Rowles and his wife, Jamie, Pat Stiles, Mike Lout, Joe Tonahill, and District Attorney Gray. The defense strategy information came from numerous telephone and several exclusive interviews with Sonny Cribbs in the days and weeks leading up to the King trial.

The fact that Blayne is Bill King's son, born out of wedlock to Kylie Greeney, is not in dispute. She has made clear that King is the father, and up until press time Greeney was still visiting King and bringing Blayne to see him.

The Confederate Knights were founded by Terry Boyce while he was in prison. The Southern Poverty Law Center Intelligence Report (North Carolina Hate Crimes Report, 1993) provided the history of the supremacist group. Some of the better-known followers of the Christian Identity movement are listed in an Anti-Defamation League Report dated December 12, 1995. Christie Marcontell confirmed in a 1999 telephone interview that her family did in fact pay for Shawn Berry's defense.

Chapter Nine: Hook, Line, and Sinker

I attended many of the pretrial hearings and interviewed Guy James Gray, Billy Rowles, and Sonny Cribbs as events were unfolding so I would not be reporting revisionist history. The excellent coverage of the pretrial hearings in the *Houston Chronicle* and the *Dallas Morning News* was also very helpful in jogging memories both of the individuals I interviewed and of this writer when it came time to reconstruct events. The account of the interplay between Cribbs and King was a result of firsthand observations and from interviews with both men. In the early days of his preparation for the defense, Cribbs said he believed that King had probably been raped in prison but he was unable to prove it. In an interview in June 2000, Cribbs demurred and said he couldn't even point to a prison rape to explain what had turned King into a killer. "He has zero remorse," said Cribbs.

City leaders, including R.C. Horn, Walter Diggles, and Nancy Nicholson, provided details to the assembled press corps about the removal of the fence at the city cemetery. R.C. Horn subsequently signed an exclusivity agreement and could not be interviewed by me.

Chapter Ten: Blood In, Blood Out

The history of the Jasper County Courthouse was constructed from a number of articles and historical documents at the Jasper County Historical Commission, including a catalog of radio pieces written by Nida Marshall, a local Jasper historian. Her book, *The Jasper Journal* (Austin, Texas: Nortex Press, 1993), was also very helpful.

Whenever possible, I tried to interview elder Jasper residents who could shed light on the debate and discussion that helped shape opinions, both past and present. The description of the crowd gathered for the King trial and the recounting of those events came from real-time reporting. I attended the trial and also interviewed King, Cribbs, and Gray while the trial was under way. Conversations in the corridors were overheard firsthand.

The Byrds were adamant from the outset that they wanted their son's killers to be sentenced to death. They made this clear in their public statements in the run-up to the three trials and in their aftermath. In an interview before the Bill King trial, Tonahill worried aloud that there would be trouble if a Jasper jury didn't give the death penalty to all three defendants. The statement by the police officer at the back door of the courthouse, where the press room was located, was made directly to me.

Matthew Hoover testified at the Bill King trial that he had been in prison for burglary, and he testified that he was a member of the Aryan Brotherhood. He had known King while they were together in the Beto I unit.

Reports of fistfights at the middle school and problems with the Letney boy were gleaned from teachers and students who witnessed it firsthand. The *Jasper Newsboy* also had an account of the controversy. The Letneys declined to be interviewed, despite several attempts to contact them; they did not want to discuss the problem with the school or their tense relationship with their neighbors. Law enforcement officers have been called to the Letneys on numerous occasions when neighbors complained about gunshots fired from the house. I visited the house, which looks like a fortress surrounded by a chain link fence, and they do indeed fly a Confederate flag. Michael Lowe of the Klan provided details on Darrell Flinn's role in the belt buckle dispute. Darrell Flinn has been missing for some time. In 2000, he was no longer a leader in the Ku Klux Klan.

Chapter Eleven: "My Little Town Stood Up"

In 2000, Texas had 110 prisons housing 150,000 prisoners. U.S. Federal Judge William Wayne Justice first took control of the Texas prisons in 1979 following a yearlong trial brought on by a civil-rights complaint filed in 1972 by prisoner David Ruiz. On March 1, 1999, Judge Justice ruled in a 167-page opinion that Texas prisons still ran a brutal system where prisoners were gang-raped, beaten, and extorted by other prisoners. "The evidence before the court revealed a prison underworld in which rapes, beatings and servitude are the currency of power," the judge said in his ruling.

"Inmates who refuse to join race-based gangs may be physically or sexually assaulted." By press time, the Texas prison system was still under federal oversight.

I attended the Bill King trial, and details in the book came from my observations at the time. William Mosley testified that he was serving time in the Texas prison system for burglary and sexual assault. He also said he had applied many of the tattoos King had on his body.

Jury foreman Joe Collins had said during jury selection that he had known King in middle school and didn't remember him as a racist. After the trial he came to believe, he said, that King had changed since then and was capable of killing Byrd simply because he was black. Collins was also black and was a guard at a local prison.

Ronald King said in an interview that his son had extreme mood swings and could have a bad temper. He said that once his wife died everyone except him seemed to be afraid of Bill King. He added that he wasn't sure why. He also acknowledged in his younger days that he himself had used racial slurs, though he denied bragging about having belonged to a Ku Klux Klan group. Two sources, who did not want to be further identified, who worked with Ronald King during his early years in Jasper said he used the word "nigger" frequently when he first arrived in the 1970s but later dropped that word from his vocabulary. Christine and Vander Carter said they did not sense that Ronald King was racist.

The account of the killing of F. Teague Jennings by Ronald King's older brother originally appeared in the *Dallas Morning News* in a story by reporter Lee Hancock. I checked the details of events with court records in Virginia and had Ronald King retell me the story so I would hear his version for myself. He was very upset that the story of his brother had been published and said it only appeared to confirm the worst that people thought about his family. He said he begged Hancock not to publish it.

I attended the Jasper High School ceremony on February 26, 1999, a day after the verdict, and saw the students file in and segregate themselves. I spoke with Walter Diggles about the episode two days later.

Chapter Twelve: Death Town, U.S.A.

Details of King's transfer to Huntsville Prison came from interviews with Billy Rowles, Mo Johnson (who sat beside him in the car), and Huntsville prison spokesman Larry Fitzgerald. The description of death row, the death chamber and Warden Jim Willett came from interviews conducted at the prison itself shortly after President George W. Bush's inauguration in January 2001. I spoke with Larry Fitzgerald, Warden Jim Willett, and Chaplain Jim Brazzil. Cruthers Alexander was the first man in Texas to be put to death after President George W. Bush took the oath of office.

Sheriff Rowles acknowledged that he had been in such a hurry to get Bill King out of Jasper, he accidentally left his paperwork at the county jail, and it took a day for the file to catch up to King.

Chapter Thirteen: The More Things Change

Details on the Brewer trial in Bryan, Texas, and Shawn Berry's trial in Jasper were gleaned from interviews with Guy James Gray, Billy Rowles, Mo Johnson, Berry's girlfriend, Christie Marcontell, and radioman Mike Lout. Newspaper articles from the *Houston Chronicle*, the *Dallas Morning News*, and the Associated Press were also useful in reconstructing events. The trial record says Brewer's wife was Hispanic, and a letter from Brewer to his wife while he was in prison was also part of the prosecution's evidence.

John Herrin was convicted of murdering Wayne Martindale in 2000. Guy James Gray said that Martindale's body had been dragged behind Herrin's truck in a killing that had echoes of the Byrd murder.

The dedication of the James Byrd Park on Easter Sunday was seen, accidentally, firsthand. I happened to be driving by, saw the balloons, and went to investigate. I also happened to attend the Democratic National Convention in Los Angeles, where the Byrds were honored by presidential candidate Al Gore. I was in the hall, sitting about a hundred feet away from Al Gore, when the Byrd introductions were made.

Epilogue

As of June 2001, there had not been any result in the wrongful death suit filed by the Byrd family against King, Brewer, and Berry. So far, only King has responded to the suit. He denied his role in the killing.

The Lamp of Hope Project was founded by Texas death row prisoners. The nonprofit organization seeks to educate the public about the death penalty and its alternatives and supports prisoners' and victims' families. The John William King Web site has a link to the Lamp of Hope Project home page.

The reporting for the book ended in mid-June 2001. The epilogue represents the whereabouts of all the characters at press time.

ACKNOWLEDGMENTS

MY DEEP THANKS to all those who took the time to help me with this task, whether it was providing information, adding insight, offering advice, or patiently listening to yet another story about my latest trip to Jasper. This project spanned three years: it began several months after the murder and was finally completed in the middle of 2001.

By definition, a book about ordinary people in a small Texas town depends on the kindness of strangers. My greatest debt is to the people of Jasper who allowed me to pepper them with pointed questions about a subject that makes everyone uncomfortable: race. They shared their feelings about the murder, prejudice, and the decline of Jasper with unsparing generosity. They took me into their houses, introduced me to their children, and allowed an outsider to rummage around in their lives. Without them, this book would never have come into being. While I know many Jasperites will not agree with the conclusions I have drawn about their town, I hope they feel that I have been fair in trying to portray their trials through a difficult time.

In particular, I would like to thank Sheriff Billy Rowles, his wife, Jamie, District Attorney Guy James Gray, Reverend Kenneth Lyons, Ronald King, Vander and Christine Carter, Joe Tonahill, C. Haden "Sonny" Cribbs, and William Seale for always making time for me when I came to town. In particular, Billy Rowles and Guy James Gray allowed me to bounce my theories off them and helped me calibrate my conclusions. I was in Jasper for a total of more than four months over the course of two years, and I appreciated very much the hospitality of Janie Sheffield and David and Pat Stiles. They treated me like a member of the family and were always excited to see me when I arrived.

My agents, Joy Tutela and David Black, provided unending enthusiasm, keeping the book alive when despair threatened to set in. Joy Tutela fell in love with the proposal from the start and was always full of ideas and encouragement as she shepherded it to its conclusion. She embodies all the qualities the best agents are supposed to have.

My editor at Henry Holt, Elizabeth Stein, is one of the smartest people I know. Her good humor, ability to guide gently, and editorial instincts were an unbeatable combination for this first-time author. Joan Didion, in her essay about her editor, Henry Robbins, said the best editors gave the writer an idea of themselves, and that image enabled the writer to sit down and write. A good editor "not only [has] to maintain a faith the writer shares only in intermittent flashes but also [has] to like the writer, which is hard to do. Writers are only rarely likable." Liz and I developed a great friendship, and she is a pleasure to work with. She is everything a great editor is supposed to be.

My copy editor, Vicki Haire, did a meticulous job in finding my errors of commission and omission. My colleague at *USA Today*, George Hager, was kind enough to read the manuscript with a copy editor's eye to ensure that I didn't make mistakes that would be an embarrassment later. He is one of the kindest, most intelligent people with whom I have ever had the pleasure to work, and his good humor throughout this project will always be appreciated.

Many friends read the manuscript, in whole or in part. Bob Mautner, Linda Kulman, Robin Meszoly, Gary Rawlins, Denise Pellegrini, George David, Skip Thurman, Campbell Brown, and Jim Angle provided helpful suggestions and guidance as this north-erner tried to capture life in the South. Encouragement and sup-port from the editors at *USA Today*, in particular Mike Clements, Jim Henderson, and John Hillkirk, who gave me time off to com-plete the manuscript, were invaluable in getting the book finished.

My deepest thanks go, finally, to the people who supported me in this project, including Bob Mautner and that friend who always makes me try harder. Last but not least, my writing professor at Northwestern University, Joseph Epstein, has my gratitude. A men-tor and a friend for more than fifteen years, he has always had a knack of saying just the right thing at just the right time. I would not be a writer today if it were not for him.

Van Winkle, Falyssa, 171
Verrett, Darrell, 193
Verrett, Mary, 193
Vidor, King, 142–43
Vidor, Texas, 29, 142
Vietnam War, 47
Visador company, 36

Wade, Annegenette, 115
Wade, Unav, 17, 57, 59, 115, 116,
    159, 160, 258, 259, 271, 286,
    289, 293
Walker, Ted, 103
Wall Street Journal, 136, 291
Washington, Gen. George, 86
Weaver, Randy, 169
Whistle in the Piney Woods (Maxwell),
    283
White Knights, 170
white(s) in Jasper. *See also* blacks in
    Jasper; civil rights movement;
    prejudice; race relations;
    racism; segregation; slavery;
    white supremacist groups
    black deputy and, 41–42
    criminal justice system and, 48,
        50–51
    denial of racism by, 171
    Diggles and, 120, 121
    drug problem and, 24, 66
    grave markers for blacks and,
        60–61
    Gray and, 102–3
    impact of murder on, 40, 115–19
    King seen as aberration by, 224

lumber industry and, 33
McQueen killing and, 8
in prison, 71
race relations and, 38–39,
    158–60, 164–65, 266
resent "special treatment" for
    blacks, 257–58
trial and, 165–66, 182, 192–93,
    201–2
unemployment, and KKK,
    143
use of "nigger" by, 38–40, 158,
    279
white supremacist groups, 71, 72,
    81, 114, 167–69, 182–83,
    216–18
Wilkinson, Betty, 243
Willett, Janice, 235, 243
Willett, Jim, 235–38, 240–43,
    272–73, 298
Williams, Clyde, 286, 293
Wilson, Ron, 148
Withers, V. J., 93, 288
workers' compensation, 33, 34
Wright, Alton, 50–51, 285
Wright, Herman, 286, 293
Wright, Willie May, 285

X, Malcolm, 127
X, Quanell, 147–48, 150, 293

Yockey, Francis, 223
Your Blues Ain't Like Mine (Campbell),
    290

ABOUT THE AUTHOR

DINA TEMPLE-RASTON was a longtime White House reporter for *Bloomberg Business News* before becoming a correspondent for *USA Today*. This is her first book. She lives in Washington, D.C.

NORTH COUNTRY LIBRARY SYSTEM

0 11 01 0286265 0

364.1523 Temple-Raston, Dina.
TEM
        A death in Texas.

$26.00

DATE			

MAR -- 2002

CENTRAL LIBRARY
WATERTOWN

NORTH COUNTRY LIBRARY SYS
Watertown NY 13601

BAKER & TAYLOR